INTERNATIONAL TRADE AND ECONOMIC RELATIONS

IN A NUTSHELL®

SIXTH EDITION

RALPH H. FOLSOM
Professor of Law
University of San Diego

MICHAEL WALLACE GORDON
John & Mary Lou Dasburg
Professor of Law Emeritus
University of Florida

MICHAEL P. VAN ALSTINE
Professor of Law
University of Maryland Francis King Carey
School of Law

WEST ACADEMIC PUBLISHING

The publisher is not engaged in rendering legal or other professional advice, and this publication is not a substitute for the advice of an attorney. If you require legal or other expert advice, you should seek the services of a competent attorney or other professional.

We dedicate this book to those who teach international trade and economic relations in all of its various forms, and especially to the many faculty who have so thoughtfully helped us over the years to improve the successive editions of our international business law books.

PREFACE

Professor Ralph Folsom has completed this sixth edition of *International Trade and Economic Relations in a Nutshell*. It remains a companion to the tenth edition of *International Business Transactions in a Nutshell* by Profs. Michael Van Alstine and Michael Ramsey. Together, these Nutshells cover all significant areas of international business, from selling goods across borders to foreign direct investments abroad, including the role of nations in regulating trade and economic relations, both unilaterally and by participation in bilateral and multilateral agreements.

International Trade and Economic Relations in a Nutshell focuses on government controls on imports and exports, customs law, free trade agreements and customs unions, trade remedies, and the law and economic relations of the World Trade Organization, the European Union, and NAFTA.

International Business Transactions in a Nutshell focuses principally on international business negotiations, sales of goods, letters of credit, E-commerce, transfers of technology, foreign investment, and international business litigation and arbitration

The two Nutshells are intended to provide readers with a broad introduction to the people and institutions that practice international business law, and the government and multilateral organizations that both encourage and restrict trade and economic relations. The allocation of chapters between the two Nutshells reflects our value judgments as to what ought to be included in introductory volumes on a very broad subject, one which is constantly affected by change. These judgments will be familiar to those who have read or adopted our *International Business Transactions: A Problem-Oriented Coursebook*, originally published in 1986, with many new editions since then.

Prof. Folsom has also written a much more detailed Concise Hornbook on *Principles of International Trade Law*. Profs. Folsom, Van Alstine and Ramsey expect to complete a new edition of the Concise Hornbook on *Principles of International Business Transactions* towards the end of 2016.

We have been aided by colleagues at our own law schools and others both in this country and abroad, by student research assistants and by persons in practice. Prof. Folsom welcomes continued suggestions for the next edition of this Nutshell.

RALPH H. FOLSOM
RFOLSOM@SANDIEGO.EDU

January 2016

ABOUT THE AUTHOR

Ralph H. Folsom has been a Professor at the University of San Diego School of Law since 1975. A graduate of Princeton University, Yale Law School and the London School of Economics (LLM), Professor Folsom teaches, writes and consults extensively in the field of international business law.

Folsom has been a Senior Fulbright resident scholar in Singapore and a Visiting Professor at the University of Hong Kong, University of Aix-Marseille, University of Brest, University of Paris, University of Toulouse, University of Puerto Rico, Monash University in Australia and Tecnológico de Monterrey in México.

Professor Folsom has authored or co-authored a range of books with West Academic Publishing. These include course books on: *International Business Transactions*; *IBT: International Trade and Economic Relations*; *IBT: Foreign Investment Law*; *IBT: Contracting Across Borders*.

He is the author or co-author of other West Academic Nutshells, including the Nutshells on *International Business Transactions* (co-authored), *NAFTA—Free Trade and Foreign Investment in The Americas*, *Foreign Investment Law (forthcoming)*, and *European Union Law*.

Professor Folsom has also written more extensively than Nutshells permit in the West

Concise Hornbook Series: *Principles of International Litigation and Arbitration, Principles of European Union Law, Principles of International Trade Law, and Principles of International Business Transactions* (co-authored).

OUTLINE

TABLE OF CASES

References are to Pages

INTERNATIONAL TRADE AND ECONOMIC RELATIONS

IN A NUTSHELL®

SIXTH EDITION

INTRODUCTION

Three hypothetical transactions, originally created by Prof. Michael Gordon, illustrate the often unanticipated role of international trade and economic relations law:

THE STATE TRANSACTION:

PARTS FROM SALEM ARE MADE INTO GOODS IN BOSTON FOR SALE IN BROCKTON

THE UNITED STATES TRANSACTION:

PARTS FROM SAN FRANCISCO ARE MADE INTO GOODS IN BOSTON FOR SALE IN BURBANK

THE INTERNATIONAL TRANSACTION:

PARTS FROM SINGAPORE ARE MADE INTO GOODS IN BOSTON FOR SALE IN BRASILIA AND BOMBAY

The Boston Client

Representing a Boston client who (1) manufactures goods, for example children's clothing and knapsacks, for sale to numerous retail store buyers in the United States, for example in Brockton and Burbank, and who (2) purchases the parts for such products from U.S. sellers, for example in Salem and San Francisco, usually does not involve the application of U.S. trade law governing imports and exports. That is true whether the transaction is exclusively in one state, or involves more than one and perhaps many states.

But if our Boston client is an "international" company—it sells and buys where it can obtain the best price. That means it sells to and buys from parties in foreign nations as well as in the United States. Consequently, U.S. trade law affecting *exports* is applicable when our Boston client sells the goods abroad, for example to buyers in Brasilia and Bombay. U.S. trade law affecting *imports* is applicable when our Boston client purchases parts for the manufacture of its products from Singapore or Sao Paulo.

In each case, importing or exporting, our client must be familiar with the characteristics of competition on an international scale. The client assumes different risks and becomes subject to different laws. Those laws are not only U.S. laws but the laws affecting imports and exports of the foreign nations in which our client does business. Such foreign laws may include rules which appear to exist solely to protect domestic industries. There may be high tariffs, or quotas, or a vast array of nontariff barriers affecting our client's exports, such as packaging or labeling requirements, safety certification or compliance with health standards.

But that also may be how the foreign buyer or seller views the laws of the United States. The United States is not exempt from creating nontariff barriers. The Boston client's importers (buyers) in

Brasilia or Bombay may be charged with dumping the Boston sourced goods on the local market, or benefitting from U.S. subsidies. The Boston client may not believe it is acting unfairly in selling to buyers in Brasilia or Bombay, but it has become subject to protective legislation in these foreign nations.

Just as it may be the target in one case, our client may shoot the arrows in another. If the Boston client is unable to sell to its old buyers in Brockton or Burbank, because Singapore or Sao Paulo sellers are not only selling parts to our client, but also selling finished products in competition directly to the Brockton or Burbank buyers, the U.S. trade laws may help our client. This is not because our client is an international trader, but because it is a *domestic* entity which is part of an industry injured or threatened with injury by the foreign goods. The same laws might help a U.S. company which has never engaged and has no intention of engaging in international trade: Enter the Bartow client.

The Bartow Client

Assume that in the small town of Bartow, Florida, a company employs about thirty people and for decades has manufactured a variety of textile products for sale solely in Florida from material produced in North Carolina. It makes children's clothing and knapsacks, just as does the Boston entity described above. But unlike our Boston client, the Bartow entity does not sell abroad. It does not even sell in Georgia! Its owners and employees work hard in meeting the demand for its products in Florida. It pays fair, but not excessive, wages. Management is very cost conscious, but believes the company can compete with anything produced by companies subject to the same rules of minimum wages, pollution controls, workshop safety, social security, etc.

Two problems have arisen in the past few months, which have involuntarily thrust this small town enterprise into being a participant in international trade. A large Florida department store chain, which had bought its clothing for years from the Bartow entity, informed the company that it was dropping its line of products and replacing them with nearly identical products manufactured by parties in Singapore and Sao Paulo. These are the same foreign sellers that the Boston client has claimed are causing it harm. The foreign made clothing costs the Florida retail chain 40 percent less than they had been paying the Bartow manufacturer.

The second concern arose when the company was asked by a local tourist attraction to bid on the manufacture of 1,000 children's knapsacks in the form of dolphins. The company wanted the job and cut its profit to a narrower margin than it normally accepted. When it presented the design and the bid to the buyer it was told the same knapsacks could be had for half the price in Singapore or Sao Paulo.

United States Import Remedies

Why is it possible that the prices could be so low? Both the Boston and the Bartow companies are clearly being injured by these imports. Further inquiry may disclose similar injury to the U.S. children's clothing and knapsack industries as a whole, rather than to just these two domestic companies. Perhaps the products were being subsidized by the foreign governments. That may allow the Boston or Bartow companies to request that the U.S. government commence an investigation under U.S. trade laws, which may conclude that subsidies were present and there was material injury, or a threat of such injury, consequently calling for the imposition of countervailing tariff duties.

Or the foreign companies may be dumping (in contrast to the foreign governments providing subsidies) the products on the U.S. market. If they are doing so, meaning selling their products for "less than fair value" (the price for which they are sold in the foreign domestic market where they are manufactured), the U.S. government may begin an investigation. If it is concluded that dumping was present and there was material injury, or a threat of such injury, there may be an imposition of antidumping duties.

If the source of the foreign goods were Shanghai, where there may be an inadequate market economy cost analysis, it may be very difficult to establish the presence of subsidies, or sales at less than fair value to establish dumping. If China is defined as a nonmarket economy, and that seems less likely with each passing year, another section of the U.S. trade laws may allow the Boston or Bartow companies to challenge the Shanghai products without proof of dumping or subsidies, essentially because they come from a nation with a political system we do not regard with favor. This action, called a "market disruption" or Section 406 action, has been used infrequently in the past for foreign policy reasons. It will diminish in use even more as nonmarket nations move along the path towards market economies with democratic governments.

If a surge of the foreign goods is from one of the vast majority of market economy nations, and if they cause or threaten *serious* as opposed to *material* injury to the U.S. industry, the Boston or Bartow company may make use of the U.S. safeguard or Section 201 "escape clause" action provision to limit their entry. But how the U.S. government responds to a domestic company's claim of injury from foreign competition may be based more on political relations with the foreign nation than an accurate interpretation of the U.S. law. The Boston or Bartow company may correctly feel it is more a pawn in international politics than a player in international business.

For example, the United States may not wish to irritate the government of Singapore if it is helping the United States open more air routes in Asia to American carriers, or to irritate the government of Brazil if the two nations are close to a settlement of a longstanding dispute over intellectual property protection, or to irritate the government of China if there are sensitive negotiations over the use of prison labor or freeing a political dissident.

The Bartow company never intended to engage in international trade. It has not. **It still sells nothing abroad.** But it is fearful that soon it will sell nothing in Florida as well. Its officials and lawyers must learn about international business and trade law if the company is to survive, or even if it is not to survive, to provide its former employees with U.S. trade adjustment assistance made available to companies which lose out to foreign competition. For more on the law of import restraints, see Chapter 3, and more on import trade remedies for domestic parties, see Chapter 4.

Global Trade Law

Although there are significant variations in the trade laws and economic relations of different nations, for most nations there are some accepted norms. Roughly 160 trading nations are members of the World Trade Organization (WTO), the successor to the General Agreement on Tariffs and Trade (GATT). Since its formation at the end of World War II, the GATT/WTO has grown in membership, significantly reduced tariffs, and worked towards abolishing many nontariff trade barriers. The rules noted above of various nations which allow countervailing duty, dumping and safeguard (escape clause) actions all have some of their roots in the GATT/WTO. Hence, exports by either of the U.S. companies may encounter exactly the same international trade remedies in, say, Brazil or India.

Beyond these areas, the WTO "package" of 1994 agreements covers many relevant issues: Customs law, trade quotas, agricultural products, health regulation of foods, textiles and clothing (hello Boston and Bartow!), technical product regulations, trade in services, trade-related intellectual property rights and dispute settlement. These agreements are reviewed in Chapter 2.

Our client, whether it is the Boston or Bartow entity, is likely to be more interested in stopping the foreign competition or foreign application of trade remedies than in how it is stopped. Domestically, it may make little difference whether the action chosen is against foreign subsidies, dumping, surges of imports, market disruption, or any other actionable activity under any part of U.S. trade law. It is the end result the client wishes to achieve, a reduction or elimination of the allegedly "unfair" foreign competition.

The path to that result will be the recommended course of action suggested by the client's counsel. Thus counsel must know about the full array of choices available under the U.S. trade laws, and (if U.S. exports are involved) how to defend against trade remedies in foreign jurisdictions.

Economic Status

The identity of the foreign country as developed or developing, and as market or nonmarket, is thus important to the application of the appropriate trade law provisions. China's economic status, often referred to as "socialism with Chinese characteristics," is especially controversial. Regarding U.S. imports, the choice may differ depending on the nature of the foreign nation's economic and political characterization. *Developed* nations do use barriers to imports and offer subsidies to exports. They tend to be fewer in number and often are more sophisticated than barriers or subsidies in developing nations. *Developing* nations may use a greater variety of trade barriers, and justify them because they are developing economically. Trade organizations such as the WTO may grant developing nations special rights to impose barriers against imports, or assist exports.

Nonmarket economy nations (NMEs) by definition lack market economy characteristics and may substantially subsidize industry. The United States originally did not allow countervailing duty actions to be brought against imports from a nonmarket economy nation because the subsidies of those nations were deemed not "countervailable" under U.S. law. That position, after several U.S. Supreme Court cases, was repudiated by an act of Congress in 2012.

There are fewer nonmarket economies today than a decade ago, and many nonmarket economies are in a stage of transition to market economies. Thus there may be a question regarding the nature of the foreign economy. It may be both a developing and a nonmarket economy. It may be an advanced developing country (ADC) or newly industrializing country (NIC), but still be a nonmarket economy. It may be a nonmarket economy trying to become a market economy, but having difficulty overcoming decades of state central planning and government involvement in the production and distribution of goods. Or it may be a nonmarket economy which finds it necessary to do business with market economies and opens the door to market economy characteristics only enough to achieve specific goals. You might ask yourself where China fits in this picture.

Export Controls

Most of these comments have involved restrictions on imports. U.S. restrictions on imports would help our Boston client in so far as it is a seller of its products within the United States to buyers in Brockton or Burbank, but might hurt that client if the imports of components for its production from Singapore or Sao Paulo are restricted and cause it to buy higher priced U.S. components from Salem or San Francisco.

Some reference has also been made to controls on exports. To the extent that such controls exist in the United States, and limit our Boston client from exporting to buyers in Brasilia or Bombay, our client would be harmed. If export controls are imposed by the governments in Singapore or Sao Paulo on the components our client needs, it may have to buy them at higher prices from Salem or San Francisco. Unlike import trade remedies, which have been harmonized through the WTO, export control laws tend to be uniquely national in character.

Export controls usually are not imposed for the same reasons as import controls, with the exception that some nations, mainly developing countries, may tax both imports and exports as a revenue raising device. But the United States and many other nations usually limit exports for such reasons as national security, foreign policy goals, or scarcity of certain domestic resources. Most nations encourage exports, often providing incentives, and often engaging in assistance which may constitute unfair trade such as subsidies.

Because export controls often are intended to serve political goals, the executive may be given considerable discretion in imposing export limitations to certain nations. In the United States, conflict between the Congress, which believes it has authority over all aspects of foreign commerce, and the President, who believes the executive has control over all aspects of foreign policy, has led to frequent conflict and an inability to enact new export laws.

Our Boston client may be prohibited from exporting some or all of its products to all nations, or may be prohibited from exporting anything to specific nations. Export controls are thus designed to limit certain goods to any nation, or limit any goods to certain nations, or certain goods to certain nations. To assure compliance, exports may have to have a license.

The export rules in the United States long divided licenses for the most part between *general* and *validated* licenses. General licenses did not require an application to and approval by the government, only furnishing certain information upon export which was useful for compiling trade statistics. Validated licenses required an application to and permission from the Department of Commerce, often with the scrutiny and sometimes inordinate delay of approval by the Department of Defense.

The end of the Cold War, the movement of many nonmarket economy nations towards democracy and market economics, and the realization by many developing nations that joining the developed world was more promising than leading the third world, encouraged the United States to adopt a simpler export control scheme. The complex matrix of licenses noted above was replaced in 1996 by a scheme intended to be more U.S. exporter-friendly. See Chapter 5.

Our Boston client may have decided that the maze of laws and regulations in those areas where it has sold its products, such as Brasilia and Bombay, or increasingly perhaps Beijing, is so extensive that the only way to penetrate that market is to establish a direct foreign investment. It might also choose to transfer technology to a domestic manufacturer in one or more of those areas. But it may feel that to maximize profits, technology transfers across borders or foreign investment abroad are the best alternatives. These alternative transactions are covered in the *IBT Nutshell*.

Regional and Bilateral Trade Law

Suppose your Boston client gets an order to ship its goods to Brussels, and your Bartow client an order to ship its goods to British Columbia. The domestic laws of Belgium and Canada will affect such trading, and so will the laws of the European Union and the

NAFTA. Preferential agreements are rapidly expanding around the globe, a veritable "spaghetti bowl" of trade laws. Did we mention that Brazil belongs to the MERCOSUR customs union and Singapore now has free trade agreements with the United States, Japan and others? And India is pushing ahead inside the South Asian Free Trade Area.

The range of laws and economic relations you must consider in advising your clients just expanded beyond domestic and international law to include bilateral and regional law, the framework within which free trade agreements and customs unions frequently operate. Naturally there are variations on the theme, with the European Union and NAFTA serving as prototypes. This Nutshell will introduce you to bilateral and regional trade law in Chapters 6, 7 and 8.

What follows in the material ahead is an introduction to the laws and policies, the organizations and entities, and the people involved in international trade and economic relations. This Nutshell will cover government imposed restrictions on imports and exports; the GATT and the WTO; free trade agreements and customs unions; and regional economic integration with an emphasis on the European Union and the North American Free Trade Agreement.

CHAPTER 1

WORLD TRADE AND MULTINATIONAL ENTERPRISES

Trade Patterns   Transfer Pricing
MNE Operations   MNE Corporate Counsel

The United States is one of a few central players in the world of international trade. It has engaged in foreign trade from the moment of its independence over two centuries ago. Indeed, one of the reasons independence was sought was England's imposition of severe restrictions on trade between the colonies and foreign nations, intended to preserve the benefits of international trade for England.

Less than two centuries from achieving independence, the United States became the leading trade power in the world. For over a decade after World War II, the United States was in the envious and economically advantageous position of being the major center of production of finished goods for export. But with extraordinary economic growth in Japan and Europe, by the 1980s the United States no longer dominated world trade. It had to compete for sales abroad, and also in the domestic market within the United States. Traditional surpluses in the balance of trade with most nations in some cases began to be reversed. The United States has had to deal with increasingly large trade deficits with

Japan, and more recently, the most challenging trade partner—China.

The trade surplus of earlier decades has become a trade deficit of disturbing proportions. The deficit status of U.S. international trade in the 1990s and into the new millennium caused trade to be a topic of common conversation. The U.S. trade deficit is often perceived as threatening jobs for American workers and the consequent diminishment of quality of life of the American people. This has generated annual Congressional proposals of an increasingly restrictive nature. U.S. exports have continued to grow, especially in the service and technology areas, but imports have grown more rapidly. Even the periodic fall of the dollar, making U.S. exports cheaper, has not reversed the deficit.

The importance of trade and its underlying economic relations should be apparent. But the huge capacity of the United States to consume foreign products is out of balance with its ability to find reciprocal consumption for its exports. That is due to many reasons, including problems of quality, real and perceived, problems of barriers to trade imposed by every nation, and problems of government leadership. Those who view the United States from abroad continually point to excessive consumption and inadequate savings, and to the budget deficit, as the principal reasons for the deteriorating U.S. trade position. Congress and the administration hear the complaints, but make few corrections. It is easier to blame other nations. After all, the United States still generates a formidable share of world trade and will continue to do so for a while longer.

Even individual states have remarkable trade statistics. California alone generates billions of dollars of world trade, making its "gross state product" greater than the gross national products of all but a few nations of the world. In the last few years, however, the per capita standard of living of several other nations has reached and exceeded that in the United States. The periodic issuance of impressive aggregate trade figures from Washington tends to mask an ebbing and equalizing status and role for the U.S. in the world community. Status as an economic power is gained slowly when the nation's energy is directed towards the production and distribution of goods, services and technology, but can be lost quickly when that energy is directed more to producing self-serving statistics than a tangible trade surplus.

PATTERNS OF WORLD TRADE AND ECONOMIC RELATIONS

Trade traditionally has been measured by the exchange of tangible goods, both raw materials and finished products. The prominence of oil as a trading commodity, and the economic power exerted in the 1970s by the Organization of Petroleum Exporting Countries (OPEC), resulted in a considerable shift of wealth caused by remarkable changes in the price of a single commodity. The power of OPEC diminished in the 1980s and 1990s due to an oversupply of oil and conflict both within the oil industry and within

OPEC. Since the millennium, OPEC power and oil prices first rose and then collapsed with the advent of "fracking" techniques that have generated substantial amounts of U.S. oil and gas production.

Energy remains the ultimately important global commodity. It played a critical role in the decision of the United States to commence the Gulf and Iraq Wars, and more recently to become engaged in the war against ISIS in the Middle East. Extractable raw materials remain the principal source of wealth for many nations. Nations which produce many natural and agricultural resources, from tin to bananas, have attempted to create cartels which will give them control of their economic destiny.

Services Trade

In recent years attention on items of trade and therefore value has shifted from an exclusive focus on tangibles and technology, to an area of trade and economic relations far more difficult to define. That area is trade in services such as advertising, banking, insurance, accounting, consulting, entertainment, construction, tourism and the vast area of computer services. Cross-border trade in legal services also makes a contribution, particularly by large multinational U.S. law firms. U.S. trade in these "invisibles" is measured in billions annually. Trade in tangibles is marred by an increasing deficit, but U.S. trade in services is marked by an increasing surplus.

Many other nations are eager to develop their own services, and to protect them from encroachment by the developed nations. The negotiations in the Uruguay Round on trade in services were an especially difficult part of the overall trade talks. The industrialized nations, led by the United States, for the most part successfully negotiated lowering trade barriers to services, over the objections of such important developing nations as India and Brazil. These nations fear dominance in ownership of services by the industrialized nations.

The final agreement, the General Agreement on Trade in Services (the GATS), reflected many restrictions and reservations by developing nations determined to establish and maintain their own service sectors. The ability of the WTO to govern trade in services is critical to keeping service-oriented nations like the United States a supporter of this important multilateral trade regulating organization.

The Rise of Asia

Viewing the constantly changing world trade patterns as they have developed to this moment, the dominance of the United States which was prevalent decades ago has diminished substantially and is unlikely to reoccur. This trend is attributable to the prominence of Japan in manufacturing and designing products which meet current consumer demands, to the entry of China and re-entry of India in the world trade arena, to the cooperation of the European nations within the European Union, and to the movement through successive stages of development of many nations, especially the "Four

Dragons" or "Four Tigers" of Asia—Hong Kong,
South Korea, Singapore and Taiwan.

Increased "world market share" is the goal of every
nation, and nations joust over international trade
issues. Asian nations, like others, closely regulate
foreign investment coming into the country, and
create trade incentives to stimulate greater exports
to other countries.

The spectacular success of Japan and China as
exporters combined with a creativity to block imports
has led to a sequence of protests and threats of
sanctions by the United States and the European
Union. However accurately Japan or China may be
accused of being unfair traders and of using a host of
regulatory nontariff trade barriers (NTBs) to keep
foreign goods and investment out, the United States
often fails to consider that trade imbalances may be
as much caused by domestic failures as by foreign
intransigence.

Nontariff Trade Barriers

Japan and China are not alone in using nontariff
regulatory barriers, such as environmental rules and
product and health safety laws. NTBs have arisen to
protect domestic industry as the earlier protection by
high tariffs has diminished via GATT, WTO and free
trade negotiations. Every nation has developed its
own methods of keeping imports at bay.

The United States, for example, has employed
agricultural quotas and environmental/conservation
regulations in this manner. The French provoked a

stream of protest by requiring that documentation for imported goods be written in French. France established a "consultative commission for international trade" charged to watch for "abnormal" and excessive imports and unfair export practices of other countries. Meaning, of course, an agency for domestic business to complain to when affected by imports, regardless of their own efficiency in production. In the United States, similar complaints are filed with the Office of the U.S. Trade Representative.

Other nations have responded in various ways to the impact of imports. Restricted by their agreements to specific tariff levels as members of the WTO, they have carried nontariff barriers to a new height of originality. These barriers may assume the form of health or safety standards, packing or labeling requirements, and many other rules which may in theory seem justified, but in practice are structured or interpreted so as to eliminate or reduce imports and benefit domestic industries.

Lawyers retained to deal with these nontariff barriers, as well as subsidies, dumping or rules of origin, have become the major beneficiaries of these complex trade laws. They alone know how to work through the maze of details in lengthy definitions included in trade laws and multilateral agreements. For example, foreign targets of a U.S. dumping charge must expend enormous resources responding to such charges, thus making these actions themselves another form of nontariff barrier.

Trade Incentives

Goods which are sold in one nation are not necessarily either goods produced domestically by locally owned manufacturers, or goods produced abroad by foreign owned manufacturers. They may be goods produced *domestically* by *foreign* owned manufacturers. Or they may be goods produced *abroad* by domestic manufacturers.

Investing abroad is an alternative to exporting goods abroad. Foreign investment shares some benefits of trade. The foreign manufacturer receives the profit, but the host nation of the foreign investment obtains jobs and technology. Raw materials or parts may be sent by the foreign manufacturer, to create what is little more than an assembly plant in the host nation, or raw materials and parts may be purchased in the host nation, adding to the benefits of permitting investment owned by foreign entities. See R. Folsom, *Foreign Investment Law in a Nutshell.*

While trying to hold imports to reasonable levels, every nation wants to be a major exporter. It is, after all, exports that provide the means to pay for imports. The urge to export leads to another scheme of laws. They are usually laws of encouragement in contrast to laws of discouragement which typify the import rules. They may be fashioned in the way of granting tax benefits, offering export financing or insurance, overlooking trade restraint elements of permitted export cartels, or tying permitted imports to the level of exports.

The United States, for example, in enacting the 1982 Export Trading Company Act (ETC) followed the practice of nations such as Japan in assisting exporters. The ETC Act was designed to permit small and medium U.S. firms to gain information about foreign trade opportunities and techniques, and to have easier access to financing for export activity. In 2015, there was strident debate over renewing U.S. Export-Import (EXIM) Bank funding, much of which has benefited U.S. multinationals such as Boeing and GE.

The Legal Framework of Trade

Every nation which engages in international economic relations develops a legal framework defining its role. That framework will consist of domestic trade laws, including its acceptance of international laws regulating cross-border transactions, and participation in international organizations which also establish trade rules. The United States has developed by legislative and executive action an extensive set of domestic rules governing international trade. It has also been a major participant in many organizations which influence or govern trade.

The World Trade Organization, successor to the GATT, is by far the most important such organization. The United Nations has played a disappointingly minor role in trade, although UNCITRAL, the United Nations Commission on International Trade Law, has become an important forum for the harmonization of rules affecting trade, such as the Convention on International Sale of Goods (CISG).

Regional economic relations have also increased trade among groups of nations. The European Union and the NAFTA are the two most important areas which have reduced barriers to internal trade, although sometimes at the expense of increasing barriers to external trade. Free trade and customs union agreements have been proliferating. But however important may be participation in bilateral or multilateral trade agreements or organizations, the will of a single participant to abide by freer trade rules will be expressed in its domestic trade laws and policies. It is under such national laws that multinational enterprises operate.

THE MULTINATIONAL ENTERPRISE (MNE)

One important and controversial business form engaging in international trade is the multinational enterprise (MNE). Indeed, "intra-corporate" trade within a family of MNE companies comprises a very significant share of "international" trade. The most visible MNEs are the largest multinational corporations engaged in business over decades in every sector of the globe. The MNE may also be one of several less structured business forms, such as partnerships and joint ventures, used in business of short duration in only a few places in the world. A transaction may be an international business transaction whether the principal players come from private enterprise, from national or local government, or from a combination of both private enterprise and government.

The MNE has aroused concern and prompted new regulatory attempts by governments, acting singly and in concert. Although history may not yet identify the MNE as having been a primary catalyst in pressing diverse and proud countries into a measure of sustained global economic order, the utility and proper role of the MNE have engendered vigorous debate involving much unclear data.

Since 1976 the industrialized member countries within the Organization for Economic Cooperation and Development (OECD) have published a Code of Conduct for Multinationals which sets forth voluntary guidelines for appropriate enterprise behavior. With interpretative assistance of the OECD Investment Committee, MNEs operating within the forty or so OECD member countries are being encouraged to speed compliance with Code provisions dealing with disclosure of enterprise information, employment and industrial relations, and taxation and transfer pricing.

Representatives from the member countries of the International Institute for the Unification of Private Law (UNIDROIT) worked on an international trade law code regarding the formation and interpretation of contracts, especially leasing agreements. The European Union favors regulating MNE activity on a sector basis, such as in areas of company law, taxation, and employment policy.

International regulation of MNEs shows every prospect of increasing, in part due to the role illicit MNE payments play in generating public demand for closer regulation. Often such payments are a fact of international commercial life, whether they are characterized as "advertising expenses", "commissions", or more simply as "grease" or "bribes". The OECD has reached agreement on rules intended to regulate this kind of behavior, significantly resulting in the U.K. Bribery Act of 2010. This Act in many ways makes the controversial U.S. Foreign Corrupt Practices Act of 1977 look tame.

Business enterprises from the United States are seriously constrained by the 1977 Foreign Corrupt Practices Act. Amendments to the Act in 1988 removed the controversial basis for liability when the MNE had "reason to know" that some of their payments through intermediaries would end up in the hands of foreign officials. Further amendments in 1998, as a result of signing the OECD Convention on Combating Bribery of Foreign Officials, tightened definitions of wrongful conduct.

MNE FINANCIAL PRACTICES, TRANSFER PRICING

Affiliated parts of a multinational enterprise often deal with each other across national borders. Since the enterprise as a whole has goals which each part seeks to assist in achieving, intra-corporate dealings may be structured to achieve favorable tax or dividend consequences ("tax efficiency"). The MNE effectively reallocates costs and revenues within its worldwide structure so that profits are increased where tax and exchange controls are considered favorable, and decreased where taxes and controls are considered most severe. This is transfer pricing.

Host nations sometimes impose limits on profits that may be remitted abroad by a foreign investor's local operations. The MNE may seek to offset the effect of these limits on profit remittances. The foreign parent may attempt to charge more for technology transferred to the affiliate, or for raw materials or components sold to the foreign affiliate. Such "trade-based" transfer pricing is estimated to facilitate an outflow of over a trillion dollars annually from developing nations. The core technique is overvaluing import or undervaluing export invoices.

The host nation may respond by limiting amounts which may be paid for technology, or by demanding that the raw materials or components be obtained locally. Developing nations have strongly objected to MNEs' transfer pricing practices when the result appears to be very low or no profits in the developing nation, but the MNE parent appears to be profitable.

Why has the MNE done this? Typically, because the developing nation imposes high taxes on profits. Or because there are limits on profit remittances due to exchange controls, which are more lenient or do not exist for technology transfers, or for permitted imports of raw materials or components. What may anger the developing nation even more, and also local shareholders when the MNE has agreed to a joint venture, is when the same transfer pricing practices lead to few profits to distribute as dividends to the local shareholders.

It is not only developing nations which object to artificial transfer pricing practices. Australia, Canada, Japan and the United States formed the Pacific Association of Tax Administrators to combat transfer pricing's possible inter-relationship with tax evasion. Developing country monitoring of transfer pricing has not been very effective, partly because of a reluctance of the developed nations to participate in joint efforts which might transfer tax revenue away from the United States, and partly because much intra-corporate transfer information is regarded as confidential.

The Organization for Economic Cooperation and Development (OECD) has been developing transfer pricing guidelines for multinational companies for decades. Transfer pricing has also been addressed by individual countries. Within the United States, the IRS has issued regulations under Section 482 of the Internal Revenue Code. These regulations impose penalties for intercompany pricing not conducted under the regulation's arm's-length standards, which adopt a "best method" rule. IRS practices have been criticized as arbitrary and unreasonable. But the IRS claims companies do not properly calculate transfer prices. The Tax Court has had to resolve these conflicts, and is likely to be a frequent player as the IRS steps up its attack on what it considers improper transfer pricing.

Mexico has transfer pricing rules affecting its assembly industries or maquiladoras. Many foreign companies have used fees for services and transfer pricing resulting in almost no Mexican profits. The government has not traditionally enforce provisions of the Mexican Tax Code which would have required maquiladoras to recognize some level of profit. The reason has been to protect jobs and the entire program itself, but the government could demand taxes on an arm's-length basis for the services performed by the maquiladoras.

More recently, Mexico has established minimum maquiladora profit levels as "safe harbors" under its Tax Code. Most firms have moved to take advantage of them, thereby reducing tax risk exposure in Mexico. The experience of the United States and Mexico illustrate how different nations may pursue problems of transfer pricing, from a vigorous attack on the practice to minimal payments to promote social goals, such as job creation.

Finally, a word about illegal multinational enterprises engaged in arms smuggling, drug trafficking, terrorism or public corruption. Like legitimate MNE, these multinationals lace the globe in their operations and extensively engage in trade-related money laundering via transfer pricing on trade in legal goods. One study, for example, suggests that Mexican on the whole exports are over-priced by 15 to 20% as a way to move dollars into the country. The Sinaloa cartel laundered some of its dollar profits by exporting toys, food and silk into the USA. Another drug operation charged $970 while exporting plastic buckets to America.

Over-pricing to get money into sanctioned countries like Iran, try $240 for a pound of sugar, helped bring hard currency to Iranian banks and unlock frozen overseas bank accounts. India's official exports to the Bahamas, went up 1000%, yes 1000%, prior to a tax transparency agreement between the two countries as assets were removed from undeclared Bahamian accounts. Exports from China to Hong Kong, and Hong Kong to China, routinely reflect the desire to move money from one to the other.

THE ROLE OF CORPORATE COUNSEL TO A MNE

The role of corporate counsel (in-house counsel) to a MNE is not fundamentally different professionally from that of any other brand of lawyer in relation to a client, though an added emphasis on legal "risk management" is common. Unlike many other lawyers, however, counsel is also in a team member relationship with MNE management personnel. Counsel has an employment obligation to support the MNE management structure. Counsel's corporate legal function may be viewed as one vehicle through which headquarters control is exercised over affiliated, sub-parts of the MNE.

The access to information and exclusive knowledge of information possessed by counsel are visible and substantial parts of the power dimension of MNE global management. For example, counsel's working relationship with foreign assisting counsel in each country where the MNE operates, and that assisting counsel's working relationship with the principal, MNE line management person within each country, play a substantial role in MNE headquarters control and financial success.

If the principal line management person within each country is willing to explore legal aspects of new business ideas with the assisting counsel in that country, and if assisting counsel has a close reporting and consultative relationship with MNE headquarters counsel, chances increase for the "preventive" side of legal practice to help in shaping management decisions and to reduce large, unanticipated legal costs at a later time. The success of counsel's communication with management may generate an ad hoc assignment to a line management function in connection with particular MNE business transactions.

Such closeness can also raise ethical considerations which intersect with counsel's professional responsibilities as a lawyer. For example, currency control measures prevent MNE revenues from being remitted. Moreover, the rate of monetary inflation may be such that revenues left there are subject to substantial devaluation. There is an acute ethical problem for counsel, as a lawyer, who considers the idea that funds might be carried secretly into neighboring countries and then exchanged for hard currency and remitted for deposit in a jurisdiction where inflation is not severe.

Corporate line managers are charged with providing needed revenues. Corporate counsel are engaged principally in minimizing legal "overhead" costs of the corporation. Did they teach you how to be an effective cost manager in law school?

In addition, requests by line management to put recurring types of company agreements into "standard form" contracts must be squared with the reality of enforcing those contracts in different legal systems with divergent views about the sanctity of contracts. Counsel may assist in securing approvals from governmental regulatory bodies or persons charged with overseeing MNE activity, and often must testify on the MNE's behalf before people who need not listen at all or who may only care to listen in an abbreviated way. Many current presidents of corporations in the United States are lawyers and have served as corporate counsel before being appointed president. You might consider how the following hypothetical day for corporate counsel helps prepare lawyers to become MNE presidents.

A HYPOTHETICAL DAY FOR MNE CORPORATE COUNSEL

By way of hypothetical illustration, a typical office day for corporate counsel to a MNE might include work on problems such as: Senegal has served notice that a MNE's revenues worldwide will be taxed unitarily irrespective of the MNE's tax posture in other countries; the MNE's use of its trade name in Mexico is impeded by a "prior use" problem; a Uruguayan appeals court has held that the MNE's trademark is generic and thus not subject to legal protection; a line management employee of the MNE's Austrian subsidiary company needs an "L" visa to spend some time at the MNE's headquarters offices in the United States; new advertising from the MNE's marketing department has possible legal implications if placed in newspapers throughout Europe; reports of resale price maintenance agreements being made by certain companies in Transylvania and Neverland need to be checked in light of antitrust implications under U.S. and EU law.

Moreover, the MNE's products stolen in Hamburg must be traced through INTERPOL; ways must be explored to get blocked currencies from New Country to the MNE's headquarters in the United States; testimony needs to be prepared for presentation to an environmental control authority in Germany; a presentation must be made to the transportation commissioner of the Province of Ontario to secure permits to increase haulage capacity of the MNE's subsidiary company in Canada; charges of employee discrimination in the Far Islands need to be answered; sale-leaseback agreements need to be negotiated in Sydney; a company needs to be formed for tax protection in the Unusual Islands; and an expropriation in Venezuela requires attention.

The Philippine and Saudi Arabian governments want to increase their equity participation in all existing MNE's joint ventures; certain inquiries by the U.S. Federal Trade Commission need to be answered; someone from the American Bar Association wants counsel to serve on an international trade committee; all standard form contracts used by the MNE and its subsidiary companies are due for another review; line management people are interested in hearing ideas about ways to avoid legal problems, especially transfer pricing and corruption issues, in connection with their proposals for new trade activity.

CHAPTER 2
GLOBAL TRADE LAW

| Trade Treaties | GATT 1947 | The WTO |
| WTO Agreements and Disputes | | The IMF |

International trade law has a long and controversial history. Many nations, especially in their early stages of development, are fearful of trade across borders. International trade is a competitive force, one that typically shakes up domestic economic interests. It is a powerful engine of change, creating winners and losers in its path. The law of international trade, for better or worse, shapes the scope and direction of this force.

The United States in its early years sheltered "infant" agricultural and industrial sectors behind protective tariffs and regulatory restraints. When the Great Depression of the 1930s arrived, the United States enacted highly protective tariffs under the Smoot-Hawley Tariff Act of 1930 intended to wall off its economy from foreign competition, in theory "saving American jobs for American citizens." Other nations around the world retreated from international trade through similarly protective laws. Fear of foreign trade (and foreigners) reached a zenith that most economists agree deepened and prolonged the Great Depression.

World War II rescued the United States from the Depression, but did nothing to remove the Smoot-

Hawley tariffs and encourage other nations to do likewise. International trade law was at a crossroads.

Despite its economic power and leadership in the development of modern trade law, the United States retains some of its early fear and concerns about international commerce. This is particularly apparent when U.S. free trade agreements are debated and undertaken, but also when the U.S. controls exports of goods and technology. Little wonder then that developing nations, many not much more than 50 years old and created out of colonial empires, hesitate to embrace the panoply of modern international trade law.

Some developed nations are unusually dependent on international trade in goods and services. The Netherlands, for example, depends on exports for over 75% of their Gross Domestic product (GDP). Roughly 50% of the GDPs of Sweden, Germany and Switzerland derive from exports. Canada, New Zealand, France and Britain come in at about 25%, with the United States at approximately 12%.

The need to balance the protection of local industries from harm by foreign competitors and the encouragement of trade across national borders is a recurrent theme in the law of international economic relations. There has been a shift in recent years toward freer international trade because of diminished restrictions on imported goods. However, trade problems associated with the movement of goods across national borders still arise because of restrictive trade devices which impede or distort trade.

Common devices include tariff barriers (e.g., import duties and export duties) as well as certain nontariff trade barriers (NTBs) such as import quotas, import licensing procedures, safety, environmental and other minimum manufacturing standards, import testing requirements, complex customs procedures (including valuation), government procurement policies, and government subsidies or countervailing measures.

For example, France once required that all video recorders entering the country had to do so through a small customs post at Poitiers and carry documentation written in French. Product distribution practices have been an effective NTB in Japan. For example, the Japanese have banned from importation food preservatives essential to preserve the edibility of certain agricultural products from abroad.

TRADE TREATIES

Early efforts by countries to limit disruptive trade practices were commonly found in bilateral treaties of friendship, commerce and navigation (FCN). More recently, bilateral and regional trade treaties, open the territory of signatory nations to imports. Such treaties are usually linked to other preferential trade agreements, most often through a reciprocal "most favored nation" (MFN) clause. In a MFN clause, both parties agree not to extend to any other nation trade arrangements which are more favorable than available under the treaty, unless the more favorable trade arrangements are immediately *also* available to the other signatory of the treaty.

At this point, the United States has moved beyond many of its FCN treaties to bilateral Trade and Investment Framework Agreements (TIFAs), Free Trade Agreements (FTAs) and Bilateral Investment Treaties (BITs). Lists of those in force can be found at www.ustr.gov. FCN trade and investment law principles, notably MFN and national treatment, carry over into these agreements. TIFAs are centered on dialogue about trade and investment issues. They often precede the more advanced legal regimes of FTAs and BITs.

The United States has numerous TIFAs with individual countries and regional economic groups. The U.S. has TIFAs with Angola, Ghana, Liberia, Mauritius, Mozambique, Nigeria, Rwanda, South Africa and the Common Market for Eastern and Southern Africa (COMESA), the East African Community, the West African Economic and monetary Union (WAEMU) and the South African Customs Union (titled as a Trade, Investment and Development Agreement).

The U.S. also has TIFAs with Algeria, Bahrain, the Caribbean Common Market (CARICOM), Egypt, the Gulf Cooperation Council, Georgia, Iceland, Iraq, Kuwait, Lebanon, Libya, Oman, Qatar, Saudi Arabia, Switzerland, Tunisia, Turkey, Ukraine, the United Arab Emirates, Uruguay and Yemen. Additional TIFAs have been concluded with Afghanistan, collectively with five Central Asian nations, the Maldives, Nepal, Pakistan, Sri Lanka, the ASEAN group (Association of South East Asian Nations), Brunei, Cambodia, Indonesia, Malaysia, New Zealand, the Philippines, Thailand and Vietnam.

In virtually all parts of the world, countries have joined in customs unions or free trade agreements in order to expand international commerce and to acquire increased bargaining power in international trade negotiations. The European Union is a prime example (see Chapter 7), as is NAFTA, (see Chapter 8). Hundreds of such treaties now lattice the globe (see Chapter 6).

THE GATT (1947): HISTORY AND PROVISIONS

Participants in the Bretton Woods meetings in 1944 recognized a post-War need to reduce obstacles to freer trade. They envisioned the creation of an International Trade Organization (ITO) to achieve the desired result. Fifty-three countries met in Havana in 1948 to complete drafting the Charter of an ITO that would be the international organizational umbrella underneath which negotiations could occur periodically to deal with tariff reductions. A framework for such negotiations had already been staked out in Geneva in 1947, in a document entitled the General Agreement on Tariffs and Trade (GATT).

Twenty-three nations participated in that first GATT session, India, Chile, Cuba and Brazil representing the developing world. China participated; Japan and West Germany did not.

Stringent trading rules were adopted only where there were no special interests of major participants to alter them. The developing nations objected to many of the strict rules, arguing for special treatment justified on development needs, but they achieved few successes in drafting GATT.

The ITO Charter was never ratified. The United States Congress in the late 1940s was unwilling to join more new international organizations, thus U.S. ratification of the ITO Charter could not be secured. By default, and moving by way of the President's power to make executive agreements, the United States joined 21 other countries in signing a Protocol of Provisional Application of the General Agreement on Tariffs and Trade (popularly called the "GATT Agreement").

One notable feature of this protocol was the exemption of existing trade restraints of the Contracting States. The GATT 1947 Agreement evolved from its "provisional" status into the premier international trade body, GATT the organization based in Geneva. It was through this organization that tariffs were steadily reduced over decades by means of increased membership and GATT negotiating Rounds. Today, the GATT 1947 Agreement has been superceded by the substantially similar GATT 1994 Agreement, part of the World Trade Organization "package" of trade agreements that took effect in 1995.

Trade in Goods: Core GATT Principles

One of the core provisions of GATT 1947 and 1994 is Article I, which makes a general commitment to the long standing practice of "most favored nation treatment" (MFN) by requiring each Contracting Party to accord unconditional MFN status to all other Contracting Parties. Thus, any privilege granted by any Contracting Party to any product imported from any other country (WTO member or not) must also be "immediately and unconditionally" granted to any "like product" imported from any Contracting Parties.

GATT Article III incorporates the practice of according "national treatment" to imported goods by providing, with enumerated exceptions, that the products of one Contracting State shall be treated in the same manner regarding taxation and regulation as domestic goods. This Article, for example, requires that the products of the exporting GATT Contracting State be treated no less favorably than domestic products of the importing Contracting State under its laws and regulations concerning sale, internal resale, purchase, transportation and use.

In addition to requiring MFN and national treatment, GATT prohibits use of certain kinds of quantitative restrictions. Article XI broadly but not completely prohibits the use of other "prohibitions or restrictions" on imports from Contracting Parties. It specifically prohibits the use of "quotas, import or export licenses or other measures" to restrict imports from a Contracting Party. When such measures are authorized, Article XIII requires non-discrimination in quantitative trade restrictions, by barring an importing Contracting State from applying any prohibition or restriction to the products of another Contracting State, "unless the importation of the like product of *all* third countries ... is similarly prohibited or restricted" (emphasis added).

The WTO has significantly reduced the number of trade quotas. The Agreement on Textiles eliminated quotas long maintained under the Multi-Fibre Arrangement. Voluntary export restraints (quotas) are severely limited by the Safeguards Agreement. In addition, the WTO removes trade quotas by pressuring for "tariffication," or replacing them with tariffs—sometimes even at extraordinarily high tariff rates. Tariffication is the approach adopted in the WTO Agricultural Agreement. It is expected that high tariff rates will be reduced in subsequent negotiating Rounds. Import licensing schemes are also being phased out under WTO agreements.

GATT Procedures

While the GATT does permit nondiscriminatory "duties, taxes and other charges," the powers of a Contracting Party are limited even as to these devices. First, GATT Article X requires that notice be given of any new or changed national regulations which affect international trade, by requiring the prompt publication by any Contracting Party of those "laws, regulations, judicial decisions and administrative rulings of general application." Second, the Contracting Parties commit themselves, under GATT Article XXVIII to a continuing series of multilateral trade negotiations MTN ("from time to time") to seek further reductions in tariff levels and other barriers to international trade.

Such negotiations are to be "on a reciprocal and mutually advantageous basis." GATT negotiated tariff rates (called "concessions" or "bindings"), which are listed in the "tariff Schedules", are deposited with GATT by each participating country. These concessions must be granted to imports from any Contracting Party, both because of the GATT required MFN treatment, and also because Article II specifically requires use of the negotiated rates.

Framers of GATT were well aware that a commitment to freer trade could cause serious, adverse economic consequences from time to time within part or all of a country's domestic economy, particularly its labor sector. The GATT contains at least seven safety valves (in nine clauses of the Agreement) to permit a country, in appropriate circumstances, to respond to domestic pressures while remaining a participant in GATT. Two prominent safety valves contained in Article VI deal with antidumping and countervailing duties. In a nutshell, these special tariffs are authorized against what the GATT deems unfair international trade practices. They are detailed in Chapter 4.

THE GATT MULTINATIONAL TRADE NEGOTIATIONS (ROUNDS)

Under the auspices of GATT Article XXVIII, the Contracting Parties committed themselves to hold periodic multinational trade negotiations (MTN or

"Rounds"). They have completed eight such Rounds to date. While the first five Rounds concentrated on item by item tariff reductions, the "Kennedy Round" (1964–1967) was noted for its achievement of across-the-board tariff reductions.

The GATT regularly held multilateral trade negotiations (MTN) seeking open up international trade. These periodic GATT "Rounds" cumulatively reduced average tariff barriers to 80 percent below those existing in the post WWII era. After the most recent multilateral negotiations, the Uruguay Round finalized in 1994, average tariff rates of developed countries on dutiable manufactured imports were cut from 6.3 percent to 3.9 percent.

The GATT completed eight such Rounds with the GATT membership steadily increasing:

Geneva (1947) with 19 countries

Annecy (1948) with 27 countries

Torquay (1950) with 33 countries

"Dillon Round" Geneva (1960–62) with 36 countries

"Kennedy Round" Geneva (1964–67) with 74 countries

"Tokyo Round" Geneva (1973–79) with 85 countries

"Uruguay Round" Geneva (1986–94) with 128 countries

The WTO Doha Round (2001–) with 162 countries is marginally ongoing.

Tariff reductions are one of the success stories of the GATT. But not all nations participated in the GATT Rounds, or are members of its replacement, the WTO. For example, Iran is still seeking membership in the WTO. China and Chinese Taipei (Taiwan) did not join until 2001, Vietnam in 2007, and Russia in 2012.

Developing Nations and Nontariff Trade Barriers

In 1961, GATT began to consider how to approach the increasing trade disparity with the developing world. In 1964, GATT adopted Part IV, which introduced a principle of "diminished expectations of reciprocity". Reciprocity remained a goal, but developed nations would not expect concessions from developing nations which were inconsistent with developmental needs. For the developing nations, non-reciprocity meant freedom to protect domestic markets from import competition. Import substitution was a major focus of developmental theory in the 1960s, and developing nations saw keeping their markets closed as a way to save these domestic industries. Although they also sought preferential treatment of their exports, that was a demand which would remain unsatisfied for another decade.

The "Tokyo Round" (1973–1979) engendered agreements about several areas of nontariff barrier (NTB) trade restraints. Nearly a dozen major (but optional) agreements on nontariff barrier issues were produced in the Tokyo Round. In the early 1970s, national and regional generalized preference schemes (GSP) developed to favor the exports of developing nations. The foreign debt payment problems of the developing nations suggested that they need to generate revenue to pay these debts, and that developmental theory must shift from import substitution to export promotion.

In 1986, the "Uruguay Round" of multilateral trade negotiations began at a Special Session of the GATT Contracting States. This Uruguay Round included separate negotiations on trade in goods and on trade in services, with separate groups of negotiators dealing with each topic. Subtopics for negotiation by subgroups included nontariff barriers, agriculture, subsidies and countervailing duties, intellectual property rights and counterfeit goods, safeguards, tropical products, textiles, investment policies, and dispute resolution. The negotiating sessions were extraordinarily complex, but were able to achieve a successful conclusion, giving birth to the World Trade Organization in 1995.

The latest Round failed to start as scheduled late in 1999. An array of "anti-globalization" interests and street protests in Seattle led by labor and environmental groups caused the delay. Regrouping in remote Qatar, the Doha Round was launched in 2001, scheduled for completion in 2005, but barely remains ongoing.

Agriculture, services, intellectual property, antidumping duties, tariffs, export subsidies, market access, implementation, electronic commerce, dispute settlement, trade and the environment, trade, debt and finance, and special and differential treatment and assistance for developing countries are on the agenda. Developed WTO countries are pushing the so-called "Singapore" issues of investment, competition policy, transparency in procurement and trade facilitation.

At Cancun in 2003, the WTO developing nations rejected these issues while focusing on agricultural trade protectionism by industrial nations. Marathon talks in July of 2008 failed to resolve agricultural trade issues, suggesting that the Doha round, except perhaps for relatively minor matters, is dead. This has caused many nations to accelerate their participation in bilateral and regional free trade agreements. See Chapter 6.

CREATING THE WORLD TRADE ORGANIZATION (WTO)

Creating the World Trade organization was not easy. Eight years in negotiation, the major issue was trade in agricultural goods, with the EU maintaining a strongly protective position and the Cairns Group led by the USA seeking to reduce agricultural trade barriers and subsidies. In the end, a modest compromise was achieved in the WTO Agreement on Agriculture, discussed below.

What drove that compromise? In this author's opinion, the United States played two critical cards: First, it aggressively undertook unilateral, totally unauthorized trade actions against "foreign country practices" under Section 301 of the Trade Act of 1974, outlined in Chapter 5. Under considerable pressure, these actions primarily opened up foreign markets to U.S. exports. Second, the United States played the NAFTA card, commencing negotiations and reaching an extensive free trade and foreign investment agreement with Mexico and Canada. NAFTA negotiations ran more or less one year ahead of the Uruguay Round, influencing the content of and pushing forward the creation of the WTO and its package of agreements.

That said, significant differences between the WTO Agreements and NAFTA exist. A chart comparing NAFTA and WTO coverage is presented below. For example, NAFTA covers business visas, state trading, competition policy, and has an entire chapter dedicated to energy, all of which are absent from the WTO package. The WTO Agreements cover customs valuation and pre-shipment inspection, which NAFTA does not. Nothing in the WTO package of agreements touches on labor or the environment, NAFTA's two side agreements.

On market access, procurement, investment and most services, NAFTA goes further and faster than the Uruguay Round WTO agreements. There is significant overlap on intellectual property where NAFTA's leading edge was particularly influential. The WTO Agreement on Agriculture, on the other hand, exceeded by a good measure NAFTA's trade opening initiatives. The WTO package also addressed basic telecommunications, which was mostly omitted from NAFTA. The WTO has (since 1997) fostered an information technology tariff reduction agreement, but Mexico does not participate.

These differences may help explain why the basic rule of NAFTA dispute settlement is that the complaining country normally has the prerogative of choosing as between NAFTA and WTO procedures. For details and examples, see R. Folsom, *NAFTA in a Nutshell.*

WTO AGREEMENTS

The WTO is the product of the Uruguay Round of GATT negotiations, which was successfully completed in 1994. The Uruguay Round produced a package of agreements. These are the Agreement Establishing the World Trade Organization and its Annexes, which include the General Agreement on Tariffs and Trade 1994 (GATT 1994) and a series of Multilateral Trade Agreements (the Covered Agreements), and a series of Plurilateral Trade Agreements.

GATT 1947 and GATT 1994 are two distinct agreements. GATT 1994 incorporates the provisions of GATT 1947, except for the Protocol of Provisional Application, which is expressly excluded. Thus, problems created by exempting existing national laws at the time of the adoption of the Protocol are avoided by this exclusion in the Covered Agreements. Otherwise, in cases involving a conflict between GATT 1947 and GATT 1994, GATT 1947 controls. The WTO will be guided by the decisions, procedures and customary practices developed under GATT.

Annexed to the WTO Agreement are several Multilateral Trade Agreements. As to trade in goods, they include Agreements on Agriculture, Textiles,

Antidumping, Subsidies and Countervailing Measures (SCM), Safeguards, Technical Barriers to Trade, Sanitary and Phytosanitary Measures (SPS), Pre-shipment Inspection, Rules of Origin, and Import License Procedures. In addition to trade in goods, they include a General Agreement on Trade in Services (GATS) and Agreements on Trade-Related Aspects of Intellectual Property Rights (TRIPs) and Trade-Related Investment Measures (TRIMs).

Affecting all of these agreements is the Understanding on Rules and Procedures Governing the Settlement of Disputes (DSU). Most importantly, *all* of the Multilateral Trade Agreements are binding on *all* Members of the World Trade Organization, now over 160 nations. Each WTO member state is obliged to incorporate these WTO legal into their national legal regimes.

In addition to the Multilateral Trade Agreements, there are also Plurilateral Trade Agreements which are also annexed to the WTO Agreement. These agreements, however, are not binding on all WTO Members, and Members can choose to adhere to them or not. They include Agreements on Government Procurement, Trade in Civil Aircraft, International Dairy (rescinded) and an Arrangement Regarding Bovine Meat (rescinded). States which do not join the plurilateral trade agreements do not receive reciprocal benefits under them.

THE WTO AGREEMENTS PACKAGE

AGREEMENT ESTABLISHING THE WORLD TRADE ORGANIZATION (WTO)

Agreements on Trade in Goods

1   General Agreement on Tariffs and Trade (GATT) 1994

    (a)   Understanding on the Interpretation of Article II:1(b) (tariff concessions)

    (b)   Understanding on the Interpretation of Article XVII (state trading enterprises)

    (c)   Understanding on Balance-of-Payments Provisions

    (d)   Understanding on the Interpretation of Article XXIV (free trade areas and customs unions)

    (e)   Understanding on the Interpretation of Article XXV (waivers)

    (f)   Understanding on the Interpretation of Article XXVIII (modification of tariff schedules)

    (g)   Understanding on the Interpretation of Article XXXV (non-application of GATT)

2   GATT 1994

3   Agreement on Agriculture

4   Agreement on Sanitary and Phytosanitary Measures (SPS)

5   Agreement on Textiles and Clothing

6   Agreement on Technical Barriers to Trade (TBT)

7   Agreement on Trade-Related Investment Measures (TRIMs)

8   Agreement on Implementation of Article VI (antidumping and countervailing duties)

9   Agreement on Implementation of Article VII (customs valuation)

10   Agreement on Pre-shipment Inspection

11   Agreement on Rules of Origin

12   Agreement on Import Licensing Procedures

13   Agreement on Subsidies and Countervailing Measures (SCM)

14   Agreement on Safeguards

General Agreement on Trade in Services (GATS) and Annexes

Agreement on Trade-Related Aspects of Intellectual Property Rights (TRIPs), including Trade in Counterfeit Goods

Understanding on Rules and Procedures Governing the Settlement of Disputes (DSU)

Trade Policy Review Mechanism

Plurilateral Trade Agreements

4(a) Agreement on Trade in Civil Aircraft

4(b) Agreement   on   Government Procurement

4(c) International Dairy Arrangement (rescinded)

4(d) Arrangement Regarding Bovine Meat (rescinded)

ADMISSION TO THE WTO

Admission to the World Trade Organization is by "consensus." In theory, this gives each member a veto over applicant countries. In reality, no nation wishing to join has ever formally been vetoed, though many have been long delayed. It took, for example, well over a decade to negotiate acceptable terms of entry for the People's Republic of China. Such negotiations are handled individually by member states, not by the WTO as an organization. United States negotiations with China were particularly lengthy and difficult, one principal issue being whether China should be admitted as a developing or developed nation. (The issue was fudged, with China treated differently within the WTO package of agreements.)

Essentially, applicant counties make an offer of trade liberalization commitments to join the WTO. This offer is renegotiated with interested member nations, some 40 nations regarding China including the European Union which negotiates as a unit

(NAFTA does not). Regarding China, the last member to reach agreement on WTO admission was Mexico, which extracted stiff promises against the dumping of Chinese goods. The various commitments made by the applicant in these negotiations are consolidated into a final accession protocol which is then approved by "consensus." Russia completed this negotiation process in 2012, Vietnam in 2007. Iran's desire to join has basically been frustrated by U.S. refusal to negotiate on WTO entry.

The existing 130 or so members of the GATT in 1994 became the founding members of the WTO. At this writing, there are approximately 160 WTO member states. Any member may withdraw with six months' notice.

WTO AGREEMENTS AND U.S. LAW

The WTO Covered Agreements concern not only trade in goods, but also trade in services (GATS), and trade-related aspects of intellectual property (TRIPS). The basic concepts that GATT applied to trade in goods (described above) are now applied to these areas through GATS and TRIPS. In the WTO Covered Agreements, the basic concepts of GATT 1947 and its associated agreements are elaborated and clarified. In addition, there is an attempt to transform all protectionist measures relating to agriculture (such as import bans and quotas, etc.) into only tariff barriers, which can then be lowered in subsequent MTN Rounds (a process known as "tariffication"). WTO also contains some superficial provisions on trade-related investment measures

(TRIMS). Some of the WTO provisions, particularly those concerning trade in goods, will be discussed in more detail below, in relation to United States trade law.

The United States enacted legislation to implement WTO and the Covered Agreements on December 3, 1994, but did not ratify them as a treaty. The Uruguay Round Implementation Act legislation was submitted to Congress under "fast track" procedures, which required that the agreement and its implementing legislation be considered as a whole, and prohibited Congressional amendments to the implementing legislation. The Congressional authority for "fast track" procedures also required that the President give ninety days' notice of his intention to enter into such an agreement.

Neither GATT 1947 nor the WTO Agreement, GATT 1994, and the other Covered Agreements have been ratified as treaties, and therefore comprise international obligations of the United States only to the extent that they are incorporated in United States' implementing legislation. GATT 1947 was not considered controlling by the courts of the United States, and these courts have always held themselves bound to the U.S. legislation actually enacted. The WTO Covered Agreements will be considered to have a non-self-executed status, and therefore are likely to be regarded in the same manner as GATT 1947.

GATT/WTO NONTARIFF TRADE BARRIER CODES

There are numerous nontariff trade barriers applicable to imports. Many of these barriers arise out of safety and health regulations. Others concern the environment, consumer protection, product standards and government procurement. Many of the relevant rules were created for legitimate consumer and public protection reasons. They were often created without extensive consideration of their international impact as potential nontariff trade barriers. Nevertheless, the practical impact of legislation of this type is to ban the importation of nonconforming products. Thus, unlike tariffs which can always be paid, and unlike quotas which permit a certain amount of goods to enter the market, nontariff trade barriers have the potential to totally exclude foreign exports.

Multilateral GATT negotiations since the end of World War II have led to a significant decline in world tariff levels, particularly on trade with developed nations. As steadily as tariff barriers have disappeared, nontariff trade barriers (NTBs) have emerged. Health and safety regulations, environmental laws, rules regulating products standards, procurement legislation and customs procedures are often said to present NTB problems.

Negotiations over nontariff trade barriers dominated the Tokyo Round of the GATT negotiations during the late 1970s. A number of optional NTB "codes" (sometimes called "side agreements") emerged from the Tokyo Round. These concerned   subsidies,   dumping,   government procurement,   technical   barriers   (products standards), customs valuation and import licensing. In addition, specific agreements regarding trade in bovine meats, dairy products and civil aircraft were also reached. The United States accepted all of these NTB codes and agreements except the one on dairy products. Most of the necessary implementation of these agreements was accomplished in the Trade Agreements Act of 1979.

Mandatory GATT codes were agreed upon under the Uruguay Round ending in late 1993. They revisit all of the NTB areas covered by the Tokyo Round Codes and create new codes for sanitary and phyto-sanitary measures (SPS), trade-related investment measures (TRIMs), pre-shipment inspection, rules of origin, escape clause safeguards and trade-related intellectual property rights (TRIPs). The United States Congress approved and implemented these Codes in December of 1994 under the Uruguay Round Agreements Act.

One problem with nontariff trade barriers is that they   are   so   numerous.   Intergovernmental negotiation intended to reduce their trade restricting impact is both tedious and difficult. There are continuing attempts through the World Trade Organization to come to grips with additional specific NTB   problems.   Furthermore,   various   trade agreements of the United States have been undertaken in this field. For example, the Canada-United States Free Trade Area Agreement and the NAFTA built upon the existing GATT agreements to further reduce NTB problems between the United States, Canada and Mexico.

Beef Hormones NTB Dispute

The *Beef Hormones* case illustrates NTB issues and a rare outcome in WTO dispute settlement. The EU banned imports of growth enhancing hormone-treated beef from the U.S. and Canada as a health hazard. The WTO Appellate Body ruled that, since the ban was stricter than international standards, the EU needed scientific evidence to back it up. However, the EU had failed to undertake a scientific risk assessment, and its scientific reports did not provide any rational basis to uphold the ban. In fact, the primary study had found no evidence of harm to humans from the growth-enhancing-hormones. The Appellate Body ruled that the ban violated the WTO Sanitary and Phytosanitary Standards (SPS) Code and required the EU to produce scientific evidence to justify the ban within a reasonable time, or to revoke the ban. Arbitrators determined that 15 months was a reasonable time, but the EU failed to produce such evidence and the U.S. retaliated with over $200 million in tariffs on EU exports.

The United States maintained that the European Union must eliminate their ban on hormone-treated beef in order to conform to the ruling. Naturally, the Europeans saw things a bit differently. If they could come up with solid scientific evidence that the administration of hormones to beef in the U.S. and Canada poses risks to human health, they hoped to escape retaliation. The EU claimed on the basis of post-dispute studies that one beef hormone was proven harmful to human health, and five others ought to be banned as a precautionary principle. The EU petitioned the WTO to seek removal of the U.S. sanctions. This petition was rejected in 2008 by the Appellate Body, again for want of scientific justification.

Finally, in 2009, a phased four year settlement of the *Beef Hormones* dispute was reached. The U.S. got a higher quota to export hormone-free beef to the EU in return for phasing out its retaliatory tariffs on EU goods. Thus the EU ban on hormone-treated beef continues.

THE WTO AGREEMENT ON AGRICULTURE

Agricultural issues played a central role in the Uruguay Round GATT negotiations. More than any other issue, they delayed completion of that Round from 1990 to 1993 and threaten the current Doha Round. The agreement finally reached was a trade liberalizing, market-oriented effort. Each country promised a number of commitments on market access, reduced domestic agricultural support levels and export subsidies. The United States Congress approved of these commitments by adopting the Uruguay Round Agreements Act.

Broadly speaking nontariff trade barriers to international agricultural trade are replaced by tariffs that provide substantially the same level of protection. This is known as "tariffication." It applies to virtually all NTBs, including variable levies, import bans, voluntary export restraints and import quotas. Tariffication applies specifically to U.S. agricultural quotas adopted under Section 22 of the Agricultural Adjustment Act. All agricultural tariffs, including those converted from NTBs, are reduced by 36 and 24 percent by developed and developing countries, respectively, over 6 and 10 year periods.

Certain minimum access tariff quotas apply when imports amount to less than 3 to 5 percent of domestic consumption. An escape clause exists for tariffed imports at low prices or upon a surge of importation depending upon the existing degree of import penetration. The efficacy of these "liberalizations" has been severely challenged by developing nations led by Brazil and India in the Doha Round. They claim that agricultural trade restraints combined with huge export subsidies from surplus producers like the U.S. and the EU undermine their agricultural production and exports.

Regarding domestic support for agriculture, some programs with minimal impact on trade are exempt from change under the WTO Agreement. These programs are known as "green box policies." They include governmental support for agricultural research, disease control, infrastructure and food security. Green box policies were also exempt from GATT/WTO challenge or countervailing duties until 2004. Direct payments to producers that are not linked to production are also generally exempt. This will include income support, adjustment assistance, and environmental and regional assistance payments. Furthermore, direct payments to support crop reductions and *de minimis* payments are exempted in most cases.

After removing all of the exempted domestic agricultural support programs, the agreement on agriculture arrives at a calculation known as the Total Aggregate Measurement of Support (Total AMS). This measure is the basis for agricultural support reductions under the agreement. Developed nations promised to reduce their Total AMS by 20 percent over 6 years, developing nations by 13.3 percent over 10 years.

Agricultural export subsidies of developed nations had to be reduced by 36 percent below 1986–1990 levels over six years and the quantity of subsidized agricultural exports by 21 percent. Except for a handful of developed members, agricultural export subsidies were subsequently reduced to zero by WTO developed nations, including the United States. Developing nations had to meet corresponding 24 and 14 percent reductions over 10 years. Late in 2015, with relatively few exceptions, developed and developing WTO members agreed to eliminate direct farm export subsidies. They also imposed rules on export credits, international food aid and state trading enterprises in the agricultural sector.

Under the 1995 agreement on agriculture, all conforming tariffications, reductions in domestic support for agriculture and export subsidy alterations were essentially exempt from challenge until 2004 within the GATT/WTO on grounds such as serious prejudice in export markets or nullification and impairment of agreement benefits. However, countervailing duties could be levied against all unlawfully subsidized exports of agricultural goods except for subsidies derived from so-called national "green box policies" (discussed above). In *U.S.-Upland Cotton,* the Appellate Body affirmed that member states must not only conform to the Agreement on Agriculture, but also the Subsidies and Countervailing Measures (SCM) Agreement. In that decision, U.S. compliance with the Agriculture Agreement was acknowledged, but its "Step-2" payments to cotton users favoring domestic over imported cotton (local content subsidies) were held to violate the SCM Agreement.

THE WTO AGREEMENT ON TEXTILES

One critical reason why developing nations opted into the WTO package is the Agreement on Textiles. It eliminated as of 2005 the quotas long maintained under the Multi-Fiber Arrangement (MFA). The demise of MFA textile quotas in 2005, as widely expected, dramatically accelerated Chinese and other Asian textile exports to the United States. Responding to domestic pressures, the United States repeatedly invoked special safeguard protections against textile and clothing imports during the ten-year phase-out period that ended in 2005. Since then the average U.S. bound and applied tariff on textile products has been around 8 percent, and consumers must search very hard to find Made-in-the-USA clothing.

THE GENERAL AGREEMENT ON TRADE IN SERVICES (GATS)

Market access for services is a major focus of the WTO General Agreement on Trade in Services (GATS). Since the United States is the world's largest exporter of services, including for example engineering, computer and professional services, it has a special interest in GATS. The U.S. Congress approved and implemented the GATS agreement in 1994 under the Uruguay Round Agreements Act. Subsequently, early in 1995, the United States refused to extend most-favored-nation treatment to financial services. The European Union, Japan and other GATS nations then entered into an interim two-year agreement which operated on MFN principles.

Financial services was revisited in 1996–97 with further negotiations aimed at bringing the United States into the fold. These negotiations bore fruit late in 1997 with 70 nations (including the United States) joining in an agreement that covers 95 percent of trade in banking, insurance, securities and financial information. This agreement took effect March 1, 1999.

A general right of most-favored-nation treatment in the services sector has been established. National laws that restrict the number of firms in a market, that are dependent upon local "needs tests" or that mandate local incorporation are regulated by the GATS. Various "transparency" rules require disclosure of all relevant laws and regulations, and these must be administered reasonably, objectively and impartially. Certain mutual recognition of education and training for service-sector licensing will occur. State monopolies or exclusive service providers may continue, but must not abuse their positions. Detailed rules are created in annexes to the GATS on telecommunications and air transport services. Under the Telecommunications annex, for example, the United States successfully argued that Telmex had abused its monopoly position in Mexico by charging discriminatory, non-cost-oriented connection fees for foreign calls.

In addition, each WTO member state made under GATS XVI specific schedule of commitments (concessions) on opening up their markets in services' sectors negotiated using the WTO Services Sectoral Classification List. They further agreed under Article XVI to provide national treatment to their services' commitment schedule. For example, to what degree may foreign banks or foreign economic consultants provide services, and are they entitled to national treatment?

The answers to those questions will be found in the GATS specific commitments of each member. The European Union, for example, has refused to make commitments in the audio-visual sector. These commitments may be modified or withdrawn after three years, subject to a right of compensation that can be arbitrated.

Much to its consternation, the United States was found to have failed to exclude Internet gambling services under its GATS commitments' schedule. This caused Antigua-Barbuda to prevail in a dispute that alleged U.S. gambling laws discriminatorily prohibited its right to export such services to the U.S. market. The United States also lost the argument that its Internet gambling services' restraints were justifiable on public morals' grounds. This argument failed as discriminatory under the "chapeau" of the GATS Article XIV general exceptions (similar to GATT Article XX general exceptions).

The GATS has reduced unilateral U.S. action under Section 301 of the Trade Act of 1974 to gain access to foreign markets for U.S. service providers. This reduction flows from U.S. adherence to the Dispute Settlement Understanding (DSU), see below). The DSU obligates its signatories to follow streamlined dispute settlement procedures under which retaliation is restrained until the offending nation has failed to conform to a WTO ruling.

WTO DECISION-MAKING

The World Trade Organization is structured in three tiers. One tier is the Ministerial Conference, which meets biennially and is composed of representatives of all WTO Members. Each Member has an equal voting weight, which is unlike the representation in the IMF and World Bank where there is weighted voting, and financially powerful states have more power over the decision-making process.

The Ministerial Conference is responsible for all WTO functions, and is able to make any decisions necessary. It has the power to authorize new multilateral negotiations and to adopt the results of such negotiations. The Ministerial Conference, by a three-fourths vote, is authorized to grant waivers of obligations to Members in exceptional circumstances. It also has the power to adopt interpretations of Covered Agreements. When the Ministerial Conference is in recess, its functions are performed by the General Council.

The second tier is the General Council which has executive authority over the day to day operations and functions of the WTO. It is composed of representatives of all WTO Members, and each member has an equal voting weight. It meets whenever it is appropriate. The General Council also has the power to adopt interpretations of Covered Agreements.

The third tier comprises the councils, bodies and committees which are accountable to the Ministerial Conference or General Council. Ministerial Conference committees include Committees on Trade and Development, Balance of Payment Restrictions, Budget, Finance and Administration. General Council bodies include the Dispute Settlement Body, the Trade Policy Review Body, and Councils for Trade in Goods, Trade in Services and Trade-Related Intellectual Property Rights. The Councils are all created by the WTO Agreement and are open to representatives of all Member States. The Councils also have the authority to create subordinate organizations. Other committees, such as the Committee on Subsidies and Countervailing Measures are created by specific individual agreements.

Of the General Council bodies, the two most important are the Dispute Settlement Body (DSB) and the Trade Policy Review Body (TPRB). The DSB is a special meeting of the General Council, and therefore includes all WTO Members. It has responsibility for resolution of disputes under all the Covered Agreements, and will be discussed in more detail below, under Dispute Resolution.

The purpose of the Trade Policy Review-Mechanism (TPRM) is to improve adherence to the WTO agreements and obligations, and to obtain greater transparency. Individual Members of WTO each prepare a "Country Report" on their trade policies and perceived adherence to the WTO Covered Agreements. The WTO Secretariat also prepares a report on each Member, but from the perspective of the Secretariat. The Trade Policy Review Body (TPRB) then reviews the trade policies of each Member based on these two reports. At the end of the review, the TPRB issues its own report concerning the adherence of the Member's trade policy to the WTO Covered Agreements. The TPRB has no enforcement capability, but the report is sent to the next meeting of the WTO Ministerial Conference. It is then up to the Ministerial Conference to evaluate the trade practices and policies of the Member.

WTO Consensus Rules

The process of decision-making in the WTO Ministerial Conference and General Council relies upon "consensus" as the norm, just as it did for decision-making under GATT 1947. "Consensus", in this context means that no Member formally objects to a proposed decision. Thus, consensus is not obtained if any one Member formally objects, and has often been very difficult to obtain, which proved to be a weakness in the operation of GATT. However, there are many exceptions to the consensus formula under WTO, and some new concepts (such as "inverted consensus", discussed below) which are designed to ease the process of decision-making under WTO.

Article IX (1) of the WTO Agreement first provides that "the practice of decision-making by consensus" followed under GATT shall be continued. The next sentence of that provision, however, states that "where a decision cannot be arrived at by consensus, the matter at issue shall be decided by voting", except where otherwise provided. The ultimate resolution of the conflict between these two sentences is not completely clear.

There are a number of exceptions to the requirement for consensus that are expressly created under the WTO Agreement. One such exception is decisions by the Dispute Settlement Body, which has its own rules (see below). Another set of exceptions concerns decisions on waivers, interpretations and amendments of the Covered Agreements. Waivers of obligations may be granted and amendments adopted to Covered Agreements only by the Ministerial Conference. Amendments of Multilateral Trade Agreements usually require a consensus, but where a decision on a proposed amendment cannot obtain consensus, the decision on that amendment is to be made in certain circumstances by a two-thirds majority vote.

In "exceptional circumstances", the Ministerial Conference is authorized to grant waivers of obligations under a Covered Agreement by a three-fourths vote. Another exception to the consensus requirement allows procedural rules in both the Ministerial Conference and the General Council to be decided by a majority vote of the Members, unless otherwise provided.

Operationally speaking, the WTO membership rarely meets in its entirety. Alliances and groups within the membership meet to undertake WTO decisions. For example, the "Cairns Group" of 18 member-states has focused on agricultural trade issues and endured as a group for some time. Groups and alliances often shift depending upon the subject matter.

DISPUTE-SETTLEMENT UNDER THE WTO

WTO provides a unified system for settling international trade disputes through the Dispute Settlement Understanding (DSU) and using the Dispute Settlement Body (DSB). The DSB is a special assembly of the WTO General Council, and includes all WTO Members. There are seven stages in the resolution of disputes under WTO: 1) Consultation; 2) Panel establishment, investigation and report; 3) Appellate review of the panel report; 4) Adoption of the panel and appellate decision; 5) Implementation of the decision adopted; (6) Settlement by compensation; and (7) Authorized retaliation.

There is also a parallel process for binding arbitration, if both parties agree to submit this dispute to arbitration, rather than to a DSB panel. In addition, during the implementation phase (5), the party subject to an adverse decision may seek arbitration as a matter of right.

Three further points are worthy of emphasis concerning proceedings before the DSB. First, since the WTO came into being in 1994, dispute settlement before the DSB, once initiated, is compulsory and binding. Second, this dispute settlement option is not open to private litigants, for only member state governments may file an action before the DSB. Finally, although formally binding, the WTO has no direct power to compel compliance with its decisions. Nonetheless, it may order compensation for the aggrieved state(s) or authorize retaliatory trade sanctions, and these may provide a significant incentive for an offending state to bring its domestic law into compliance.

Although the DSU offers a unified dispute resolution system that is applicable across all sectors and all WTO Covered Agreements, there are many specialized rules for disputes which arise under them. Such specialized rules appear in the Agreements on Textiles, Antidumping, Subsidies and Countervailing Measures, Technical Barriers to Trade, Sanitary and Phytosanitary Measures, Customs Valuation, General Agreement on Trade in Services, Financial Services and Air Transport Services. The special provisions in these individual Covered Agreements govern, where applicable, and prevail in any conflict with the general provisions of the DSU.

Under WTO, unlike under GATT 1947, the DSU practically assures that panels will be established upon request by a Member. Further, under WTO, unlike under GATT 1947, the DSU virtually ensures the adoption of unmodified panel and Appellate Body decisions. It accomplishes this by requiring the DSB to adopt these decisions automatically and without amendment unless they are rejected by a consensus of all Members. This "inverted consensus" requires that all Members of the DSB, including the Member who prevailed in the dispute, decide to reject the dispute resolution decision; and that no Member formally favors that decision. Such an outcome seems unlikely. This inverted consensus requirement is imposed on both the adoption of panel reports or Appellate Body decisions and also on the decision to establish a panel.

The potential resolutions of a dispute under DSU range from a "mutually satisfactory solution" agreed to by the parties under the first, or consultation phase, to authorized retaliation under the last, or implementation, phase. The preferred solution is always any resolution that is mutually satisfactory to the parties. After a final decision, there are three types of remedies available to the prevailing party, if a mutually satisfactory solution cannot be obtained. One is for the respondent to bring the measure found to violate a Covered Agreement into conformity with the Agreement. A second is for the prevailing Member to receive compensation from the respondent which both parties agree is sufficient to compensate for any injury caused by the measure found to violate a Covered Agreement.

Finally, if no such agreement can be reached, a prevailing party can be authorized to suspend some of its concessions under the Covered Agreements to the respondent. These suspended concessions, called "retaliation," can be authorized within the same trade sector and agreement; or, if that will not create sufficient compensation, can be authorized across trade sectors and agreements.

The entire WTO dispute resolution process, from filing a complaint to authorized retaliation, can take roughly three years. One perspective on WTO dispute settlement seeks a rule-oriented use of the "rule of law". The other seeks a power-oriented use of diplomacy. The United States and less developed countries have traditionally sought to develop a rule-oriented approach to international trade disputes. The European Union and Japan have traditionally sought to use the GATT/WTO primarily as a forum for diplomatic negotiations, although the EU now ranks second in number of WTO dispute proceedings.

These different views created part of the conflict at the December 1999 Seattle WTO meeting (which failed to launch the Millennium Round). If the DSB is a court, its proceedings should be open and "transparent." However, if it is just another form of government-to-government diplomacy, that has always been held in secret.

Phase 1: Consultation

Any WTO Member who believes that the Measures of another Member are not in conformity with the Covered Agreements may call for consultations on those measures. The respondent has ten days to reply to the call for consultations and must agree to enter into consultation within 30 days. If the respondent does not enter into consultations within the 30 day period, the party seeking consultations can immediately request the establishment of a panel under DSU, which puts the dispute into Phase 2.

Once consultations begin, the parties have 60 days to achieve a settlement. The goal is to seek a positive solution to the dispute, and the preferred resolution is to reach whatever solution is mutually satisfactory to the parties. If such a settlement cannot be obtained after 60 days of consultations, the party seeking consultations may request the establishment of a panel under DSU, which moves the dispute into Phase 2.

Third parties with an interest in the subject-matter of the consultations may seek to be included in them. If such inclusion is rejected, they may seek their own consultations with the other Member. Alternatives to consultations may be provided through the use of conciliation, mediation or good offices, where all parties agree to use the alternative process. Any party can terminate the use of conciliation, mediation or good offices and then seek the establishment of a panel under DSU, which will move the dispute into Phase 2.

Phase 2: Panel Establishment, Investigation and Report

If consultations between the parties fail, the party or parties seeking the consultations (the complainant) may request the DSB to establish a panel to investigate, report and resolve the dispute. It is not uncommon to have several member states, sometimes a dozen or more, join together as complainants. This often creates high profile WTO disputes. The DSB must establish such a panel upon request, unless the DSB expressly decides by consensus not to establish the panel. Since an "inverted consensus" is required to reject the establishment of the panel and the complainant Member must be part of that consensus, it is very likely that a panel will be established. Hundreds of panels have been established since 1995.

The WTO Secretariat maintains a list of well-qualified persons who are available to serve as panelists. The panels are usually composed of three individuals from that list who are not citizens of either party. If the parties agree, a panel can be composed of five such individuals. The parties can also agree to appoint citizens of a party to a panel. Panelists may be either nongovernmental individuals or governmental officials, but they are to be selected so as to ensure their independence. Thus, there is a bias towards independent individuals who are not citizens of any party. If a citizen of a party is appointed, his government may not instruct that citizen how to vote, for the panelist must be independent. By the same reasoning, a governmental official of a non-party Member who is subject to instructions from his government would not seem to fit the profile of an independent panelist.

The WTO Secretariat proposes nominations of the panelists. Parties may not normally oppose the nominations, except for "compelling reasons." The parties are given twenty days to agree on the panelists and the composition of the panel. If such agreement is not forthcoming, the WTO Director-General is authorized to appoint the panelists, in consultation with other persons in the Secretariat.

The "cases" brought to DSB panels can involve either violations of Covered Agreements or non-violation nullification and impairment of benefits under the Covered Agreements. A prima facie case of nullification impairment arises when one Member infringes upon the "obligations assumed under a Covered Agreement." Such infringement creates a presumption against the infringing Member, but the presumption can be rebutted by a showing that the complaining Member has suffered no adverse effect from the infringement.

The panels receive pleadings and rebuttals and hear oral arguments. Panels can also engage in fact development from sources outside those presented by the parties. Thus, the procedure has aspects familiar to civil law courts. A panel can, on its own initiative, request information from anybody, including experts selected by the panel. It can also obtain confidential information in some circumstances from an administrative body which is part of the government of a Member, without any prior consent from that Member. Finally, a panel can establish its own group of experts to provide reports to it on factual or scientific issues.

A panel is obligated to produce two written reports—an interim and a final report. A panel is supposed to submit a final written report to the DSB within six months of its establishment. The report will contain its findings of fact, findings of law, decision and the rationale for its decision. Before the final report is issued, the panel provides an interim report to the parties. The purpose of this interim report is to apprise the parties of the panel's current analysis of the issues and to permit the parties to comment on that analysis. The final report of the panel need not change any of the findings or conclusions in its interim report unless it is persuaded to do so by a party's comments. However, if it is not so persuaded, it is obligated to explain in its final report why it is not so persuaded.

The decisions in panel reports are final as to issues of fact. The decisions in panel reports are not necessarily final as to issues of law. Panel decisions on issues of law are subject to review by the Appellate Body, which is Phase 3, and explained below. Any party can appeal a panel report, and as is explained below it is expected that appeals will usually be taken.

Phase 3: Appellate Review of the Panel Report

Appellate review of panel reports is available at the request of any party, unless the DSB rejects that request by an "inverted consensus." There is no threshold requirement for an appellant to present a substantial substantive legal issue. Thus, most panel decisions are appealed as a matter of course. However, the Appellate Body can only review the panel reports on questions of law or legal interpretation.

The Appellate Body is a new institution. GATT 1947 had nothing comparable to it. The Appellate Body is composed of seven members (or judges) who are appointed by the DSB to four year terms. Each judge may be reappointed, but only once, to a second four year term. Each judge is to be a recognized authority on international trade law and the Covered Agreements. Appointments to the Appellate Body have included a number of distinguished judges, law professors, government trade officials and trade lawyers from a range of developed and developing countries.

The review of any panel decision is performed by three judges out of the seven. The parties do not, however, have any influence on which judges are selected to review a particular panel report. There is a schedule, created by the Appellate Body itself, for the rotation for sitting of each of the judges. Thus, a party might try to appear before a favored judge by timing the start of the dispute settlement process to arrive at the Appellate Body at the right moment on the rotation schedule, but even this limited approach has difficulties.

The Appellate Body receives written submissions from the parties and has 60, or in some cases 90, days in which to render its decision. The Appellate Body review is limited to issues of law and legal interpretation. The panel decision may be upheld, modified, or reversed by the Appellate Body decision. Appellate Body decisions are anonymous, and ex parte communications are not permitted, which makes judge-shopping by parties more than usually difficult. Appellate Body decisions do not represent binding precedent. That said, many have observed a desire on the part of the Appellate Body to achieve consistency and a willingness to discuss its prior rulings when rendering decisions.

Phase 4: Adoption of the Panel or Appellate Body Decision

Appellate Body determinations are submitted to the DSB. Panel decisions which are not appealed are also submitted to the DSB. Once either type of decision is submitted to the DSB, the DSB must automatically adopt them without modification or amendment at its next meeting unless the decision is rejected by all Members of the DSB through the form of "inverted consensus" discussed previously.

An alternative to Phases 2 through 4 is arbitration, if both parties agree. The arbitration must be binding on the parties, and there is no appeal from the arbitral tribunal's decision to the DSB Appellate Body.

Phase 5: Implementation of the Decision Adopted

Once a panel or Appellate Body decision is adopted by the DSB, implementation is a three-step process. In the first step, the Member found to have a measure which violates its WTO obligations has "a reasonable time" (usually 15 months) to bring those measures into conformity with the WTO obligations. That remedy is the preferred one, and this form of implementation is the principal goal of the WTO dispute settlement system. To date, most disputes have resulted in compliance in this manner.

Phase 6: Settlement by Compensation

If the violating measures are not brought into conformity within a reasonable time, the parties proceed to the second step. The parties negotiate to reach an agreement upon a form of "compensation" which will be granted by the party in violation to the injured party. Such "compensation" will usually comprise trade concessions, which are over and above those already available under the WTO and Covered Agreements. The nature, scope, amount and duration of these additional concessions is at the negotiating parties' discretion, but each side must agree that the final compensation package is fair and is properly related to the injury caused by the violating measures.

Few such compensation agreements have ever been achieved, though the United States compensated most of the membership after losing a dispute to Antigua about whether it had "reserved" (excepted) Internet gambling from coverage under the GATS. The United States also compensated the EU in a copyright dispute involving small business use of music, and Brazil after losing a subsidies dispute concerning cotton.

Phase 7: Authorized Retaliation

If the parties cannot agree on an appropriate amount of compensation within twenty days, the complainant may proceed to the third step. In the third step, the party or parties injured by the violating measures seek authority from the DSB to retaliate against the party whose measures violated its WTO obligations (the respondent). Thus, complainant seeks authority to suspend some of its WTO obligations benefitting the respondent. The retaliation proposed must ordinarily be within the same sector and agreement as the violating measure. "Sector" is sometimes broadly defined, as all trade in goods, and sometimes narrowly defined, as in individual services in the Services Sectoral Classification List. "Agreement" is also broadly defined. All the agreements listed in Annex IA to the WTO Agreement are considered to be a single "agreement." If retaliation within the sector and agreement of the violating measure is considered insufficient compensation, the complainant may seek suspension of its obligations across sectors and agreements.

Within 30 days of the complainant's presentation of the request to retaliate, the DSB must grant the request, unless the request is rejected by all the members through an "inverted consensus." However, the respondent may object to the level or scope of the retaliation. Upon such an objection, the issues raised by the objection will be examined by either the Appellate Body or by an arbitrator. The respondent has a right, even if arbitration was not used in Phases 2 through 4, to have an arbitrator review in Phase 5 the appropriateness of the complainant's proposed level and scope of retaliation. The arbitrator will also examine whether the proper procedures and criteria to establish retaliation have been followed. The Phase 5 arbitration is final and binding and the arbitrator's decision is probably not subject to DSB review.

In addition to objecting to the level of authorized retaliation, the responding WTO member may simultaneously challenge the assertion of noncompliance. This challenge will ordinarily be heard by the original panel and must be resolved within 90 days. Thus the request for authorized retaliation and objections thereto could conceivably be accomplished before noncompliance is formally determined. In practice, WTO dispute settlement has melded these conflicting procedures such that compliance and retaliation issues are decided together, typically by the original panel.

Retaliation in Action

Retaliation has rarely been authorized, and even less rarely imposed. The amount of a U.S. retaliation permitted after the WTO *Bananas* and *Beef Hormones* decisions were not implemented by the EU was contested. The arbitration tribunals for this issue were the original WTO panels, which did not allow the entire amount of the almost $700 million in retaliatory tariffs proposed by the United States. The U.S. was authorized and levied retaliatory tariffs amounting to about $100 million (*Bananas*) and $200 million (*Beef Hormones*) against European goods because of the EU failure to implement those WTO decisions. Since 2000, Congress has authorized rotating these tariffs in "carousel" fashion upon different European goods. The threat of carousel retaliation contributed to an April 2001 settlement of the *Bananas* dispute and a 2009 settlement of the *Beef Hormones* dispute.

Perhaps the most dramatic use of retaliation occurred in a tax subsidy dispute. The amount of EU retaliation permissible after the U.S. lost (for the second time) under WTO subsidy rules concerning Internal Revenue Code extraterritorial export tax preferences (FISCs) was disputed. A WTO panel, serving as an arbitrator, authorized approximately $4 *billion* in EU retaliation against U.S. exports. This retaliation commenced in March of 2004 and escalated monthly until the U.S. capitulated by amending the I.R.C. late in 2004.

Cross-Sector Retaliation

In a landmark ruling, a WTO panel acting as an arbitrator authorized Ecuador to remove protection of intellectual property rights regarding geographical indicators, copyrights and industrial designs on European Union goods for sale in Ecuador. This authorization was part of Ecuador's $200 million compensation in the *Bananas* dispute. The WTO panel acknowledged that Ecuador imports mostly capital goods and raw materials from the European Union and that imposing retaliatory tariffs on them would adversely harm its manufacturing industries. This risk supported "cross-retaliation" outside the sector of the EU trade violation and likewise contributed to settlement of the *Bananas* dispute. Cross-sector retaliation has also been authorized against the U.S. after losing a GATS dispute to Antigua on Internet gambling restraints.

U.S. INVOLVEMENT IN WTO DISPUTE RESOLUTION

The WTO dispute resolution process has been invoked more frequently than many expected. The United States has been the leading complainant and respondent in WTO disputes. Early on, the U.S. lost a dispute initiated by Venezuela and Brazil concerning U.S. standards for reformulated and conventional gasoline. The offending U.S. law was amended to conform to the WTO ruling. It won on a complaint initiated jointly with Canada and the European Union regarding Japanese taxes on alcoholic beverages. Japan subsequently changed its law. When Costa Rica complained about U.S. restraints on imports of underwear, the U.S. let the restraints expire prior to any formal DSB ruling at the WTO. Similar results were reached when India complained of U.S. restraints on wool shirts and blouses.

The United States won a major dispute with Canada concerning trade and subsidies for periodicals. This celebrated *Sports Illustrated* dispute proved that WTO remedies can be used to avoid Canada's cultural industries exclusion under NAFTA.

In the longstanding *Bananas* dispute noted above, the United States joined Ecuador, Guatemala, Honduras and Mexico in successfully challenging EU import restraints against so-called "dollar bananas." The EU failed to comply with the Appellate Body's ruling, and retaliatory measures were authorized and imposed. A patent law complaint by the U.S. against India prevailed in the DSB and ultimately brought changes in Indian law regarding pharmaceuticals and agricultural chemicals. In *Beef Hormones,* also noted above, the European Union lost twice before the Appellate Body for want of a "scientific basis" to ban hormone beef imports. It refused to alter its import restraints and was hit with about $200 million in retaliatory tariffs on selected exports to Canada and the United States.

In 2009, an arguably pro-European settlement was reached. The U.S. effectively got a higher quota to export hormone-free beef to the EU, in return for phasing out over four years its retaliatory tariffs on EU goods. The U.S. threat of carousel sanctions, i.e. rotating goods subject to retaliation, was instrumental to this settlement. Meanwhile, because the U.S. beef industry failed to timely ask for a continuation of the retaliatory tariffs, the Federal Circuit ruled in 2010 that they expired in 2007.

Refunds were given to importers of EU products who paid those tariffs.

The United States prevailed against Argentina regarding tariffs and taxes on footwear, textiles and apparel. It lost a challenge (strongly supported by Kodak) to Japan's distribution rules regarding photo film and paper. In this dispute the U.S. elected *not* to appeal the adverse WTO panel ruling to the Appellate Body. In contrast, the European Union took an appeal which reversed an adverse panel ruling on its customs classification of computer equipment. The U.S. had commenced this proceeding. Opponents in many disputes, Japan, the United States and the European Union united to complain that Indonesia's National Car Program was discriminatory and in breach of several WTO agreements. They prevailed and Indonesia altered its program.

India, Malaysia, Pakistan and Thailand teamed up to challenge U.S. shrimp import restraints enacted to protect endangered sea turtles. The WTO Appellate Body generally upheld their complaint and the U.S. has moved to comply. The adequacy of U.S. compliance was unsuccessfully challenged by Malaysia. The European Union and the United States jointly opposed Korea's discriminatory taxes on alcoholic beverages. This challenge was successful and Korea now imposes flat non-discriminatory taxes. The United States also complained of Japan's quarantine, testing and other agricultural import rules. The U.S. won at the WTO and Japan has changed its procedures.

In a semiconductor dumping dispute, Korea successfully argued that the U.S. was not in compliance with the WTO Antidumping Agreement. The United States amended its law, but Korea has instituted further proceedings alleging that these amendments are inadequate. The United States did likewise after Australia lost a subsidies dispute relating to auto leather exports. The reconvened WTO panel ruled that Australia had indeed failed to conform to the original adverse DSB decision. A U.S. challenge concerning India's quotas on imports of agricultural, textile and industrial products was upheld. India and the United States subsequently reached agreement on a timeline for removal of these restraints.

Closer to home, New Zealand and the United States complained of Canada's import/export rules regarding milk. Losing at the WTO, Canada agreed to a phased removal of the offending measures. The United States also won against Mexico in an antidumping dispute involving corn syrup, but lost a "big one" when the DSB determined that export tax preferences granted to "Foreign Sales Corporations" of U.S. companies were illegal. The United States expanded the FSC regime by removing the requirement that eligible goods be manufactured in the U.S. It claimed that this change made the FSC program not contingent upon exports, and thus WTO-legal. The European Union challenged this assertion of compliance before the WTO and won. Retaliation finally brought U.S. compliance.

Another "big one" went in favor of the United States. The European Union challenged the validity under the DSU of unilateral retaliation under Section 301 of the Trade Act of 1974. Section 301 has been something of a *bete noire* in U.S. trade law, but the WTO panel affirmed its legality in light of Presidential undertakings to administer it in accordance with U.S. obligations to adhere to multilateral WTO dispute settlement. The WTO Appellate Body ruled against the United States regarding the legality of the Antidumping Act of 1916 and the royalty free provisions of the 1998 Fairness in Music Licensing act. The Appellate Body also ruled against Section 211 of the Omnibus Appropriations Act of 1998 denying trademark protection in connection with confiscated assets (the "HAVANA CLUB" dispute). U.S. compliance with these rulings has been slow in forthcoming, although the Antidumping Act of 1916 has been repealed.

A WTO panel ruled that the Byrd Amendment violates the WTO antidumping and subsidy codes. The Byrd Amendment (Continued Dumping and Subsidy Act of 2000) authorizes the Customs Service to forward AD and CVD duties to affected domestic producers for qualified expenses. Eleven WTO members including the EU, Canada and Mexico challenged the Amendment. This ruling was affirmed by the WTO Appellate Body and retaliation was authorized. Late in 2005, the U.S. repealed the Byrd Amendment, subject to a contested two-year phase-out.

U.S. involvement in WTO dispute settlement continues to be extensive. The Appellate Body ruled that U.S. countervailing duties against British steel based upon pre-privatization subsidies were unlawful. U.S. complaints against Korean beef import restraints and procurement practices were upheld. Canada's patent protection term was also invalidated by the WTO under a U.S. complaint. European Union complaints concerning U.S. wheat gluten quotas have been sustained. The *Wheat Gluten* dispute questions the legality of U.S. "causation" rules in escape clause proceedings under Section 201 of the Trade Act of 1974. See Chapter 4.

The United States and other complainants prevailed in a WTO proceeding against Indian local content and trade balancing requirements for foreign auto manufacturers. These requirements violated the TRIMs agreement. In a David and Goliath dispute, Antigua-Barbuda won a WTO panel ruling under the GATS against U.S. Internet gambling restraints, the Appellate Body affirming in part.

The U.S. won a panel decision against Mexico's exorbitant telecom interconnection rates, but lost a cotton subsidy challenge by Brazil. Retaliation was authorized by the Appellate Body. In 2009, a WTO panel ruled that Airbus had received $20 billion in illegal EU "launch" subsidies. By 2010, that same panel found Boeing the recipient of $5 billion in federal research contract subsidies that violated the WTO Subsidies Code. These disputes, long in the making, remain ongoing.

After losing a cotton export subsidy dispute, the United States agreed to pay $147 million annually to provide technical assistance to Brazilian cotton farmers. In return, Brazil has suspended retaliatory tariffs and cross-sector IP sanctions authorized by the WTO. The U.S. also lost a country of origin labeling (COOL) dispute raised by Mexico and Canada challenging mandatory retail meat origin packaging rules. Over $1 billion in annual retaliatory tariffs on U.S. exports to Canada and Mexico were authorized late in 2015. The U.S. moved swiftly towards repeal of its COOL regulations.

Major U.S. safeguard tariffs against steel were invalidated by the Appellate Body. The U.S. won a SPS dispute against Japanese quarantine of U.S. apples, while losing an important softwood lumber "zeroing" methodology complaint brought by Canada. In 2006, the Mexico-United States "sugar war" came to a head before the Appellate Body. Mexico's 20% soft drink tax on beverages not using cane sugar, its 20% distribution tax on those beverages, and related bookkeeping requirements were found to violate GATT Article III and not exempt under Article XX(d). Subsequently, the two countries settled their dispute by agreeing, effective in 2008, to free trade in sugar and high fructose corn syrup.

The U.S. failed to persuade the Appellate Body to require the European Union under GATT Article X (3) to undertake a major overhaul of its customs law system targeting inconsistencies therein among the 27 member states. Lastly, the United States lost another "zeroing" dispute under its antidumping law.

In 2008, the WTO Appellate Body, for the second time, ruled against the EU *Beef Hormones* ban (discussed above). U.S. retaliatory tariff sanctions remained in place. In 2009, a settlement was reached. The U.S. effectively gets a higher quota to export hormone-free beef to the EU, in return for phasing out over four years its retaliatory tariffs on EU goods. The U.S. threat of carousel sanctions, i.e. rotating goods subject to tariff retaliation, was instrumental to this settlement.

The United States continues to lose WTO disputes about its zeroing methodology in antidumping proceedings. Despite over 12 decisions against zeroing, the U.S. has moved slowly to alter its rules to comply with WTO rulings. See Chapter 4. As the U.S. winds down its "Byrd Amendment" (repealed, 2006) distributions of prior antidumping and countervailing duty revenues to U.S. industries, Japan and the EU continue retaliatory tariffs that correspond in amount to those distributions, $8 million and $95 million in 2010 respectively.

The United States has also settled a number of disputes prior to WTO panel decisions, and remains in consultation on other disputes that may be decided by a WTO panel. For the latest summary of all WTO disputes, including many not involving the United States, see www.wto.org.

CHINA INVOLVEMENT IN WTO DISPUTES

China, a member since 2001, is involved in a growing number of WTO disputes. Here is a sampling of those disputes.

Canada, the European Union and the United States complained against Chinese duties on imported auto parts (10 percent) that rose to those on complete autos (25 percent) if the imported parts exceeded a fixed percentage of the final vehicle content or price, or if specific combinations of imported auto parts were used in the final vehicle. In addition, extensive record keeping, reporting and verification requirements were imposed when Chinese auto companies used imported parts. In July of 2008, a WTO panel ruled that these "internal charges" violated Articles III (2) and III (4) of the GATT and China's accession commitments.

The core panel ruling, affirmed by the Appellate Body, found China's auto parts measures discriminatory in favor of domestic producers, a violation of the national treatment standard for taxes and regulations. This ruling marked the first time since China's admission in 2001 that it was held in breach of its WTO commitments and obligations.

Less than one month after losing this dispute, China enacted a clever "green tax" on gas-guzzling autos, most of which just happen to be imported. The sales tax on cars with engine capacities over 4.1 litres has been doubled to 40%. Autos with engines between 3 and 4.1 litres are taxed at 25%, up from 15%. Most Chinese-made cars have engines with 2.5 litres or less. Autos with engines between 1 and 3 litres remain taxed at 8% and 10%. The smallest cars with engines below 1 litre have their sales tax reduced from 3 to 1 percent. This green tax could achieve protective results similar to China's Auto

Parts tariff structure and could be challenged under GATT Article III.

Other disputes challenging China's compliance with WTO law are pending. They concern China's auto export subsidies and CVDs on auto imports, protection and enforcement of intellectual property rights (2009 WTO panel ruled against China), trade and distribution of publications and audiovisual entertainment products and services (2009 Appellate Body ruled against China), commodity export tariffs and restrictions (2012 WTO Appellate Body ruled against China), application of Chinese AD to U.S. grain-oriented flat rolled steel (GOES) (2012 WTO Appellate Body ruled against China), discriminatory treatment of foreign electronic payment services (2012 WTO panel ruled against China), rare earth export controls (2014 Appellate Body rules against China) and AD and CVD duties on U.S. electrical steel exports (2015 WTO panel rules against China). The United States has been a complaining party to all of these disputes.

China, in turn, has challenged U.S. safeguard measures applied to Chinese steel exports (2010 WTO Panel rejected challenge) and tires (2011 WTO Panel rejected challenge). It has challenged U.S. antidumping and countervailing duties on paper products from China (2011 WTO Panel ruled against U.S. dual assessment of AD and CVD duties), as well as U.S. AD on Chinese solar panels. China has also applied AD duties to U.S. exports, e.g. chicken.

THE INTERNATIONAL MONETARY FUND (IMF)

Most nations have a national currency and pursue an internal monetary policy to meet their own political and economic goals. Fifteen EU nations have joined in a common currency, the Euro, managed by the European Central Bank. No central authority controls a world monetary system; monetary policy is decentralized. Since 1944, nations have coordinated national monetary policies principally through the International Monetary Fund (IMF).

Both the IMF and the International Bank for Reconstruction and Development (the "World Bank") arose out of the Bretton Woods Conference in 1944. The World Bank was to facilitate loans by capital surplus countries (e.g., then the United States) to countries needing foreign investment for economic redevelopment after World War II. The IMF was to stabilize currency exchange rates, assist countries in their balance of payments, and repair other war damage to the international monetary system. Twenty-nine countries including the United States became party to the IMF Articles of Agreement in 1945. Today, over 150 countries are members of the IMF.

IMF Operations

The IMF goals are to facilitate the expansion and balanced growth of international trade, to assist in the elimination of foreign exchange restrictions which hamper the growth of international trade, and to shorten the duration and lessen the disequilibrium in the international balances of payments of members. The mitigation of wide currency fluctuations is achieved through a complex lending system which permits a country to borrow money from other Fund members or from the Fund (by way of "Special Drawing Rights" or "SDRs") for the purpose of stabilizing the relationship of its currency to other world currencies. These monetary drawing arrangements permit a member country to support its national currency's relative value when compared with national currencies of other countries, especially the "hard" ("reserve") currencies such as the Swiss franc, the Euro, Japanese yen, and United States dollar.

In recent years, IMF loans have normally been "conditioned" upon adoption of specific economic reforms by debtor states, especially in Asia and Latin America. This has led to the perception that the IMF is the world's "sheriff", setting the terms for refinancing national debts and protecting the interests of commercial bank creditors. The IMF has functioned as the first line of negotiation in an international "debt crisis," and commercial and national banks often conform their loans to IMF conditions. These IMF conditions can have dramatic political and social repercussions in debtor nations.

From 2006 onwards, nations paid their IMF debt in record numbers. Argentina did so with an assist from Venezuela. Brazil, Russia, Bolivia, Uruguay, Indonesia, the Philippines and others joined in the flight from IMF loan conditions. The IMF's loan portfolio stood at $100 billion in 2003. By 2009, that portfolio was approaching zero, the IMF was running a budget deficit, and proposing sales of gold to make up the difference. Many commentators wondered aloud, what is the role of the IMF without loans? Then the world financial and economic meltdown arrived in the fall of 2008. By year's end and thereafter the IMF was back in the loan business, with increased funds and notable participation in conditioned bail-outs of Iceland, Greece, Portugal, Ireland and other European nations.

The IMF, like any bureaucracy in search of a mission, drafted a Code of Best Practices for "Sovereign Wealth Funds" (SWFs). Such Funds are said to hold over $3 trillion, and are expanding rapidly. Abu Dhabi, Saudi Arabia, Kuwait, Singapore, Russia, China and Norway (for example) all have large SWFs, many of which played an important role in bailing out U.S. banks and securities firms during the 2007–08 sub-prime lending crisis. The primary concern is that SWFs might use their power for political purposes. Their emergence further diminishes the need for IMF loans. As yet the SWFs have not "conditioned" their lending or investment decisions.

Special Drawing Rights (SDRs)

The International Monetary Fund has established a form of international money which is not a national currency and is called a Special Drawing Right (SDR). Certificates of deposit are denominated in SDRs; short-term SDR loans may be obtained commercially; and some OPEC nations have begun to value their national currencies in SDRs. Mechanically, an SDR is an international medium of exchange having a 2016 composite value based 42% percent on the U.S. dollar, 31 percent on the Euro, 11% on the Chinese renminbi, 8 percent on the Japanese yen, and 8 percent on the British pound. Each exchange rate fluctuation in any one of these "basket currencies" produces commensurately only a smaller, fractional fluctuation in the value of an SDR.

Although the SDR has been talked about as if it is a supranational currency, and China has advocated as much, the SD "Right" is more technically a "unit of account" created by an IMF process. When an IMF member country, having a negative balance of payments position, runs short of its currency "reserves" (which may be its stocks of "hard" "reserve" currencies or gold), the member country may exercise its "Right" to make a "Special Drawing" from the IMF (e.g., the country may ask the IMF to arrange for that country to receive $40 million worth of currency). Upon receipt of the Drawing "request", the IMF approaches another member country having a fuller stock of "reserves" (which "back up" its national currency), and requests that country to provide currency to the requesting country (e.g., to provide $40 million worth of currency other than gold). In return for having supplied the currency, the supplying country acquires additional Special Drawing Rights (e.g., worth $40 million) which it may revoke if ever its currency "reserves" get too low.

Each IMF Member Country participating in the SDR scheme has a finite allocation of SDRs available for its possible use. A net result of the SDR scheme is that countries "swap" currencies to help other countries from time to time in maintaining existing, relative values between their national currency and other currencies of the world. Greece in 2015, for example, used its SDR quota to "repay" IMF debt associated with its bailouts.

CHAPTER 3
IMPORTS

Tariffs	Nontariff Trade Barriers
Customs Law	Duty Free Entry
Fast Track	U.S. Free Trade Agreements

Virtually all governments regulate the entry of goods into their jurisdiction. Customs tariffs may be collected, and conformity of the imported goods to local product standards will be reviewed. Much of the law related to restrictions on imports is derived from agreements governing international economic relations, notably those of the World Trade Organization. In this chapter, we will focus on United States law, which is broadly representative of the regulation of imports.

UNITED STATES TRADE LAWS

Rules and sources of law for United States international trade are mostly found in a sequence of specific trade acts which make up the basic framework for import and export trade. To these, however, must be added numerous provisions of other laws which are directed to specific trade issues. For example, the Export Administration Act of 1979 details U.S. export controls, the subject of Chapter 5. United States trade case law tends to be limited. Trade rules have evolved in legislative chambers and multilateral organizations rather than in the courts. There is really no common law of trade; the decisions which do exist are almost exclusively interpretations of the statutory rules.

For U.S. international trade law, there is no easy single statutory source of law. New trade statutes do two things. They create some new trade rules and thus have some permanency standing alone. But they also modify earlier trade statutes. Thus a search often requires checking several U.S. trade laws, although certain subjects tend to be identified with a single trade Act. For example, the Tariff Act of 1930 is where the tariff schedules are located along with several U.S. "trade remedies" for domestic interests impacted by imports.

The Trade Act of 1974 is where rules governing trade with less favored nations, those not benefitting from "normal" MFN status, are found. It is a source of trade rules for more than most favored nations, for example those benefitting duty free entry under the Generalized System of Preferences (GSP) program. The Trade Agreements Act of 1979, the Omnibus Trade and Competitiveness Act of 1988, the Uruguay Round Implementation Act of 1994, and the Trade Act of 2002 cover a number of GATT/WTO trade rules. Trade is thus governed principally by a matrix of separate U.S. trade laws ranging from the Tariff Act of 1930 to the Trade Preferences Extension Act of 2015.

These are not the only laws which govern United States trade. There are many other acts which regulate trade, some of which appear as amendments to other laws. For example, the Foreign Corrupt Practices Act, intended to reduce the making of improper payments to government officials abroad, is a relatively brief act which modifies the securities laws. The Caribbean Basin Economic Recovery Act, and the Africa Growth and Opportunity Act extend special duty free import rights to goods from those developing areas. The Buy American Act of 1933 grants government procurement preferences to U.S. manufacturers and service providers to the exclusion of many foreign suppliers.

All of these laws provide the basic domestic law framework governing United States trade. When combined with United States obligations in international and regional organizations and agreements such as the WTO and NAFTA, one begins to understand the complexity and diversity of United States international trade and economic relations law.

U.S. IMPORT LAWS

The first of the principal laws regulating imports to the United States is the Tariff Act of 1930. This is the famous Smoot-Hawley Tariff Act, which raised tariff walls to substantial heights and worsened the world depression of the 1930s. The severe tariffs of Smoot-Hawley have since been largely diminished for those nations which benefit from most favored nation (MFN) status, but remain for those less favored. One reason the 1930 Act remains in force is that it is the location of the hundreds of pages of tariffs—the tariff schedules.

In addition to tariffs, the 1930 Act includes the organization and functions of the International

Trade Commission. It controls some of the actions which the Commission may take, including of considerable importance, what are commonly referred to as Section 337 actions challenging unfair practices in import trade. There are extensive provisions for the promotion of foreign trade, and also a major provision protecting American trademarked goods from the entry of counterfeit products, Section 526. Finally, the Tariff Act of 1930 includes the United States rules governing countervailing and antidumping duties.

Although other trade acts were enacted subsequent to the 1930 Act, the next which includes major provisions important to U.S. international trade law is the Trade Act of 1974. This Act includes executive negotiating authority for trade agreements with other countries, the creation of the office of the United States Trade Representative, and provisions governing the interrelationship of Congress and the President with regard to trade relations. Furthermore, it includes provisions regulating relief from injury caused by surging import competition, particularly Section 201 actions, known as "escape clause" or "safeguards" actions. Part of the relief from injury includes adjustment assistance for workers, renewed in 2015. Another title of the 1974 act addresses the enforcement of United States rights under trade agreements, which are reflected in Section 301.

A separate title governs trade relations with countries not currently receiving nondiscriminatory treatment, meaning essentially nonmarket economies. These provisions are becoming less significant as many nonmarket economies have attempted to shed such status for participation in the world market. They include the little used but potentially important Section 406, allowing "market disruption" actions. Finally, the 1974 Trade Act includes the generalized system of preferences (GSP) scheme, which gives to certain developing nations duty free tariff status.

The Trade Agreements Act of 1979 is the third important trade act. This Act was passed principally to implement several of the NTB codes negotiated in the Tokyo Round of the GATT, concluded in the mid-1970s. Thus, it has sections dealing with government procurement and technical barriers to trade (standards). Changes to the rules governing countervailing and antidumping duties, and to customs valuation, both part of newly adopted GATT codes, were implemented by this Act, but as amendments to the Tariff Act of 1930 rather than enduring provisions identified with the 1979 Act.

The fourth important act is the Trade and Tariff Act of 1984. In addition to making amendments to the earlier acts, this Act extended "fast track" negotiating authority (discussed below) to the President, which provided for the development of a free trade agreement with Israel and Canada. The fifth act is the Omnibus Trade and Competitiveness Act of 1988. This Act authorized the President to enter into the Uruguay Round of GATT negotiations. It also implemented the Harmonized Tariff Schedule of the United States. Special attention was devoted in the 1988 Act to amending Section 301 of the 1974 Trade Act. It is the source of the notorious "Super 301" and "Special 301" procedures whereby the United States could target nations with which it has major trade or intellectual property disputes.

When the United States became a signatory to the North American Free Trade Agreement in 1993, Congress soon thereafter enacted the North American Free Trade Implementation Act, which made NAFTA part of U.S. trade law. Similarly, when the United States became a signatory to the Agreement Establishing the World Trade Organization in 1994, and its extensive package of agreements and understandings, Congress enacted the Uruguay Round Agreements Act, which made the WTO a part of U.S. trade law.

The Trade Act of 2002 renewed, after a notable lapse during the Clinton administration, "fast track" international trade negotiating authority for the President. It is under this authority that President George W. Bush concluded free trade agreements with Chile, Singapore, five Central American nations and the Dominican Republic (CAFTA/DR), Oman, Bahrain, Peru, Colombia, Panama, Morocco, South Korea and Australia. He also pursued agreement on other bilateral free trade deals, a Free Trade Area of the Americas, and the Doha Round of World Trade Organization negotiations, none of which were completed prior to the expiration of fast track in July 2007.

After an extended lapse, President Obama received fast track authority in 2015, notably to pursue negotiations on the Trans-Pacific Partnership (TPP) and the Transatlantic Trade and Investment Partnership (TTIP). In addition, the Trade Preferences Extension Act of 2015 renewed various U.S. duty free entry programs, and also reauthorized trade adjustment assistance for impacted U.S workers and firms.

THE ORIGINS OF UNITED STATES TARIFFS

Article I, Section 8, of the United States Constitution authorizes Congress to levy uniform tariffs on imports. Tariff legislation must originate in the House of Representatives. Although tariffs were primarily viewed as revenue-raising measures at the founding of the nation, it was not long before tariffs became used for openly protectionist purposes. The Tariff Act of 1816 initiated this change in outlook.

During much of the 19th Century, the United States legislated heavy protective tariffs. These were justified as necessary to protect the country's infant industries and to force the South to engage in more trade with the North (not with Europe). Exceptions were made to the high level of tariffs for selected United States imports. These typically flowed from conditional most-favored-nation reciprocity treaties. The first of these treaties involved Canada (1854) and Hawaii (1875).

As the United States moved into the 20th Century, additional tariffs in excess of the already high level of protection were authorized. "Countervailing duty" tariffs were created in 1890 to combat export subsidies of European nations, particularly

Germany. After 1916, additional duties could also be assessed if "dumping practices" were involved. Early American dumping legislation was largely a reaction to marketplace competition from foreign cartels.

Throughout all of these years the constitutionality of protective tariffs was never clearly resolved. In 1928, however, the United States Supreme Court firmly ruled that the enactment of protective tariffs was constitutional. This decision, followed by the crash of the stock market in 1929, led to the enactment of the Smoot-Hawley Tariff Act of 1930. This Act set some of the highest rates of tariff duties in the history of the United States. It represents the last piece of tariff legislation that Congress passed without international negotiations. These tariffs remain part of the United States law and are generally referred to as "Column 2 tariffs" under the U.S. Harmonized Tariff Schedule (HTS).

Since 1930, changes in the levels of tariffs applicable to goods entering the United States have chiefly been achieved through international trade agreements negotiated by the President and affirmed by Congress. During the 1930s and 40s, the Smoot-Hawley tariffs generally applied unless altered through bilateral trade agreements. The Reciprocal Trade Agreements Act of 1934 gives the President the authority to enter into such agreements, and under various extensions this authority remains in effect today. An early agreement of this type was the Canadian Reciprocal Trade Agreement of 1935.

UNITED STATES TARIFF RATES

United States tariffs generally take one of three forms. The most common is an *ad valorem* rate. Such tariffs are assessed in proportion to the value of the article. Tariffs may also be assessed at specific rates or compound rates. Specific rates may be measured by the pound or other weight. A compound rate is a mixture of an *ad valorem* and specific rate tariff. Tariff rate quotas involve limitations on imports at a specific tariff up to a certain amount. Imports in excess of that amount are not prohibited, but are subject to a higher rate of tariff. Thus tariff rate quotas tend to restrict imports that are in excess of the specified quota for the lower tariff level.

These are three sets of United States tariff rates: Column 1 General, Column 1 Special and Column 2. Column 1 General tariff rates, known as most favored-nation (MFN) or "normal" tariffs, are the lower and most likely to be applicable. Column 2 tariff rates, originating in the Smoot-Hawley Tariff Act of 1930, are the higher and least likely to be applicable.

In addition, there are a variety of selective Column 1 Special provisions, usually duty free entry programs to which the U.S. subscribes. These include the Generalized System of Tariff Preferences of the United States (GSP), the Caribbean Basin Initiative, the Andean Trade Preference Act, the Africa Growth and Opportunity Act, the Hope for Haiti program, and Section 9802.00.80 of the HTS. The North American Free Trade Agreement (NAFTA), and a growing number of bilateral U.S. free trade agreements, also generally provide for duty free access.

Column One Tariffs and the GATT

The Trade Agreements Extension Act of 1945 authorized the President to conduct multilateral negotiations in the trade field. It was out of this authority that the General Agreement on Tariffs and Trade (GATT) was negotiated. The GATT became effective on January 1, 1948 and was implemented in the United States by executive order. Indeed, despite its wide-ranging impact on United States tariff levels since 1948, the GATT has never been ratified by the United States Congress.

Nevertheless, it is the source of the principal tariffs assessed today on imports into the United States. These duties, known as most-favored-nation (MFN) tariffs or "Column 1 tariffs," have been dramatically reduced over the years through successive rounds of GATT/WTO trade negotiations. See Chapter 2. They are unconditional MFN tariffs, meaning that reciprocity is not required in order for them to apply to WTO member nations.

Column 1 (MFN) tariff status for exports to the United States can also be obtained under U.S. bilateral trade agreements. Chinese goods enjoyed such status long before WTO membership, but were subject to the "Jackson-Vanik Amendment." This provision of the 1974 Trade Act requires tolerably liberal emigration policies of nonmarket economy nations for U.S. Column 1 tariff status to apply. Chinese and Vietnamese goods qualified under the

Jackson-Vanik for MFN treatment prior to WTO membership for China in 2001 and Vietnam in 2007. Each year the President issued a "waiver" to facilitate these outcomes.

The term "most-favored-nation" is misleading in its suggestion of special tariff arrangements. It is more appropriate and officially correct to think of MFN tariffs as the "normal" level of U.S. tariffs, to which there are exceptions resulting in the application of higher, lower or zero tariffs. At this point, the average MFN tariff applied to manufactured imports into the United States is approximately 3.5 percent.

Special U.S. Tariffs

In addition to its GATT/WTO negotiated MFN tariffs, the United States and other WTO member states are authorized in appropriate circumstances to assess special tariffs. Antidumping duties are authorized to counteract dumping practices (sales of goods abroad at prices below those in the country of export). Countervailing tariffs are authorized in response to selected foreign government subsidies that benefit their exports. Occasionally, as well, additional tariffs may be assessed under escape clause (safeguard) proceedings when imports surge. All of these special, additional U.S. tariffs are covered in Chapter 4 on Trade Remedies.

Foreign Trade Zones

"Free trade zones" are located throughout the U.S., many of them near ports and airports. While imported goods remain in the zones, they are not subject to U.S. tariffs. The imported goods are subject to U.S. tariffs when they leave the zones, but only if they are then brought into the United States. If they are exported from the free trade zone to another country, they will never be subjected to U.S. tariffs.

Such zones serve as distribution centers, encourage assembly of certain manufactured items for export, provide local employment, and may lessen overall tariffs which must be paid before an assembled item crosses the zone for routine importation into the country. In the U.S., zones are supervised by the Foreign Trade Zones Board (located within the Commerce Department) and by the Customs Service.

U.S. CUSTOMS LAW

Trillions of dollars of imports enter the United States each year. To calculate U.S. import duties, you must first determine the classification, country of origin and the customs valuation of imported goods. In other words, what is it, where is it from, and what is its customs value?

Customs Classification

Imported goods must "pass customs". Usually, the passage through customs and physical entry into a country occur simultaneously. When goods arrive at the United States border, the consignee (or an agent, such as a customs broker) files both "entry" and "entry summary" forms which are used to determine the classification, valuation, origin and conformity to product standards of the imported goods. At the same time, a deposit of the amount of estimated customs duties is made with customs officials. A procedure for immediate release of imported goods is available, as is the use of consolidated periodic statements for all entries made during a billing period.

The classification problem may be illustrated as follows: Are parts of a wooden picture frame, imported piece by piece in separate packages for later assembly within a country, to be assessed duties prescribed for wood picture frames or for strips of wood molding? Is "wood picture frame" even an appropriate nomenclature, or should what is commonly known to be a wood picture frame have a tariff nomenclature of "art object" or "forest product" or simply "personal belonging"?

For decades, most of the countries in the world, except the United States and Canada, classified imports according to the Brussels Tariff Nomenclature (BTN), which identifies items along a progression from raw materials to finished products. The United States had its own system of classification set out in the Tariff Schedule of the United States (TSUS). However, beginning in 1982, the United States initiated steps to convert the TSUS into a Harmonized Commodity Description and Coding System (HS) of classification, in common with the classification system used by most other countries and developed by the World Customs Organization in Brussels.

The United States adopted the Harmonized System as the Harmonized Tariff Schedule (HTSUS) for classification of all imports by enactment of the Omnibus Trade and Competitiveness Act of 1988, with an effective date of Jan. 1, 1989. Most nations have adopted HTS and use it to classify U.S. exports.

The HTS "nomenclature" has twenty sections, the majority of which group articles from similar branches of industry or commerce. For example, Section I covers live animals and animal products, Section II vegetable products, Section III animal or vegetable fats, Section IV prepared foodstuffs, and Section V mineral products. The twenty sections are subdivided into 99 chapters, which in total list approximately 5,000 article descriptions in the heading and sub-heading format. These provisions apply to all goods entering the customs territory of the United States.

Most problems arise when it is possible to classify imported goods under more than one heading. If the importer and the United States customs officials disagree about the proper classification of an imported item, and appeals within the U.S. customs service fail to resolve the dispute, the United States Court of International Trade (CIT) has exclusive jurisdiction to resolve their dispute.

In cases decided under TSUS, the CIT has followed its own logic, without reference to decisions of other courts, because the approach of the U.S. TSUS was so unique. In the cases decided under HTSUS, the CIT has continued this tradition in its decisions under the new classification system, rather than viewing the decisions of foreign courts or the Rules accompanying the HTS as persuasive.

The U.S. Supreme Court notably held in *United States v. Mead Corp.*, 533 U.S. 218 (2001) that Customs Service classification rulings are not entitled to full administrative deference. Rather, such rulings are entitled to limited deference depending on their "thoroughness, logic and expertness, fit with prior interpretations, and any other sources of weight."

Rules of Origin

Tariff schedules often provide that duties on an imported item vary depending upon the country from which the item comes. Hence, where goods are from, legally speaking, matters. To resolve this issue, "rules of origin" come into play. Two common situations raising questions of origin involve products shipped to the United States from Country "X" that have been manufactured in Country "Y," and products shipped to the United States from Country "X", in which the product was made, but certain component parts of the product have originated in Country "Y".

Under U.S. "rules of origin" an article is a product of a country if it is *wholly* the growth, product, or manufacture of that country. In the case of an article which consists in whole or in part of materials from another country, it originates where it has been substantially transformed into a new and different article of commerce with a name, character, or use distinct from that of the article or articles from which it was so transformed. This core "substantial transformation" test is relevant in determining the rate at which U.S. customs duty is charged (MFN or not). The substantial transformation test is generally the fallback rule of origin for goods absent specific U.S. provisions to the contrary, which are numerous.

Special rules of origin apply to the various U.S. duty free entry programs (see below) which rely principally on changes in tariff classifications and regional value content to determine which goods may freely be traded. For NAFTA rules of origin, see Chapter 8. The Court of International Trade requires importers seeking preferential tariff treatment to verify the country of origin of their goods. "Reasonable care" must be exercised, not just simple reliance on the exporter's assertions of origin. Failures in this regard can result in collection of lost duties and penalties.

Under the proposed WTO Agreement on Rules of Origin, there is an effort to harmonize the rules of origin on a world-wide basis. A committee of experts is charged with creating rules which are "objective, understandable, and predictable." Some 20 years later, no WTO agreement on rules of origin has emerged. This leaves each nation in charge of developing its own rules of origin for goods. Not surprisingly, there are significant differences.

Customs Valuation

Even though an imported item may be classified, have an ascertainable legal origin, and a clear-cut percentage rate of duty, difficulty may still arise in getting the importer and customs authorities to agree upon the item's value to which that percentage applies. For decades, United States customs valuation of an imported item was gauged by the American Selling Price (ASP) of the item—i.e., the usual wholesale price at which the same item manufactured in the United States was offered for sale.

However, Article VII of GATT 1947 requires that "value for customs purposes . . . should not be based on the value of merchandise of national origin or on arbitrary or fictitious values." The 1979 Tokyo Round produced a Customs Valuation Code, which established the details of an approach which was quite different from ASP. This approach was incorporated into the U.S. Trade Agreements Act of 1979.

United States customs valuation is now calculated by the "transaction value" of the imported item. "Transaction value" is "the price actually paid or payable for the merchandise when sold for exportation to the United States" plus "certain amounts reflecting packing costs, commissions paid by buyer, any assist, royalty or license fee paid by buyer, and any resale, disposal, or use proceeds that accrue to seller."

If a transaction value cannot be determined, certain fallback methods are used. In descending order of eligibility these methods are: The transaction value of identical merchandise, the transaction value of similar merchandise, the resale price of the merchandise with allowances for certain factors, or the cost of producing the imported item.

These approaches to valuation form the core of the new Agreement on Implementation of Article VII of GATT 1994 (WTO Customs Code). Hence, unlike rules of origin, WTO member states have adopted a uniform approach to customs valuation law.

U.S. IMPORT QUOTAS

Goods imported into the United States may have to qualify within numerical quota limitations imposed on that item or upon that kind of item. "Tariff-rate quotas" admit a specified quantity of goods at a preferential rate of duty. Once imports reach that quantity, tariffs are normally increased.

The United States has employed import quotas for many years. Tariff-rate quotas have been applied to dairy products, olives, tuna fish, anchovies, brooms, and sugar, syrups and molasses. Quite a few absolute quotas originate under Section 22 of the Agricultural Adjustment Act. These quotas are undertaken when necessary to United States farm price supports or similar agricultural programs. They have been used on animal feeds, dairy products, chocolate, cotton, peanuts, and selected syrups and sugars.

Some U.S. agricultural quotas are being converted into tariffs under the WTO Agreement on Agriculture. Some quotas imposed by the U.S. are sanctions for unfair trade practices, as against tungsten from China. Other quotas originate in international commodity agreements. Major quota restraints on textile imports were achieved as a result of the international Multi-Fiber Arrangement, which expired in 2005 under the WTO Textiles

Agreement. Global trade in textiles and apparel is now normally quota free, significantly benefitting China and other Asian producers.

The Agricultural Act of 1949 requires the President to impose global import quotas on Upland Cotton. Whenever the Secretary of Agriculture determines that its average price exceeds certain statutory limits, unlike the ordinary restrictive import quota, the importation of Upland Cotton is duty free. Like the U.S. Meat Import Act, this provision tends to be countercyclical to market forces for cotton in the United States. A U.S. cotton subsidy system has been ruled invalid by the WTO Appellate Body in a dispute brought by Brazil, but the U.S. is essentially paying Brazil not to retaliate as authorized.

Lastly, the United States sometimes imposes import restraints for national security or foreign policy reasons. Many of these restraints originate from Section 232 of the Trade Expansion Act of 1962. This provision authorizes the President to "adjust imports" whenever necessary to the national security of the country. Trade embargoes (zero quotas) are sometimes imposed on all the goods from politically incorrect nations (e.g., North Korea). Product-specific import bans also exist for selected goods, e.g., narcotic drugs and books urging insurrection against the United States.

The importation of "immoral" goods is generally prohibited, even for private use, and the obscenity of such items is decided by reviewing the community standards at the port of entry. Generally, goods

produced with forced, convict or indentured or
bonded child labor are excluded from the United
States. The ban against goods produced by convicts
has been applied to certain items from the People's
Republic of China.

If a quota system is created, a fundamental
subsidiary issue is: How will the quotas be allocated?
The U.S. Customs Service generally administers
quotas on a first-come, first-served basis. This
approach creates a race to enter goods into the
United States. The President is authorized to sell
import licenses at public auctions. One advantage of
an auction system is its revenue raising potential.
Instead of an auction system, the U.S. has ordinarily
used a Presidentially-managed system of import
allocations, especially in regard to agricultural
import quotas.

The U.S. Tariff Act of 1930 provides that to the
extent practicable and consistent with efficient and
fair administration, the President is to insure against
inequitable sharing of imports by a relatively small
number of the larger importers. In fact, allocating
quotas among U.S. importers rarely happens. In the
past, quotas were often part of a "voluntary export
restraint" (VER) or orderly market agreement (OMA)
between the U.S. and one or more foreign
governments, and represented adherence by those
governments to U.S. initiatives. The negotiations
typically concentrated on obtaining foreign
government agreement to limitations on exportation
of their products into the U.S. market, and did not
pursue rules on who might use the resulting

allocations. A classic example for many years was Japanese "voluntary" restraints on exporting autos to the United States. The WTO Agreement on Safeguards severely limits the use of VERs and OMAs.

U.S. PUBLIC PROCUREMENT

Where public procurement is involved, and the taxpayer's money is at issue, virtually every nation has some form of legislation or tradition that favors buying from domestic suppliers. In federal nations like the United States, these rules can also be found in state and local purchasing requirements.

The principal United States statute affecting imports in connection with government procurement is the Buy American Act of 1933. This Act requires the government to buy American unless the acquisition is for use outside the U.S., there are insufficient quantities of satisfactory quality available in the U.S., or domestic purchases would be inconsistent with the public interest or result in unreasonable costs.

Buy American

As currently applied, the United States Buy American Act requires federal agencies to treat a domestic bid as unreasonable or inconsistent with the public interest only if it exceeds a foreign bid by more than six percent (customs duties included) or ten percent (customs duties and specific costs excluded). Exceptions to this general approach exist for reasons of national interest, certain designated small business purchases, domestic suppliers operating in areas of substantial unemployment and demonstrated national security needs. Bids by small businesses and companies located in labor surplus areas are generally protected by a 12 percent margin of preference. Bids from U.S. companies are considered foreign rather than domestic when the materials used in the products concerned are below 50 percent American in origin. These rules apply to civil purchasing by the United States government, but are suspended for purchasing subject to the WTO Procurement Code.

The Department of Defense has its own Buy American rules. Generally speaking, a 50 percent price preference (customs duties excluded) or a 6 or 12 percent preference (customs duties included) whichever is more protective to domestic suppliers is applied. However, intergovernmental "Memoranda of Understanding" (MOU) on defense procurement provide important exceptions to the standard Department of Defense procurement rules.

A practice known as "unbalanced bidding" has arisen in connection with the Buy American Act. Unbalanced bidding involves the use of United States labor and parts by foreigners in sufficient degree so as to overcome the bidding preferences established by law for U.S. suppliers. This occurs because the United States value added is *not* included in the calculations of the margin of preference for the U.S. firms. Thus foreign bids minus the value of work done in the U.S. are multiplied by the 6, 12 or 50 percent Buy American Act preference. If the U.S. bids are above the foreign bids but within the margin of preference, the U.S. company gets the contract. If the U.S. bids are higher than the foreign bids plus the margin of preference, the foreigners get the contract.

Additional procurement preferences are established by the Small Business Act of 1953. Under this Act, federal agencies may set aside certain procurement exclusively for small U.S. businesses. In practice, the federal government normally sets aside about 30 percent of its procurement needs in this fashion. Special set-aside rules apply to benefit socially and economically disadvantaged minority-owned businesses. These preferences are generally excepted from U.S. adherence to the WTO Procurement Code.

A number of federal statutes also contain specific Buy American requirements. These include various GSA, NASA and TVA appropriations bills, the AMTRAK Improvement Act of 1978, the Public Works Employment Act of 1977, various highway and transport acts, the Clean Water Act of 1977, and the Rural Electrification Acts of 1936 and 1938. Many of these statutes involve federal funding of state and local procurement. All are generally excepted from the WTO Procurement Code as applied by the United States.

In addition to the Buy American Act, state and local purchasing requirements may inhibit import competition in the procurement field. For example, California once had a law which made it mandatory to purchase American products. This law was declared unconstitutional as an encroachment upon the federal power to conduct foreign affairs. A Massachusetts ban on contracting with companies with investments in Myanmar (Burma) was likewise struck down. *See Crosby v. National Foreign Trade Council,* 530 U.S. 363 (2000).

State statutes which have copied the federal Buy American Act, on the other hand, and incorporated public interest and unreasonable cost exceptions to procurement preferences, have generally withstood constitutional challenge. For example, courts have upheld New Jersey laws fashioned in this manner. Courts have also declared lawful a Pennsylvania statute that requires state and local agencies to ensure that contractors do not provide products containing foreign steel.

GATT Procurement Code and U.S. Response

The Buy American Act was conformed to the optional GATT Procurement Code negotiated during the Tokyo Round. That Code did not apply to state and local purchasing. Congress expressed its displeasure with the degree to which that Code opened up sales opportunities for United States firms abroad. It therefore amended the Buy American Act in 1988 to deny the benefits of the GATT Procurement Code when foreign governments are not in good standing under it. United States government procurement contracts are also denied to suppliers from countries whose governments "maintain ... a significant and persistent pattern of practice or discrimination against U.S. products or services which results in identifiable harm to U.S. businesses."

Presidential waivers of these statutory denials may occur in the public interest, to avoid single supply situations or to assure sufficient bidders to provide supplies of requisite quality and competitive prices.

The European Union was one of the first to be identified as a persistent procurement discriminator by the USTR. This identification concerned longstanding heavy electrical and telecommunications disputes that were partly settled by negotiation with the EU. The remaining disputes led to U.S. trade sanctions and EU retaliation. This did not occur with Greece, Spain and Portugal (where the EU procurement rules did not apply), and with Germany which broke ranks and negotiated a path breaking bilateral U.S. settlement. Japan has also been identified as a persistent procurement discriminator in the construction, architectural and engineering areas.

The Tokyo Round GATT Procurement Code was not particularly successful at opening up government purchasing. Only Austria, Canada, the twelve European Union states, Finland, Hong Kong, Israel, Japan, Norway, Singapore, Sweden, Switzerland and the United States adhered to that Procurement Code. This was also partly the result of the 1979 Code's many exceptions. For example, the Code did not apply to contracts below its threshold amount of $150,000 SDR (about $171,000 since 1988), service contracts, and procurement by entities on each country's reserve list (including most national defense items).

Because procurement in the European Union and Japan is often decentralized, many contracts fell below the SDR threshold and were therefore GATT exempt. By dividing up procurement into smaller contracts national preferences were retained. United States government procurement tended to be more centralized and thus more likely to be covered by the GATT Code. This pattern may help explain why Congress restrictively amended the Buy American Act in 1988.

WTO Procurement Code

The WTO Procurement Code took effect in 1996 and replaced the 1979 Tokyo Round Code. It remains optional for WTO members. The WTO Code expanded the coverage of the prior Code to include procurement of services, construction, government-owned utilities, and some state and local (sub-central) contracts. The U.S. and the European Union applied the new Code's provisions on government-owned utilities and sub-central contracts as early as 1994.

Various improvements to the procedural rules surrounding procurement practices and dispute settlement under the WTO Code attempt to reduce tensions in this difficult area. For example, an elaborate system for bid protests is established. Bidders who believe the Code's procedural rules have been abused will be able to lodge, litigate and appeal their protests. The Procurement Code became part of

U.S. law in 1994 under the Uruguay Round Agreements Act.

The United States has brought, with few exceptions, all procurement by executive agencies subject to the Federal Acquisition Regulations under the Code's coverage. This has the effect of suspending application of the normal Buy American preferences to such procurement. That said, thirteen U.S. states have not conformed to the WTO Procurement Code.

Further, the United States, amid considerable controversy, adopted "Buy American" steel rules in the Obama administration economic stimulus plan (the American Recovery and Reinvestment Act of 2009), exempting WTO Procurement Code participants and U.S. free trade agreements. Additional Buy American preferences were created by the Obama administration auto bail-out plans and other legislation.

U.S. PRODUCT STANDARDS

There are numerous nontariff trade barriers applicable to United States imports. Many of these barriers arise out of federal or state safety and health regulations. Others concern the environment, consumer protection, product standards and government procurement. Many of the relevant rules were created for legitimate consumer and public protection reasons. They were often created without extensive consideration of their international impact as potential nontariff barriers. Nevertheless, the practical impact of legislation of this type is to ban the importation of nonconforming products from the

United States market. Thus, unlike tariffs which can always be paid and unlike quotas which permit a certain amount of goods to enter the United States market, nontariff barriers have the potential to totally exclude foreign exports.

The diversity of U.S. regulatory approaches to products and the environment makes it extremely difficult to generalize about nontariff trade barriers. In 2008, all imports of plants and wood products (even toothpicks) were subjected to new disclosure duties that may inhibit trade. All foods imported into the United States are subject to inspection for their wholesomeness, freedom from contamination, and compliance with labeling requirements (including the 1993 nutritional labeling rules). This examination is conducted by the Food and Drug Administration using samples submitted to it by the United States Customs Service. If these tests result in a finding that the food products cannot be imported into the United States, they must be exported or destroyed.

The Consumer Products Safety Act bars the importation of consumer products which do not comply with the standards of the Consumer Products Safety Commission. Exporters of consumer products must certify that their goods conform to applicable United States safety and labeling standards. Any product that has a defect which is determined to constitute a "substantial product hazard" or is imminently hazardous may be banned from the United States market. The Customs Service may seize any such nonconforming goods. These goods may be modified in order to conform them to U.S. Consumer Products Safety Commission requirements. Otherwise, such goods must be exported or destroyed, an end result notably applied in 2007 to children's toys from China.

The Bioterrorism Act of 2002 requires all U.S. and foreign food companies selling in the United States to register with the Food and Drug Administration. Importers must notify the FDA in advance and in detail of food shipments, and keep records of suppliers and customers. The FDA can detain any food deemed a risk, including late or missing notice items.

Generally speaking, the United States maintains an open market for competitive trade in services. One major exception is maritime transport. In this area, the U.S. protects its domestic industry from import competition under the Merchant Marine Act of 1920 ("Jones Act") and other statutes. For example, the shipment of Alaskan oil is reserved for U.S.-flag vessels as is the supply of offshore drill rigs. The Jones Act most notably prohibits foreign vessels from transporting goods or passengers between U.S. ports and on U.S. rivers, lakes and canals. The reservation of goods for U.S.-flag ships (such trade is known as cabotage) is very significant economically, amounting to some billions annually with a heavy concentration in petroleum products.

United States environmental or conservation laws notably affecting international trade include:

- The Endangered Species Act of 1973 prohibiting import/export of endangered species.

- The "Pelley Amendment" authorizing import restraints against fish products of nations undermining international fisheries or wildlife conservation agreements.

- The High Seas Driftnet Fisheries Enforcement Act of 1992 banning imports of fish, fish products and sport fishing gear from countries violating the United Nations driftnet moratorium.

- The Sea Turtle Conservation Act prohibiting shrimp imports harvested with adverse effects on sea turtles first used in 1993 against shrimp from several Caribbean nations and now applicable globally to Thailand, India, China and Bangladesh among others.

- The Wild Bird Conservation Act banning imports of tropical wild birds.

- The Antarctic Marine Living Resources Convention Act prohibiting import/export of living resources.

- The African Elephant Conservation Act restricting ivory imports.

WTO Product Standards Law

Under United States law, state and federal agencies may create standards which specify the characteristics of a product, such as levels of quality, safety, performance or dimensions, or its packaging and labeling. However, in accordance with the WTO Technical Barriers to Trade Agreement (Standards Code), these "standards-related activities" must not create "unnecessary obstacles to U.S. foreign trade," and must be demonstrably related to "a legitimate domestic objective" such as protection of health and safety, security, environmental or consumer interests.

Sometimes there is a conflict between federal and state standards. For example, federal law licensing endangered species' articles preempted California's absolute ban on trade in such goods. The Office of the USTR is charged with responsibility for implementation of the WTO Standards Code within the United States.

United States standards have been attacked as nontariff trade barriers violating international obligations. Sometimes the standards have been upheld, sometimes not. For example, a binational arbitration panel established under Chapter 18 of the Canada-U.S. FTA issued a decision upholding a United States law setting a minimum size on lobsters sold in interstate commerce. The panel found that, since the law applied to both domestic and foreign lobsters, it was not a disguised trade restriction.

In 2012, the WTO Appellate Body determined that the United States ban on flavored cigarettes, as applied to clove cigarettes from Indonesia, breached the WTO Technical Barriers to Trade (TBT) Code national treatment standard. The Appellate Body noted particularly the discriminatory allowance for sale in the U.S. of menthol flavored cigarettes.

Tuna, Shrimp and Beef Disputes

In 1991, a GATT panel found that United States import restrictions designed to protect dolphin from tuna fishers violated GATT 1947. The panel ruled that GATT did not permit any import restrictions based on extraterritorial environmental concerns, whether they were considered disguised trade restrictions or not. This decision suggested difficulty with a number of United States laws which concern health, safety and environmental conditions in exporting nations.

A 1994 decision by a second GATT 1947 panel recognized the legitimacy of environmental regulations, but ruled against the tuna boycott by the U.S. because of its focus on production methods and the unilateral imposition of standards by the U.S. In 1997, Congress enacted legislation that replaced the domestic controls on imported tuna with international restrictions stated in the Declaration of Panama. This Declaration, with internationally accepted standards, finally placed U.S. tuna legislation in conformity with its GATT/WTO obligations.

Nevertheless, in 2008, Mexico initiated WTO proceedings against U.S. "dolphin-safe" label rules and a Ninth Circuit decision requiring zero use of purse seine nets for such labels. In 2010, the U.S. commenced NAFTA proceedings seeking to force Mexico to withdraw its WTO complaint and re-file it under NAFTA. "Standards" disputes are supposed to be resolved exclusively under NAFTA Chapter 20 procedures and trade rules that strongly favor national laws. In 2011, a WTO panel held in favor of Mexico's complaint, which Mexico declined to re-file under NAFTA. The WTO Appellate Body affirmed, ruling that the U.S. dolphin-safe label rules violated the national treatment standard of the WTO TBT Code.

In 1998 the WTO Appellate Body ruled against a U.S. ban on shrimp imports from nations that fail to use turtle exclusion devices comparable to those required under U.S. law. The Appellate Body found the U.S. ban undermined the multilateral GATT 1994 trading system because the security and predictability of the system would be compromised if other Members adopted similar measures. The unilateral use of extraterritorial measures to protect exhaustible natural resources was not "justifiable." The Appellate Body believed international agreement on the subject should be sought.

The standards of other nations have also been challenged as violations of WTO obligations. For example, the United States has challenged European Union bans of imports of meat from the United States, first for containing certain hormones, later for unsanitary conditions in U.S. meatpacking facilities. In the former controversy, the United States retaliated. In 1997 and again in 2008, the WTO Appellate Body ruled against the EU ban on hormone-treated beef, citing the lack of an adequate scientific basis for the ban as required under the WTO Sanitary and Phytosanitary (SPS) Agreement.

Import Labeling Disputes

The United States requires clear markings of countries of origin on imports. This can be perceived, especially by those abroad, as a nontariff trade barrier intended to promote domestic purchases. Section 304 of the Tariff act of 1930 establishes the basic rules for origin markings. Every imported article of foreign origin (or its container) must be marked conspicuously, legibly, indelibly and as permanently as practical in English so as to indicate to ultimate purchasers its country of origin. Violation of these rules can result in additional tariffs of up to 10 percent. Intentional removal or alteration of markings is a crime.

In 2008, as part of the Farm Bill, new Lacey Act import disclosure and country of origin requirements were broadly created for plants and wood products. Additional import disclosure and origin "COOL" rules for meat and meat products were also legislated in the 2008 Farm Bill. The COOL rules were successfully challenged by Canada and Mexico before the WTO. The Appellate Body declared them discriminatory, and violations of TBT Code national treatment obligations.

TRANSBORDER DATA FLOWS

Because information transfers are linked with employment and trade patterns, many countries have taken a keen interest in regulating transborder data flows (TBDFs). Technical strides in satellite communications and the digital age make regulation a challenge. In 1981, the OECD approved fourteen principles as Guidelines on the Protection of Privacy and TransBorder Flow of Personal Data. In 1998, Europe finalized a data privacy directive that is noticeably more protective of individual privacy than U.S. law. Any information relating to natural persons must be secure, current, relevant and not excessive in content. In most cases, personal data may be processed only with individual consent. Individuals have broad rights of disclosure, access, correction and erasure of data, particularly before it is used in direct marketing.

Transfers of data to non-EU countries are prohibited unless the recipient jurisdiction provides an "adequate level of protection." Whether the United States does so is hotly debated. To remove risks of liability under the European law, "safe harbors" have been created by EU-USA agreement for firms willing to abide by the EU rules on data privacy. The primary safe harbor involves participation in self-regulating privacy groups (e.g., BBB Online) supervised by the U.S. Federal Trade Commission. EU law on data privacy has thus become a global standard.

The EU has proposed tighter revisions to its data privacy rules, and after a major adverse European Court of Justice ruling, has suggested it may eliminate the "safe harbor" cooperation agreement with the United States.

U.S. DUTY FREE GENERALIZED
TARIFF PREFERENCES (GSP)
FOR DEVELOPING NATIONS

The Generalized System of Preferences (GSP) recognizes that economic development of the third world requires the assistance of industrialized nations, and grants preferences to products of developing countries without demanding reciprocity. In addition to obtaining MFN tariff rates, developing countries can ship goods **duty free** into U.S. and other major industrial markets under GSP. These special arrangements for developing countries are permitted by the provisions of GATT/WTO. They have been implemented by the U.S., the EU, Japan and other major "donor" nations, although each GSP program differs in structure and approach.

It was not until the Trade Act of 1974 that a GSP system was incorporated into United States tariff law. The Trade Act authorized GSP tariff preferences for ten years. Various GSP renewals have followed. The United States GSP system, as presently operated, designates certain nations as "beneficiary developing countries." Unless a country is so designated, none of its imports can enter duty free under the GSP program. In addition, only selected goods are designated "eligible articles" for purposes of the GSP program. Thus, for duty free entry under the GSP program to occur, the goods must originate from a beneficiary nation and qualify as eligible articles.

Any United States producer of an article that competes with GSP imports can file a petition with the United States Trade Representative (USTR) to have a country or particular products withdrawn from the program. This petitioning procedure can also be used in the reverse by importers and exporters to obtain product or beneficiary country status under the United States GSP program. The President is given broad authority to withdraw, suspend or limit the application of duty free entry under the GSP system.

The GSP program lapsed in 2013 but was renewed by the Trade Preferences Extension Act of 2015. At this point, tens of billions worth of goods from well over 100 countries enter the U.S. market duty free under the GSP program, but it is estimated that more imports could achieve this status if traders better understood the GSP.

GSP Country Eligibility

The designation of developing countries as eligible for the GSP benefits has always been to some extent politicized—e.g., by declaring all communist states and all but three OPEC member states to be ineligible. In addition, under 1984 amendments, the President must evaluate whether a country recognizes "internationally recognized worker's rights" and adequately protects intellectual property rights before that country can be designated as a GSP beneficiary. the President must also evaluate whether nations give more preferential treatment to imports from other developed nations than to U.S. products, assist terrorists, expropriate U.S. owned investments, refuse to cooperate in drug enforcement, or deny recognition of international arbitration awards.

In applying these country eligibility criteria, past Presidents have disqualified a variety of nations from the U.S. GSP program. For example, Romania, Nicaragua, Paraguay, Chile, Burma, the Central African Republic and Liberia have all been disqualified in the past for failure to meet the workers' rights standards. Argentina and Honduras have lost GSP benefits for perceived failures to adequately protect U.S. pharmaceutical patents. Panama under General Noriega was rendered ineligible because of the failure to cooperate on narcotics. Intellectual property piracy led to the suspension of Ukraine's country eligibility in the GSP program.

The President's review of a country's eligibility under the GSP program is ongoing. This led to the reinstatement of GSP beneficiary nations. Russia was made a GSP beneficiary by President Clinton, later removed by President Obama. China is not a GSP beneficiary. Any country designated as a beneficiary nation under the GSP program that is subsequently disqualified by exercise of Presidential discretion, or "graduated" (see below), must receive 60 days' notice from the President with an explanation of this decision. This, in effect, presents the opportunity to reply and negotiate.

GSP Product Eligibility

For each designated GSP beneficiary country, the President also issues a list of products from that country eligible for duty free entry into the United States. The statutory authorization for the United States GSP program generally excludes leather products, textiles and apparel, watches, selected electronics and, certain steel, footwear and categories of glass from being designated as eligible articles. All these goods are thought to involve particular "import sensitivity."

Products of particular GSP beneficiary countries can be added or removed to the list of GSP qualified goods by petition of interested persons. The petitions, and the resultant certification or de-certification, are determined by the U.S. Trade Representative, with the advice of the U.S. International Trade Commission (ITC). The criterion used is "import sensitivity," which means that American industry or labor must actively seek protection from this foreign competition. The tendency of the decisions has been not to displace American interests, and to regard the GSP benefits as a "gift" to developing countries.

The GSP rule of origin requires that the product be shipped directly from the beneficiary developing country to the United States. Where the goods are locally produced from local resources, there is no further problem. However, where the goods exported by the beneficiary country are produced from materials imported into the developing country, further analysis is necessary.

In such cases, the present GSP rule of origin requires that at least 35 percent of the value of an item be added within a developing country for the item to be considered as "originating" in that

developing country. Thus, Toyotas manufactured in
Japan, but shipped to the U.S. through a GSP
beneficiary country, would not qualify for GSP duty
free treatment. But Toyotas manufactured in the
GSP beneficiary country from parts manufactured in
Japan could so qualify, if the value of the parts
aggregated only 60 percent of the value of the final
product. In addition, the Federal Circuit Court of
Appeals has ruled that the processing of goods in the
GSP   country   must   create   two   substantial
transformations in the identity of the goods for GSP
treatment to be available. *See Torrington Company
v. United States,* 764 F.2d 1563 (Fed.Cir.1985).

A separate principle is known as "graduation" from
the GSP list. While the principle can be applied to an
entire country, it is also used to "graduate" specific
products from specific countries from the GSP list to
the MFN list. In one case, for example, the
President's decision to withdraw GSP benefits for
"buffalo leather and goat and kid leather (not fancy)"
from India was affirmed. *See Florsheim Shoe Co. v.
United States,* 744 F.2d 787 (Fed.Cir.1984). In
another decision, the President's discretionary
authority to deny GSP benefits to cut flowers from
Colombia was similarly upheld. *See Sunburst Farms,
Inc. v. United States,* 797 F.2d 973 (Fed.Cir.1986).

The 1984 amendments required the President to
complete a general review of all GSP products to
determine whether they were "sufficiently
competitive" to graduate. Graduation has had its
greatest impact on so-called "newly industrialized
countries." In 1989, South Korea, Taiwan, Hong

Kong and Singapore were graduated entirely from the GSP list. At the same time, Bahrain, Brunei, Nauru and Bermuda were dropped from the list because their per capita GNP exceeded the statutory "competitive need" limit for country eligibility. In 2015, Seychelles, Uruguay and Venezuela were excluded for the same reason from GSP benefits. In 1995, the Bahamas and Israel were similarly dropped, and in 1997 Malaysia was entirely graduated. Russia was likewise graduated in 2014.

All developing nation U.S. free trade partners, for example Mexico, Jordan, Morocco, Colombia and Peru, have been removed from the GSP list of eligible countries.

U.S. DUTY FREE CARIBBEAN BASIN, ANDEAN AND AFRICAN TRADE PREFERENCES

In addition, and sometimes overlapping with the GSP, the United States grants duty free entry under a number of other special programs.

Caribbean Preferences

The European Union has had for many years a policy which grants substantial duty free entry into its market for goods originating in Mediterranean Basin countries. The United States has duplicated this approach for the Caribbean Basin. This is accomplished through the Caribbean Basin Economic Recovery Act of 1983 (CBI). For these purposes, the Caribbean Basin is broadly defined to include nearly all of the islands in that Sea, and a significant number of Central and South American nations bordering the Caribbean. So defined, there are 28 nations (not including Cuba) which could qualify for CBI treatment.

As with the GSP program, the Caribbean Basin Initiative (CBI) involves presidential determinations to confer beneficiary status upon any of these eligible countries. U.S. Presidents have typically required of each potential beneficiary a concise written presentation of its policies and practices directly related to the issues raised by the country designation criteria listed in the Caribbean Basin Economic Recovery Act. Wherever measures were in effect which were inconsistent with the objectives of these criteria, U.S. presidents have sought assurances that such measures would be progressively eliminated or modified. For example, the Dominican Republic promised to take steps to reduce the degree of book piracy and the Jamaican and Bahamian governments promised to stop the unauthorized broadcast of U.S. films and television programs.

Unlike the GSP, there are no presidential determinations as to which specific products of these countries shall be allowed into the United States on a duty free basis. All Caribbean products except those excluded by statute are eligible for duty free entry. Moreover, there are no "competitive need" or annual per capita income limits under the CBI.

Lastly, unlike the GSP program which must be renewed periodically, the Caribbean Basin Initiative is a permanent part of the U.S. tariff system. For U.S.

free trade partners in the region, Panama and CAFTA/DR for example, the CBI and GSP duty free regimes are no longer applicable.

Special duty free U.S. treatment has been granted to Haitian apparel under the Hope for Haiti program, renewed in 2015.

Andean Preferences

The Andean Trade Preference Act (ATPA) of 1991, renewed in the Trade Act of 2002, authorizes the President to grant duty free treatment to imports of eligible articles from Colombia, Peru, Bolivia and Ecuador. Venezuela is not included as a beneficiary under this Act. The Andean Trade Preference Act is patterned after the Caribbean Basin Economic Recovery Act of 1983. Goods that ordinarily enter duty free into the United States from Caribbean Basin nations will also enter duty free from these four Andean countries. The same exceptions and exclusions discussed above in connection with the Caribbean Basin Initiative generally apply.

While the CBI is a permanent part of United States Customs law, the ATPA was only authorized initially for a period of ten years. Furthermore, the guaranteed access levels for Caribbean Basin textile products, separate cumulation for antidumping and countervailing duty investigations, and the waiver of the Buy American Act for procurement purposes are not authorized by the ATPA. Broadly speaking, the passage of the ATPA represents assistance to these nations in return for their help in containing narcotics. U.S. free trade agreements with Peru and

Colombia supersede the ATPA, whose continued application to Ecuador and Bolivia is in doubt.

African Preferences

The Africa Growth and Opportunity Act of 2000 (AGOA) granted duty-free and quota-free access to the U.S. market for apparel made from U.S. fabric and yarn. Apparel made from African fabric is capped for duty free entry. The least developed sub-Saharan countries enjoy duty-free and quota-free apparel access regardless of the origin of the fabric. The Act also altered U.S. GSP rules to admit certain previously excluded African products on a duty-free basis, including petroleum, watches and flat goods.

Sub-Saharan countries can export almost all products duty-free to the United States. These countries are encouraged to create a free trade area with U.S. support. African exports are subject to import surge (escape clause) protection and stringent rules against transshipments between countries for purposes of taking advantage of U.S. trade benefits.

AGOA was renewed in 2015 subject to eligibility rules concerning market-based economies, poverty reduction, rule of law, and anti-corruption and human rights efforts, including internationally recognized workers' rights.

GOODS INCORPORATING DUTY FREE UNITED STATES COMPONENTS

Section 9802.00.80 of the Harmonized Tariff Schedule of the United States (formerly Section

807.00 of the Tariff Schedule of the United States) is an unusual "duty free" provision. This section allows for the duty free importation of United States fabricated components that were exported ready for assembly abroad. If qualified, goods assembled abroad containing U.S. components are subject only to a duty upon the value added through foreign assembly operations.

In order for this to be the case, Section 9802.00.80 requires that the components be fabricated and a product of the United States, that they be exported in a condition ready for assembly without further fabrication, that they not lose their physical identity by change in form, shape or otherwise, and that they not be advanced in value or improved in condition abroad except by being assembled and except by operations incidental to the assembly process such as cleaning, lubricating and painting.

If all of the Section 9802.00.80 criteria are met, the tariff that will be assessed upon the imported assembled product will be limited to a duty upon the full value of that product less the cost or value of U.S. made components that have been incorporated into it. Those who seek to take advantage of Section 9802.00.80 must provide the United States Customs Service with a Foreign Assembler's Declaration and Certification. The assembly plant operator certifies that the requirements of Section 9802.00.80 are met, and the importer declares that this certification is correct.

Billions of dollars of ordinarily tariffed value have been excluded as a result of this Customs law provision. Motor vehicles, semiconductors, office machines, textiles and apparel, and furniture are good examples of the kinds of products assembled abroad with fabricated U.S. components so as to meet the requirements of Section 9802.00.80. Historically, many of these products were assembled in Japan, Germany or Canada. In recent times, the assembly operations (maquiladoras) to which Section 9802.00.80 frequently applies have more commonly been found in the developing world.

U.S. FREE TRADE AGREEMENTS

Removing trade barriers is usually done on a reciprocal basis, and requires lengthy bargaining and negotiations between the sovereigns. Congress is not adapted to carry on such negotiations, so it routinely delegates limited authority to the President to negotiate agreements reducing trade restrictions. Recent efforts to reduce trade restrictions have been multilateral and bilateral. Congress has intermittently given quite broad authority to the President, or his Trade Representative (USTR), to reduce or eliminate United States tariffs on a reciprocal "fast track" basis, discussed below.

The USTR

In response to Section 1104 of the Trade Agreements Act of 1979, the President reviewed the structure of the international trade functions of the Executive Branch. Although this did not lead to the establishment of a new Department of International Trade and Investment, it did lead to enhancement of the Office of the Special Representative for Trade Negotiations, which has since been renamed the United States Trade Representative (USTR). The powers of the USTR were expanded and its authority given a legislative foundation. The USTR is appointed by the President, with the advice and consent of the Senate.

The Office of the USTR has been the principal vehicle through which tariff and trade negotiations have been conducted on behalf of the United States. Among other things, the USTR has had continuing responsibility in connection with implementation of the WTO Agreements and U.S. free trade agreements. The USTR is the contact point for persons who desire an investigation of instances of noncompliance with any trade agreement. The USTR has negotiated about 20 free trade agreements for the United States, noted below.

"Fast Track" U.S. Trade Negotiations

Fast track originated in 1974 as a compromise after Congress refused to ratify two major components of the Kennedy Round of GATT negotiations. When in place, fast track requires Congress to vote within 90 legislative days up or down, without amendments, on U.S. trade agreements. In return, Congress receives substantial notice and opportunity to influence U.S. trade negotiations conducted by the USTR. Congress also sets nonbinding trade negotiation objectives under fast track enabling legislation.

NAFTA and the Uruguay Round WTO agreements were negotiated and implemented under fast track procedures in place from 1991–1996. The bipartisan Trade Act of 2002 authorized President George W. Bush to negotiate international trade agreements on a fast track basis for five years. President Bush and the USTR quickly completed, and Congress quickly approved, free trade agreements (FTAs) with Chile and Singapore. Thereafter U.S. FTAs with Morocco, Australia, Central America/Dominican Republic (CAFTA), Peru, Jordan, Oman, and Bahrain followed. Just prior to the expiration of fast track authority in July of 2007, President Bush signed FTA agreements with Colombia, Panama and Korea. Several years later these agreements were implemented by Congress under the Obama administration.

Nevertheless, recognizing that China is a rapidly developing economic superstar, the United States under the Obama administration has been pursuing what resembles a "containment" strategy by promoting a "Trans-Pacific Partnership (TPP)." This strategy seeks to bring the U.S., Australia, New Zealand, Chile, Peru, Malaysia, Brunei, Singapore and notably Vietnam, Japan, Canada and Mexico into a broad trade, technology and investment alliance. Late in 2015, the TPP agreement was finalized, and now awaits ratification by all participating states.

In addition, in 2013, the USTR commenced negotiations with the European Union on a "Transatlantic Trade and Investment Partnership

(TTIP)" agreement. Both of these negotiations were notably commenced without fast track authority.

After an extended lapse, President Obama eventually received fast track authority in 2015, notably to pursue TPP and TTIP negotiations. For U.S. free trade partners, fast track suggests that once they reach a deal with the USTR Congress cannot alter it. That said, in recent years Congress has effectively tacked on additional requirements via letters of intent, notably regarding labor and the environment.

DUTY FREE ACCESS TO MULTIPLE MARKETS

The end-game so far as exporters and importers to the United States are concerned is unlimited duty free access. Except for raw materials and goods from U.S. free trade partners, few exports will ordinarily qualify for such treatment. However, products of GSP-eligible developing nations, and especially Andean, Caribbean or African countries, may significantly achieve this goal. This is possible because of United States adherence to the duty-free entry programs discussed above.

There are, of course, exceptions and controls (quotas, NTBs) that may apply under these duty free programs. Nevertheless, the United States market is so lucrative that careful study of these external trade rules is warranted. Such studies can realize unusually advantageous trade situations. For example, many developing nations have duty free rights of entry into the European Union under the

Lomé/Cotonou Conventions, the Union's Mediterranean Basin Policy or the EU version of the GSP program. The goods of some of these nations may also qualify for duty free access to the United States market.

A producer strategically located in such a nation (e.g., Jamaica) can have the best of both worlds, duty free access to the European Union and the United States. Mexico, which in addition to NAFTA has free trade agreements with the European Union, Japan and dozens of other countries, is another premier duty-free export location.

CHAPTER 4

TRADE REMEDIES: RESPONSES TO IMPORT COMPETITION

Antidumping Duties	Countervailing Duties
Trade Safeguards	Gray Market Trading
Counterfeit Goods	IP Infringing Imports

The core of the GATT (1947) and (1994) agreements is the principle of binding tariffs applied equally to all WTO member states, the most-favored-nation (MFN) principle. These tariffs, negotiated in the various GATT/WTO Rounds, are commonly referred to as MFN tariffs. The national tariff levels of the approximate 165 WTO member states reflect these negotiated MFN tariffs. In the United States tariff code, MFN tariffs are referenced as Column 1 tariffs.

The GATT/WTO system allows, however, certain exceptions to MFN tariff levels. The two most important are "antidumping duties" (ADs) and "countervailing duties" (CVDs). Such duties are intended to "remedy" what the GATT/WTO has agreed are unfair international trade practices. Think of them as special tariffs which, in authorized circumstances, are additional to MFN tariffs.

None of the trade remedies in favor of domestic producers is based on any notion of reciprocity. That is, none has any relation to restricting goods from a country because that country does not allow or restrains entry of goods into its markets. Antidumping and countervailing duties deal only with unfair selling prices for dutiable imported goods, and the safeguard "escape clause" mechanism deals only with temporarily protecting a domestic industry from unexpected surges in competition arising from imported goods.

AD and CVD Basics

Antidumping duties are a permissible trade response where an enterprise prices its goods for sale in the country of importation at a level that is less than that charged for comparable sales in the home country (*i.e.*, at "less than fair value" (LTFV)). Hence AD generally counteract private sector discriminatory pricing. Countervailing duties are a permissible response to certain "subsidies" given in another country that favor its exports in the international marketplace. Hence CVD counteract governmental subsidies. AD and CVD cannot simultaneously be applied.

The WTO system recognizes and permits both antidumping duties and countervailing duties, providing of course the respective requirements are satisfied. Each "trade remedy" also is governed by a separate Agreement ("Code") that provides more detail on the circumstances under which member states may impose these exceptional duties. Because the AD and CVD Codes are mandatory in the WTO system, they provide the foundation for a reasonably uniform body of legal rules for trade remedies among the roughly 160 WTO member states.

Under the WTO Antidumping Agreement (AD Code) and the WTO Subsidies and Countervailing Measures Agreement (CVD Code), a country may impose a special duty on products of another WTO member state only if two requirements are met. First, the country must find sufficient evidence of an unfair trade practice, either dumping (sales at less than fair value) or prohibited or actionable subsidies.

Second, the practice must cause a sufficiently significant injury to a domestic industry. In the case of dumping or subsidies, this requires proof that the practice has caused or threatens to cause "material injury" to a domestic industry, or that it has "materially retarded" the establishment of such an industry. Thus, the substantive grounds for the determination of the existence of "dumping" and of a "countervailable (actionable) subsidy" are different, but the domestic injury standard is essentially the same.

Safeguard Basics

Under the WTO Safeguards Agreement, the imposition of temporary protective relief from imports does not require a showing of any unfair trade practice, such as dumping or subsidies. As a result, the injury standard is higher: Under U.S. law, "escape clause" duties or other protective measures authorized by the President are only permitted where increased imports ("surges") are a "substantial cause" of "*serious* injury, or threat of *serious* injury" (emphasis added) to a domestic industry.

A careful understanding of causation issues is critical to all three trade remedies for import competition.

U.S. PROCEDURES RELATING TO THE IMPOSITION OF TRADE REMEDIES

The procedures for the imposition of ADs or CVDs under U.S. law in general terms are the same and involve a complicated interaction between two administrative agencies: The International Trade Administration (ITA), and the United States International Trade Commission (ITC). The ITA is an executive branch agency that is part of the Commerce Department (DOC). Its general mandate is to promote and develop world trade, and to help American companies sell overseas by providing them with information concerning the "what, where, when, and how" of imports and exports.

The ITC, in contrast, is an independent, quasi-judicial, and bipartisan agency created to provide trade expertise to both Congress and the Executive. The ITC, a successor to the U.S. Tariff Commission, was formally established by the Trade Act of 1974, and consists of six commissioners appointed by the President with the advice and consent of the Senate.

The ITA and ITC also are the two principal agencies responsible for the administration of U.S. trade remedy laws. Such trade remedy cases may be initiated either by the Department of Commerce or by a group or association of aggrieved domestic interests. The ITA's function is to assess claims of a substantive unfair trade practice—*i.e.*, to determine whether there has been a countervailable subsidy or a sale at less than fair value ("dumping"). The ITC has a separate responsibility to assess causation and injury issues—*i.e.*, to determine whether a practice has substantially caused or threatens to cause material injury to a domestic industry.

In general, AD and CVD trade remedy procedures involve the ITA first making a determination that a petition adequately alleges the relevant statutory requirements. Before initiating an investigation, the ITA also must find that a sufficient percentage of the affected domestic industry supports the petition. Generally, this requires that the industry or workers who support the petition account for (a) at least 25 percent of the total industry, and (b) at least 50 percent of those that have actually expressed an opinion for or against the petition.

After an initial investigation, the ITA then makes a "preliminary determination"—based on the "best information available at the time"—on whether there is "a reasonable basis to believe" that dumping or a countervailable subsidy exists. Use of the "best information available" approach has been upheld by the WTO Appellate Body. This approach has the effect of incentivizing foreign party participation in U.S. antidumping and countervailing duty proceedings lest their absence increase the likelihood of AD or CVD duties being imposed on their exports.

The ITC conducts its proceedings in parallel with those of the ITA. The ITC also makes a preliminary determination "based on the best information available" as to whether there is "a reasonable indication" that the challenged practice presents a real or threatened material injury to the affected domestic industry. An affirmative preliminary determination by the ITC is required *before* the ITA may proceed to make its own preliminary determination.

The DOC's discretion to impose extremely high AD duties using the best facts available rule strongly incentivizes foreign exporters to participate in U.S. antidumping proceedings. If both the ITC and the ITA make affirmative preliminary determinations, then each conducts a further investigation and ultimately makes a "final determination" in its respective area of responsibility. The ITA has final authority over the appropriate extra AD or CVD duty to offset any proven unfair trade practice.

Thus the U.S. chain of decision-making in antidumping proceedings (and also most countervailing duty proceedings) runs as follows:

ITC Preliminary Injury Determination

ITA Preliminary Dumping Determination

ITA Final Dumping Determination

ITC Final Injury Determination

Congress has repeatedly amended U.S. antidumping law so as to accelerate the rate at which these determinations are made and tighten the administrative rules used in them. For example, the so-called Level Playing Field Act of 2015 notably did so. At this point, it is common for the proceeding to be completed within one year. U.S. antidumping duties are then and in the future assessed retrospectively for each importation such that the amount payable varies for each importer and transaction.

Only the ITC is involved in safeguard (escape clause) proceedings. Upon the filing of a petition by a representative of an affected industry the Trade Act of 1974 requires the ITC to conduct an investigation into whether the statutory standard is satisfied. If it makes an affirmative determination on substantial causation and serious injury standards, the ITC submits its findings and any recommendation for relief to the President.

The Trade Act then grants the President broad discretion in determining the appropriate temporary safeguard measures to protect the affected domestic industry. These may range from increased tariffs to import quotas to "trade adjustment assistance" for workers.

The Importance of the ITA Preliminary Determination

As a practical matter, the ITA's *preliminary* determination that dumping or a countervailable subsidy has occurred will place significant, often overwhelming, pressure on the importers of the relevant goods. This is because at that point any covered goods become subject to the CVD or AD duties that are ultimately determined to apply once the ITA and ITC complete their investigations.

Hence the preliminary ITA determination tends to discourage or even cut off the imports. At that point importers generally must post cash or bonds to cover any AD or CVD duties preliminarily determined by the ITA. At a minimum, importers likely will have to raise their prices—unless and until either the ITA or the ITC makes a contrary final determination once the agencies have completed their administrative proceedings.

Once an antidumping petition is filed, importers will not know what their liabilities for duties are going to be, and may be required to post an expensive bond in the meantime to gain entry. Foreign exporters frequently raise their "United States prices" to the level of home market prices soon after such a preliminary determination. If they do, antidumping law will have accomplished its essential purpose. However, the U.S. Tariff Act disfavors termination of the proceeding on the basis of voluntary undertakings of compliance.

United States antidumping proceedings may be settled by the ITA if the respondents formally agree to cease exporting to the United States within six months or agree to revise their prices so as to eliminate the margin of the dumping. Because price revision agreements are hard to monitor, they are disfavored by the ITA. But an agreement to cease exports also cancels any outstanding suspension of liquidation. The total time secured in this manner may allow foreigners a window of opportunity to establish market presence prior to shifting production to the United States.

If requested, the ITA and ITC may proceed to their final determinations after a settlement is agreed. If the respondents prevail, normal trading will resume; but if the petitioners prevail, the settlement agreement will remain in effect. The ITA monitors all settlement agreements and may assess civil penalties (in addition to antidumping duties) in the event of a breach.

The U.S. Court of International Trade

A party to an administrative proceeding on an AD or CVD matter may appeal an adverse final determination of the ITA or ITC to the U.S. Court of International Trade (CIT). The CIT also hears appeals from ITC determinations in escape clause proceedings, but in these cases review is limited to procedural irregularities or clear statutory misconstructions.

The CIT was established in 1980 as the successor to the U.S. Court of Customs. The CIT is an Article III court, and its nine judges are appointed by the President with the advice and consent of the Senate. The CIT possesses all the powers in law and equity of a U.S. District Court, including the authority to enter money judgments against the United States, but with three general limitations. These limitations (a) prohibit its issuance of injunctions or writs of mandamus in challenges to trade adjustment rulings, (b) allow it to issue only declaratory relief in suits for accelerated review of pre-importation administrative actions, and (c) limit its power to order disclosure of confidential information to a narrowly defined class of cases.

The CIT has "exclusive" subject matter jurisdiction over suits against the United States, its agencies, or its officers arising from any law pertaining to revenue from imports, tariffs, duties or embargoes, or the enforcement of such laws and related regulations. The court's exclusive jurisdiction also includes any civil action commenced by the United States that arises out of an import transaction, as well as the authority to review final agency decisions concerning antidumping duties and countervailing duties, along with eligibility for trade adjustment assistance.

The geographical jurisdiction of the CIT is nationwide, and it is even authorized to hold hearings in foreign countries. However, the CIT does not have jurisdiction over disputes involving public safety or health restrictions on imports because of the need in such cases for uniformity of treatment of both domestically produced goods and imports. That can best be ensured by referring such issues to U.S. District Courts.

CIT decisions may be appealed first to the Court of Appeals for the Federal Circuit (formerly the Court of Customs and Patent Appeals), and ultimately to the United States Supreme Court.

International Tribunals

International institutions also play an increasingly significant role in the resolution of trade disputes. The most important of these is the WTO's Dispute

Settlement Body ("DSB"). Dissatisfied parties in domestic administrative proceedings may convince their government to challenge an adverse CVD, AD, or safeguard decision before the DSB based on alleged violations of a WTO Agreement. A large number of such complaints have been filed against the United States. As Chapter 2 examines in detail, proceedings before the DSB are governed by a separate WTO Agreement, the Dispute Settlement Understanding (DSU).

Separately, a unique international institution exists for trade remedy disputes involving the three member states—the U.S., Canada, and Mexico—of the North American Free Trade Agreement (NAFTA). NAFTA provides for resolution of antidumping and countervailing duty disputes through "binational panels." Such panels apply the domestic law of the importing country, and provide a substitute for judicial review of the decisions of administrative agencies of the importing country. Indeed, the initiation of a review under NAFTA divests the CIT of jurisdiction over the same dispute.

Although the decisions of such binational panels are not formally binding in U.S. law, the ITA or ITC may decide to review any administrative action to conform to an adverse panel decision, including through a revocation or reduction of CVDs or ADs.

DUMPING AND ANTIDUMPING DUTIES

The economics of dumping arise from a producer's opportunity to compartmentalize the overall market for its product, thus permitting it to offer the product for sale at different prices in different geographic areas. Only if trade barriers or other factors insulate each market sector from others is there opportunity to vary substantially the product's price in different sectors of the global market. For example, a producer can securely "dump" products in an overseas market at cheap prices and high volume only if it can be sure that the market in its home country is immune from return of these products. The objectives of dumping range include increasing marginal revenues, ruining a competitor's market position, and developing a new market on an expeditious basis.

On the other hand, a sale at less than the home price may not necessarily represent an unfair trade practice. It may instead merely result from a short-term need to introduce new products, sell off excess inventory, or conduct a distress sale in difficult financial circumstances. Indeed, "dumping" products in order to establish a foothold in a new foreign market or to raise brand awareness may make sense as a marketing technique. Consumers, at least in the short term, are typically enthusiastic about obtaining goods at "dumped" prices.

Hence there is considerable debate about the economic rationality of categorizing dumping an unfair trade practice. Nevertheless, a substantial body of international trade law seeks to identify dumping and counteract it through AD tariffs.

THE WTO ANTIDUMPING AGREEMENT

GATT Article VI grants WTO member states the right to impose antidumping duties. But the more detailed standards for such duties are set forth in a separate WTO Agreement: "The Agreement on Implementation of Article VI of GATT 1994." This "Antidumping Agreement" provides that a member state may impose antidumping duties if a product's export price is less than the "normal value." It defines the "normal value" of a good as the comparable price, in the ordinary course of trade, for the same or a similar product "when destined for consumption in the exporting country." Thus, in evaluating whether an export price constitutes dumping, the best baseline for comparison is the domestic sales price of comparable goods in the exporting country (*i.e.*, the home country).

However, such comparable sales may not be available, either because comparable products are not sold domestically, or because the usual retail transaction there is not comparable (*e.g.*, leasing rather than a sale). In that situation, the Antidumping Agreement provides a hierarchy of alternative computation methods to achieve an approximate valuation. Among these alternatives, the preferred one uses the price for the same or a similar product in the ordinary course of trade for export to a third country. The next alternative is to calculate the cost of production of the exported goods in the country of origin, plus a reasonable amount for profits and for administrative, selling and any general costs, and then compare that to the price of the product when sold for export to the foreign country.

The WTO Antidumping Agreement, adopted from the earlier Tokyo Round GATT "Antidumping Code," focuses upon dumping determinations (particularly criteria for allocating costs) and material injury determinations (particularly causation). The Agreement also has a few special rules that are worthy of emphasis. First, it forbids duties for *de minimis* dumping, defined as less than two percent of the product's export price, and in such cases member states must terminate any AD investigations immediately. Second, it permits "cumulation" of imports—*i.e.*, imports of the same goods from more than one country—if the dumping from each is more than *de minimis* and this is otherwise appropriate under the circumstances.

Third, it recognizes, but does not expressly allow or disallow, AD petitions by employees and their union representatives. Fourth, member states must notify the WTO of any changes to their domestic antidumping laws as well as any related administrative actions. More generally, a special WTO "Committee on Anti-Dumping Practices" oversees implementation of the Agreement by member states. Finally, when another member state challenges the imposition of ADs before the WTO, the DSB panel may rely on the facts developed in the domestic administrative proceedings and must accept those facts if the domestic evaluation "was unbiased and objective, even if the panel might have reached a different conclusion."

THE ORIGINS OF U.S. ANTIDUMPING LAW

Controversies over dumping of goods in the United States go back as far as complaints by Secretary of the Treasury Alexander Hamilton in 1791. The subject continues to excite interest and even passion. In general, U.S. antidumping statutes have long compared the price at which articles are imported or sold in the United States with the actual market value or wholesale price of such articles in the principal markets of the country of their production. This approach was established by the Antidumping Act of 1916, a rarely used criminal statute. Considered a form of unfair competition law, the Act provided for criminal prosecution and treble damages for certain types of dumping.

The European Union, Japan, and other states successfully challenged these aspects of the 1916 Act in WTO dispute settlement proceedings as inconsistent with the Antidumping Agreement. The pressure of the adverse rulings by the WTO's DSB ultimately led the United States to repeal the 1916 Act in 2004.

U.S. LAW ON ANTIDUMPING DUTIES

The modern U.S. rules and procedures governing antidumping duties are set forth in a statute that is still known as the Tariff Act of 1930. But, significantly, the U.S. amended this Act in 1994 to implement the WTO Antidumping Agreement. In conformance with that Agreement, the fundamental determination under U.S. law is whether a sale is at "less than fair value" (LTFV). This in turn requires a comparison of the U.S. price of imported goods with their "normal value."

ITA Dumping Determinations

"Normal value" is usually determined by the price charged for the goods in the exporter's *domestic* market (the home market) in the ordinary course of business. If the ITA determines that the home market is not "viable" (*i.e.*, is not sufficiently large or otherwise inappropriate), it may use the price in sales in a comparable third country. Finally, if neither of those measures is appropriate, the ITA may use a "constructed value" based on the cost (properly adjusted) to produce the goods (not the price).

The ITA then compares this price with the price of the goods for export to the United States. Generally, for this measure the ITA uses the "export price," which means the price at which the goods are first sold *outside* of the United States to an unaffiliated person *for exportation to* the United States. If, however, the foreign exporter first sells the goods to an affiliated person outside the United States—such that this "export" price is not a reliable one—then the ITA may use the "constructed export price," which means the price at which the goods are first sold to an unaffiliated person *in* the United States.

Ultimately, the ITA compares the appropriate "normal value" (again, generally the home country price) with the U.S. price (again, generally the export price for goods destined for the U.S.) to determine whether there has been a sale at "less than fair value" (*i.e.*, "dumping").

ITC Injury Determinations

As noted, the ITC separately makes determinations on causation and injury in AD proceedings. In order to impose ADs, the statute requires an affirmative determination by the ITC that a challenged practice presents an actual or threatened "material injury" to a domestic industry or that the practice has "materially retarded" the establishment of such an industry. Much, therefore, depends upon a workable definition of "material injury."

The statute defines the term as "harm which is not inconsequential, immaterial, or unimportant." It further provides that, in making a determination of "material injury," the ITC "shall" consider the volume of imports involved, the effect of the imports on U.S. prices for "like products," and the impact of the imports on U.S. producers of "like products," but only in relation to production operations in the United States. The ITC is directed to evaluate both the actual and potential declines not only in production, sales and profits, but also in the market share and productivity of the domestic industry. It is also directed to evaluate actual and potential negative effects on employment and growth, and on the ability to raise capital and investment.

All effects are to be measured on an industry-wide basis, and not in relation to an individual company. But a threat to a "major portion" of a national industry is sufficient. In order to assess "material injury," the ITC also must identify the relevant domestic industry affected by an alleged dumping practice. It does so by, first, defining the relevant "the domestic like product" that competes with the imported goods. From this, it then defines the relevant "domestic industry" as those domestic producers, "as a whole," of a "domestic like product" or as those producers "whose collective output of a domestic like product constitutes a major proportion" of the total domestic production.

Antidumping Duties

If the sales of imported goods both are at LTFV and cause or threaten "material injury" to a domestic industry, or retard the development of a domestic industry, then the statute provides that an antidumping duty "shall" be imposed. In other words, AD are statutory remedies which neither the President nor others may deter.

The antidumping duty levied is in addition to the usual tariffs charged on such products. But because the duties are not imposed to support any specific domestic price, they may not exceed the "margin of dumping"—*i.e.*, the amount of the difference between the normal price and the price at which the goods are sold for export to the United States. The antidumping duty is to remain in force only as long as the dumping occurs.

U.S. Antidumping Rules and Nonmarket Economies

Congress has enacted special rules to govern antidumping duty analysis of imports from nonmarket economy countries (NMEs). The Department of Commerce gets to decide which countries have NMEs. Russia was "graduated" from this status in 2002. China, under its WTO accession protocol, has been promised graduation late in 2016. However, 2015 amendments to U.S. antidumpimg law vest considerable discretion in the DOC "in particular market situations" to apply NME rules in AD proceedings where the producer's costs do not accurately reflect ordinary trade costs. These amendments were apparently adopted with China's antidumping graduation in mind.

The NME rules are based on the assumption that "normal value" cannot be determined by NME prices, which are bureaucratically determined and therefore not sufficiently subject to the forces of competition to form an accurate standard for comparison. Whether that assumption is accurate for all NMEs, notably China, is a matter of some debate.

When applicable, the ITA will "construct" a NME "normal value" by determining the factors of production (labor, materials, energy, capital, etc.) actually used by the NME to produce the goods destined for export to the United States. The ITA then assigns a value for each of those factors using prices prevailing in a suitable market economy (in a "surrogate" country). In one proceeding, for example, Paraguay served as a surrogate for China. Finally, the ITA adds appropriate amounts from values in the surrogate market economy country for factory overhead, sales expenses, general and administrative expenses, packing, and profit.

The result is a "constructed value" for goods from the exporting NME. Although the statutory definition refers to a "nonmarket economy country," which implies use of a single standard for a whole political unit, the ITA has differentiated between imports from specific NME countries based on whether particular factors of production in specific fields are considered to be market driven or not.

Other Provisions of U.S. Law Designed to Conform to the WTO Antidumping Agreement

When it accepted the substantial changes to the WTO system in 1994, the U.S. also made a variety of more specific changes to domestic law to conform to the WTO Antidumping Agreement. First, the U.S. amended the Tariff Act of 1930 to provide for an exclusion of *de minimis* dumping margins. Specifically, the ITA, in making its preliminary dumping determinations, must disregard any weighted average dumping margin that is less than two percent *ad valorem* or the equivalent specific rate for the subject merchandise. The ITA likewise must disregard any weighted average dumping margin that is *de minimis* when making final determinations.

Other changes to the Tariff Act have reduced the discretion previously available by imposing strict statutory time limits. In the case of an antidumping petition, the ITA must make an initial determination on whether the petition alleges the required statutory elements within twenty days after the petition is filed. This time limit may, in exceptional circumstances, be extended to forty days if it becomes necessary to poll or otherwise determine support for the petition in the affected domestic industry. The statute also imposes a 45 day deadline from the filing of the petition for the ITC to make a preliminary determination on injury and a 140 day deadline for the ITA to make a preliminary determination on whether the challenged sales are at less than fair value.

Further WTO-derived amendments authorize an adjustment to sales-below-cost calculations for start-up costs, thought to be particularly beneficial to high-tech products. The 1994 amendments also included a controversial "captive production" section intended to remove intra-enterprise sales from ITC injury determinations. The United States, however, failed to implement fully the average-to-average or transaction-to-transaction dumping calculations mandated by the Antidumping Agreement.

The 1994 amendments permit the use of weighted average approaches in the investigatory phase, but the traditional U.S. practice of comparing individual U.S. sales to average home (or third country) sales will continue in subsequent administrative reviews. Adjustments for profits from further manufacturing, selling, and distribution of products in the U.S. are authorized. And the amendments strengthened existing U.S. anti-circumvention provisions despite their absence from the WTO Antidumping Agreement.

Still more WTO-driven changes require the ITC to provide all parties to the proceeding with an opportunity to comment, prior to the Commission's vote, on all information collected in its investigations. In addition, a 1994 amendment requires that an antidumping investigation cease if the volume of dumped imports from a single country is negligible—that is, less than three percent of total imports of a product in the most recent 12-month period preceding the filing of the petition.

Separately, the ITC is ordinarily required to consider "cumulation" of imports from two or more countries if the imports are subject to investigations as a result of petitions filed on the same day. It may continue an investigation, notwithstanding the rule on negligible dumping, if the volume of imports of a product from several countries, each accounting for less than three percent of the imports, together account for more than seven percent of total imports. The Commission must make any cumulative analysis on the basis of the same record, even if the simultaneously filed investigations end up with differing final deadlines.

The ITC also must consider the magnitude of the dumping margin in making material injury determinations. Lastly, the Commission must conduct a review no later than five years after an antidumping or countervailing duty order is issued to determine whether revoking the order would likely lead to continuation or recurrence of dumping or subsidies and material injury. Known as the "sunset" provision, this WTO rule requires a review of all existing antidumping and countervailing duty orders at regular intervals.

U.S. Anti-Circumvention Rules

In 1988, Congress enacted important amendments to Tariff Act to address the "circumvention" of antidumping and countervailing duties. These "anti-circumvention" rules entered into force while the subject was under discussion in the GATT Uruguay Round negotiations. Ultimately, the WTO Antidumping Agreement included no substantive rules on anti-circumvention, but also did not forbid the practice.

The Tariff Act addresses circumvention in a variety of ways. First, it allows the ITA to ignore fictitious markets in the source country when calculating the foreign market "normal value." Moreover, the ITA may include within the scope of an antidumping order merchandise "completed or assembled" in the United States if such merchandise includes "parts or components produced in the foreign country" that is the original subject of the order. The principal requirements are that the process of completion or assembly in the United States is "minor or insignificant" and the value of the components themselves is a "significant portion of the total value of the merchandise.

Similarly, when the exporter ships the components to a third country for assembly and subsequent exportation to the United States, such circumvention efforts can be defeated by extending an antidumping order to those goods as well. Again, such an action is appropriate if the assembly in the third country is "minor or insignificant" and the components themselves represent the principal value of the merchandise.

U.S. ANTIDUMPING PROCEEDINGS REVIEWED BY THE WTO

The WTO Appellate Body has taken a restrictive view of what constitutes permissible antidumping duties.

Zeroing

In a series of decisions, the WTO's Appellate Body ruled against "zeroing," a methodology used in dumping margin calculations by the United States and other countries. This practice involved disregarding any sales in the home market that were below the export price. The Appellate Body has reasoned, however, that a proper understanding of the home market price should involve a weighing of both positive and negative numbers in calculating weighted average dumping margins.

Notwithstanding these decisions, the Federal Circuit repeatedly upheld the zeroing methodology as a reasonable interpretation of the actual language in the Tariff Act and described the analysis of the Appellate Body as not "sufficiently persuasive." *See, e.g., Corus Staal BV v. Department of Commerce*, 395 F.3d 1343 (Fed.Cir.2005). In response to the repeated adverse rulings by the WTO, however, the Commerce Department has adjusted its approach to discontinue zeroing in antidumping investigations, but maintain the practice in antidumping duty reviews.

Causation and Other Issues

More generally, the Appellate Body (AB) has rejected cursory material injury determinations and stressed that member state governments must consider all relevant economic factors in making such decisions. Thus, in the *United States-Hot-Rolled Steel from Japan* dispute, the AB found bias in the determination of normal value when low-priced sales from a respondent to an exporter were automatically excluded. The AB also indicated that injury determinations must include an analysis of captive production markets in addition to merchant markets. Causation in such determinations must be rigorously scrutinized.

A WTO panel also has ruled that the Commerce Department's refusal to revoke an antidumping order against South Korean DRAMS was inconsistent with Article 11.2 of the Antidumping Agreement. Hence, U.S. regulations regarding the likelihood of continued dumping after a three-year hiatus are suspect under the Antidumping Agreement. The Court of International Trade, on the other hand, found the U.S. regulations in question consistent with the WTO Antidumping Agreement. The Court took the position that the WTO panel ruling was not binding precedent, merely persuasive.

The Byrd Amendment

The WTO Appellate Body also repeatedly ruled against the U.S. with respect to the Continued Dumping and Subsidy Offset Act of 2000 (CDSOA, the so-called "Byrd Amendment"). The controversial aspect of that Act was a mechanism under which the U.S. government funneled the antidumping duties that it collected back to the members of the affected domestic industry. In this way, millions of dollars were collected by the U.S. government and distributed to U.S. companies in, among others, the steel, bearings, candy, candle, cement, computer chip, and lumber industries.

Other countries promptly filed challenges against the Act with the WTO's DSB, and the Appellate Body ultimately determined that the CDSOA was inconsistent with the Antidumping Agreement (as well as various provisions of other WTO Agreements). When the U.S. failed to comply with this decision, the WTO authorized the claimant countries to retaliate in their domestic trade laws as permitted under the WTO's Dispute Settlement Understanding. On this basis, the European Union, Canada, Japan and others imposed WTO-authorized retaliatory trade sanctions on U.S. exports to their markets. Ultimately, Congress bowed to the pressure created by the WTO decisions and repealed the CDSOA in a late 2005 budget bill.

SUBSIDIES AND COUNTERVAILING DUTIES

A WTO member state may impose an increased tariff payable on an imported item beyond the regular tariff schedule as a "countervailing duty." Such duties are based not on a foreign exporter selling goods as less than fair value, but rather on a foreign government providing "subsidies" that support production for exportation and thus permit the exporter to sell at lower prices in exports to other countries. Subsidies come in many forms, including, among others, tax reductions or rebates; tax credits; loan guarantees; subsidized financing; equity infusions; and outright grants.

In theory, a countervailing duty offsets exactly the unfair subsidy. Proponents of countervailing duties argue that they are necessary to keep imports from being unfairly competitive based on foreign government support. Opponents of countervailing duties argue that there is no coherent standard of "fairness" vs. "unfairness" to justify a rational assessment of such duties. Such opponents argue that it is often difficult to identify precisely when a subsidy exists as compared with general governmental actions to support beneficial commercial activity.

Rapidly developing countries also routinely offer to give some form of subsidy for initial foreign investments designed to produce exports. But subsidies are not only a phenomenon for developing countries. In the United States, for example the Export-Import Bank (EXIMBANK) has routinely offered low cost loans to overseas buyers of Boeing and GE products exported from the United States. Other developed countries have similar programs. In all cases, the critical legal issue is which subsidies may be countervailed by CVD duties under the rules of the WTO Agreement on Subsidies and Countervailing Measures (SCM).

THE WTO AGREEMENT ON SUBSIDIES AND COUNTERVAILING MEASURES

International concern with unfair subsidies and countervailing duties is reflected in Articles VI, XVI, and XXIII of the GATT 1994 and in the 1994 WTO "Agreement on Subsidies and Countervailing Measures" (SCM Agreement). A WTO member state may impose an increased tariff on an imported item beyond the regular tariff schedule as a "countervailing duty." Such duties are an authorized response to a foreign government providing a "prohibited" or "actionable" subsidy that permits their exporters to sell at lower prices in other countries. In all cases, the critical legal issue is which subsidies may be countervailed by CVD duties under the rules of the WTO SCM Agreement.

Under the SCM Agreement, the authorities of the importing member state may impose a countervailing duty (CVD) in the amount of the subsidy for as long as the subsidy continues. The SCM Agreement also provides substantive rules governing when, and under what circumstances, a member state may impose CVDs to offset a claimed governmental or "public body" subsidy. State-owned-enterprises (SOEs) are not generally treated as public bodies unless performing governmental functions.

The CVD may only be imposed after an investigation, begun on the request of an affected industry, has demonstrated the existence of a prohibited or actionable "specific" subsidy that has adverse trade effects, such as injury to a domestic industry or "serious prejudice" to the interests of the importing state. Finally, there must be a causal link between the subsidy and the alleged injury.

The SCM Agreement attempts to shift the focus of subsidy rules from a national forum, as was the exclusive case under GATT, to the multinational forum provided by the WTO. As a result, disputes over subsidies may occur either in the national forum or before the WTO's DSB (or both). In addition, a special WTO "Committee on Subsidies and Countervailing Measures" supervises the implementation of the SCM Agreement by the member states.

Countervailable Subsidies

The SCM Agreement established three classes of subsidies: (1) prohibited subsidies (also known as "red light" subsidies); (2) actionable subsidies, *i.e.*, those that are permissible unless they cause adverse trade effects ("yellow light"); and (3) non-actionable and non-countervailable subsidies ("green light").

Under the terms of the SCM Agreement, however, the "green light" category expired in 2000. The SCM Agreement also granted special exemptions for developing countries that permitted them to phase out their export subsidies and local content rules on a gradual basis. These exemptions were to have expired by 2003, but as of 2015, eighteen countries—principally in the Caribbean and Central America—continue to operate under an extension of this deadline granted by the WTO's Committee on Subsidies and Countervailing Measures.

SCM Dispute Procedures

The SCM Agreement also prescribes procedural rules for the investigation and imposition of CVDs by domestic authorities. It addresses, among other things, the initiation of CVD proceedings, the conduct of investigations, the calculation of the amount of subsidy, and the right of all interested parties to present information. The Agreement also has special rules relating to subsidies that cause a "serious prejudice" to the interests of another member state (although some of these rules have lapsed). The SCM also has rules on the gathering of evidence in CVD proceedings, on the imposition and collection of CVDs, on provisional measures, and on the permitted length of any allowed CVDs (typically five years).

As noted above, an aggrieved country may challenge another member state's CVD laws or actions before the WTO's DSB, but the SCM also has special dispute settlement procedures regarding such actions. Those procedures first provide for consultations between the complaining member state and the subsidizing member state. If these do not resolve the dispute within 30 days for a "prohibited subsidy" (red light) or 60 days for an "actionable subsidy" (yellow light) either party may request that the DSB establish a panel to investigate the dispute and issue a written report.

The DSB panel will have 90 days (red light) or 120 days (yellow light) to investigate and prepare its report. The panel report is appealable on issues of law to the Appellate Body. The Appellate Body has 30 days (red light) or 60 days (yellow light) to decide the appeal. Panel and Appellate Body decisions are adopted without modification by the DSB unless rejected by an "inverted consensus." *See* Chapter 2 for more detail on DSB procedures.

If a prohibited or actionable subsidy is found to exist, the subsidizing state is obligated under WTO to withdraw the subsidy. If the subsidy is not withdrawn within a six month period, the WTO may authorize the complaining member state to take countermeasures. Such countermeasures may not be countervailing duties, but may instead comprise increased tariffs by the complaining member on exports from the subsidizing state.

Boeing v. Airbus

A classic, longstanding pair of subsidy disputes concerning Boeing and Airbus aircraft have been decided by the WTO Appellate Body. In 2011, the European Union and various member states were found to have illegally subsidized Airbus, mainly through "launch aid", by $22 billion. In 2012, the Appellate Body determined that the U.S. and various state governments had subsidized Boeing by about $4.3 billion under procurement contracts and tax loopholes.

At this writing, neither side seems inclined to comply with these rulings. No settlement is in sight and hence mutual trade retaliation could occur. See Chapter 2 on WTO remedies.

U.S. COUNTERVAILING DUTY LAW

United States law has long considered the grant of a subsidy by a foreign government to aid its exporters to be an unfair trade practice. Laws granting a right to impose countervailing duties to counter unfair subsidies have existed since 1897, long before the creation of the GATT. The origin of U.S. laws against export "bounties" or "grants" can be traced to Section 5 of the Tariff Act of 1897.

For many years, this law vested almost complete discretion in the Treasury Department to levy CVDs as it saw fit. Several early CVD tariffs targeted tax subsidies on sugar exports. The U.S. Supreme Court essentially gave the Treasury Department *carte blanche* to impose CVDs whenever foreign government regulations favored exports reaching the United States.

Prior to the Trade Act of 1974, U.S. law on CVDs was largely administered as a branch of U.S. foreign policy, not as a private international trade remedy. Indeed, it was not until 1974 that negative bounty or grant determinations by the Treasury Department became subject to judicial review. The Trade Act of 1974 also gave private parties a number of procedural rights, notably time limits for Treasury decisions on their petitions for CVD relief and mandatory publication of Treasury rulings. It is from this point, therefore, that a systematic body of case law interpreting and applying U.S. bounty, grant, and CVD provisions began to develop.

The next major development in the U.S. statutes governing this field arrived in the Trade Agreements Act of 1979. This Act, *inter alia,* codified the rules on the use of CVDs to counteract unfair "export subsidies" as agreed in the Tokyo Round GATT Subsidies Code. In addition, the 1979 Act authorized limited use of CVDs against foreign *domestic* subsidies, a subject the GATT Subsidies Code did not address. Furthermore, the 1979 Act adopted the GATT requirement of proof of an actual injury to a domestic industry.

The Uruguay Round Agreements Act of 1994 implemented the numerous changes of the WTO SCM Agreement into U.S. law. Most important, the URAA amended the Tariff Act of 1930 to reflect a rough arrangement similar to the "red light," "yellow light," and "green light" (now lapsed) categories of the SCM Agreement. The requirements of the Tokyo Round Subsidies Code relating to material injury continued in substantially the same form.

Two U.S. Statutory Tests

The United States currently has two statutory structures on countervailing duties: Section 1671 of the Tariff Act of 1930 provides a test for products imported from countries that participate in the WTO SCM Agreement (or its equivalent), as compared to products imported from other countries.

The most important difference between the two is that for imports from a "Subsidies Agreement Country," CVDs may be imposed only upon an affirmative determination that a U.S. industry is "materially" injured, or threatened with such injury, or its development is materially retarded. For the relatively few other countries, CVDs may be imposed *without* any finding of injury to a domestic industry.

In most other significant respects, the two tests are the same. Nonetheless, with the continuing growth in the membership of the WTO (roughly now 160 member states), the possibility of imposing CVDs without a showing of material injury is rapidly decreasing in significance.

The Tariff Act of 1930 contains the U.S. statutory provisions on countervailing duties for products imported from WTO member states. Those provisions permit the imposition of duties if the ITA and the ITC find that a product is subsidized, and that as a result a U.S. industry is materially injured or threatened with such injury or its development is materially retarded.

The U.S. amended its rules on countervailing duties in 1994 to conform to the SCM Agreement. The amendments changed many concepts under U.S. law. Although mostly consistent in substance, however, the U.S. rules follow a slightly different structure as compared to the SCM Agreement.

In general, the U.S. rules state that "there shall be imposed . . . a countervailing duty" if the ITA determines that an exporting country is providing, "directly or indirectly," a disallowed subsidy, and the ITC makes an affirmative injury determination. Thus, U.S. law defines essentially three elements for the imposition of a CVD: (1) a "countervailable subsidy," (2) that is "specific," and (3) that causes or threatens a material injury to a domestic industry.

Once again, as in antidumping proceedings, the ITA's preliminary determination that a countervailable subsidy exists has important practical consequences for importers and exporters. See the discussion of these consequences above in the coverage of U.S. antidumping law.

The Subsidy Requirement

A "subsidy" is defined in U.S. law as a "financial contribution" by a governmental entity that confers a "benefit" on the exporter of the subsidized product. It includes governmental grants, loans, equity infusions and loan guarantees, as well as tax credits and the failure to collect taxes. It can also include the governmental purchase or providing of goods or services on advantageous terms.

Further, direct governmental action is not required: A subsidy may also arise if a government provides any of the above through a private body. A financial contribution provides a "benefit" if it grants an exporter a better deal than would be available through normal market mechanisms.

The Specificity Requirement

In addition to a financial contribution and a benefit, under U.S. law a subsidy must be "specific" to a particular industry or enterprise. This is where U.S. law uses a slightly different structure, or at least different terminology, as compared to the structure of the SCM Agreement (although the latter also refers to specificity).

U.S. law employs the notion of "export subsidies" to correspond to the "prohibited" (red light) subsidies under the SCM Agreement. These are deemed to be specific as a matter of law. Similarly, U.S. law employs the notion of "domestic subsidies" to correspond to "actionable" (yellow light) subsidies under the SCM Agreement. These may be subject to CVDs if they cause "adverse trade effects" based on a variety of further factual considerations.

Export Subsidies

U.S. CVD law provides that a subsidy is an "export subsidy," and thus is specific as a matter of law, if "in law or in fact" it is "contingent upon export performance," even where that condition is only one of several. The same applies for a subsidy that is "conditioned upon the use of domestic goods over imported goods" ("import substitution subsidy"). As noted, these rules correspond to the "prohibited" (red light) subsidies under the SCM Agreement. (Annex I to the SCM Agreement also provides an "Illustrative List of Export Subsidies.")

A footnote to the SCM Agreement explains that a subsidy also is contingent on exports if it is "in fact tied to actual or anticipated exportation or export earnings." A 2011 WTO Appellate Body decision in the long-running dispute between the E.U. and the U.S. over aircraft subsidies explained that this concept applies "[w]here the evidence shows, all other things being equal, that the granting of the subsidy provides an incentive to skew anticipated sales towards exports." Although U.S. law does not expressly incorporate the language of the SCM Agreement footnote, a fair interpretation of the definition of an "export subsidy" would seem to capture it as well.

Domestic Subsidies

U.S. CVD law covers the category of "actionable" (yellow light) subsidies under the concept of a "domestic subsidy." Such a subsidy exists if as a matter of law or fact it is provided to a specific enterprise or industry, even if not linked to export performance.

The law lists four "guidelines" for determining whether a subsidy so qualifies as a domestic subsidy:

(1) If the subsidizing country "expressly limits access" to the subsidy to an enterprise or industry, then it is "specific as a matter of law."

(2) If the subsidy is in fact automatically granted to all enterprises or industries that meet written and objective criteria or conditions, it is "not specific as a matter of law."

(3) A subsidy may be "specific as a matter of fact" where the actual recipients are limited in number; one enterprise or industry is the predominant user or receives a "disproportionately large amount" of the subsidy; or the manner in which the granting authority exercises its discretion indicates that one enterprise or industry is favored over others.

(4) Finally, a subsidy is specific if it is limited to an enterprise or industry in a "designated geographic region" and is granted by the governmental authority of that region.

Two other categories originally recognized under the SCM Agreement, and incorporated into U.S., have lapsed. A so-called "dark amber" subsidy was one that exceeded five percent of the cost basis of the product, or provided debt forgiveness, or covered the operating losses of a specific enterprise industry more than once. The dark amber provisions lapsed in 2000. As noted above, the "green light" category of allowed subsidies—for industrial research and development, regional development, and adaptation of existing facilities to new environmental standards—also lapsed after five years and was not renewed.

The Injury Requirement

In parallel with the rules for antidumping duties, the ITA and ITC have separate responsibilities for making determinations on countervailing duties. The ITA makes determinations on whether a "countervailable subsidy" exists and whether it is "specific." The ITC's separate responsibility is to determine whether such a subsidy meets the statutory requirements for causation and injury.

As with ADs, the ITC must determine whether "by reason of" the sale of subsidized goods, (a) a domestic industry producing like products "is materially injured," (b) such an industry "is threatened with material injury," or (c) "the establishment of an industry . . . is materially retarded." The definition of the relevant "domestic industry" likewise parallels that for AD proceedings (see above).

U.S. CVD Enforcement Procedures

The procedures for investigating and imposing CVDs generally are the same as those for ADs. In general, the ITA first makes a determination that a petition adequately alleges the statutory requirements. After an initial investigation, the ITA then makes a "preliminary determination" on whether there is a "reasonable basis to believe" that the statutory definition of a countervailable subsidy is met. At the same time, the ITC conducts its own investigation and then makes a preliminary determination on whether there is "a reasonable indication" that a subsidy presents a real or threatened material injury to the affected domestic industry.

If both make affirmative preliminary determinations, the goods are immediately subject to any countervailing duties imposed later; as noted above, this usually has the effect of reducing imports of such goods. Following more detailed investigations, the ITA and ITC then proceed to final determinations in their respective areas of responsibility and, if both determinations are affirmative, the ITA determines and imposes an appropriate CVD. Final determinations may be appealed to the CIT, then to the Federal Circuit, and ultimately to the Supreme Court.

Subsidies, CVDs, and Non-Market Economies

The subject of subsidies is particularly difficult with respect to non-market economies (NMEs). The longstanding view was that such duties were not appropriate because the NME government in effect is responsible for the entire economy. In accordance with this view, the Federal Circuit Court of Appeals ruled in 1986 that economic incentives given to encourage exportation by the government of an NME cannot create a countervailable "subsidy." *Georgetown Steel Corp. v. United States*, 801 F.2d 1308 (Fed.Cir.1986).

The court's rationale was that, even though an NME government provides export oriented benefits, the NME can direct sales to be at any set price, so the benefits themselves do not distort competition. The court also suggested that imports from NMEs with unreasonably low prices should be analyzed under the rules for antidumping duties.

Beginning in the early part of this century, the Commerce Department has pushed against this view. In 2008 and 2010, it thus imposed CVDs against imports of certain products from China and Vietnam respectively. In 2011, the Federal Circuit rejected this effort based on its reading of congressional intent in the substantial amendments of CVD law in 1994. *See GPX Intern. Tire Corp. v. United States*, 666 F.3d 732, 745 (Fed.Cir.2011).

In 2012, however, Congress annulled that decision by special legislation, with the result that countervailing duties also may be imposed on goods from non-market economies such as China and Vietnam. China's challenge of this legislation in WTO proceedings failed.

SAFEGUARD (ESCAPE CLAUSE) MEASURES

GATT Article XIX permits—even in absence of an unfair trade practice in the form of a subsidy or dumping—temporary suspension of agreed tariff concessions if increased quantities of imports cause or threaten to cause *serious* injury to a domestic industry. A member state may only undertake such an "emergency action" after consultation with the affected WTO exporting country. Similar to ADs and CVDs, a special WTO "Agreement on Safeguards" concluded during the Uruguay Round of negotiations governs the imposition of safeguard measures.

On this authority, the United States has authorized suspension of tariff concessions through "escape clause proceedings" (also known as Section 201 proceedings) under the Trade Act of 1974. Similar to all other WTO Covered Agreements, Congress amended this Act to implement the Safeguards Agreement in December of 1994 as part of the Uruguay Round Agreements Act.

The rationale for such "escape clause" measures is that the reduction of trade barriers under the WTO/GATT system may cause serious dislocations for certain industries and workers. If sudden increases in imports thus cause or threaten to cause a "serious injury" to a domestic industry, protective duties are allowed on a *temporary* basis to permit the industry to adjust to the unexpected international competition.

In addition, "market disruption proceedings" can also provide temporary relief from import competition. Market disruption proceedings concern imports from "communist" nations and are authorized by Section 406 of the 1974 Trade Act. They are similar but not identical to escape clause proceedings. Either may result in the imposition of U.S. import restraints.

Import injury relief available under the Trade Act of 1974 is basically of two kinds: (1) Presidential relief designed to temporarily protect domestic producers of like or directly competitive products; and (2) governmental assistance to workers and firms economically displaced by import competition. This assistance is intended to enhance job opportunities and competitiveness.

Protective relief tends to be awarded when the President believes that U.S. industry needs time to adjust. Governmental assistance is seen as a means to accommodate the injury caused by import competition. In either case, adjustment to import competition is the longer term goal, hopefully resulting in more competitive U.S. industries and markets.

THE WTO AGREEMENT ON SAFEGUARDS

The WTO's Safeguards Agreement defines the substantive and procedural requirements for the imposition of protective relief by a member state in response to increased import competition. Most important, the Agreement states as a fundamental rule that such measures are only allowed for a "serious" injury or a threat of a "serious" injury. In addition, it permits safeguard measures "only to the extent necessary" to prevent or remedy such an injury and to "facilitate adjustment."

Such measures are allowed for a maximum of four years, and on a progressively decreasing basis (although, upon a further investigation, a member state may extend the measures, but not beyond a total period of eight years). The exporting countries whose goods are covered by allowed safeguard measures also may not retaliate for the first three years. Special rules limit the use of safeguard measures against imports from developing countries and allow such countries to impose safeguard measures to protect domestic industries for up to ten years.

Perhaps the most important provision of the Safeguards Agreement is that it expressly prohibits a member state from seeking, undertaking, or maintaining voluntary export or import restraint agreements (VERs or OMAs). These were quite common, especially by developed countries to protect against unwanted imports, prior to the adoption of the Safeguards Agreement in 1994.

U.S. ESCAPE CLAUSE (SAFEGUARDS) LAW

As noted above, the United States has implemented the authority for safeguard measures granted by GATT Article XIX and the Safeguards Agreement through "escape clause proceedings" in Section 201 of the Trade Act of 1974. Decisions about such import adjustments are made by the President upon the recommendation of the International Trade Commission (ITC).

Any entity that is "representative of an industry," including a "trade association, firm, certified or recognized union, or group of workers," may file a petition requesting such import relief. The petition must state the "specific purposes" for any requested action "which may include facilitating the orderly transfer of resources to more productive pursuits, enhancing competitiveness, or other means of adjustment to new conditions of competition." The petitioner industry or worker group may—and is well advised to—submit its own specific plan "to facilitate positive adjustment to import competition" during the term of any protective relief.

The ITC also must initiate an escape clause proceeding at the request of the President, the United States Trade Representative, and certain congressional committees, and may do so "on its own motion." The ITC then investigates to determine whether the import competition meets the statutory standard for temporary escape clause relief.

The Statutory Standard

The ITC traditionally has divided the statutory standard into three separate criteria. In order to make an affirmative determination on an escape clause petition, the ITC must find, as it stated in the famous (or infamous) *Steel Safeguards* case, that:

"(1) imports of the subject article are in *increased quantities . . .* ;

(2) the domestic industry producing an article that is like or directly competitive with the imported article is *seriously injured or threatened with serious injury*; and

(3) the article is being imported in such increased quantities as to be a *substantial cause* of serious injury or threat of serious injury to the domestic industry."

The 1974 Trade Act also provides more detail on these elements.

(a) On the requirement of *increased quantities of imports*, the Act provides that the increase may be "either actual or relative to domestic production," and in consideration of imports from all sources.

(b) In determining whether *serious injury* exists, the ITC may consider "all economic factors which it considers relevant," including a significant idling of productive facilities in the domestic industry, an inability of a significant number of firms to carry out domestic production operations at a reasonable level of profit, and significant unemployment or underemployment within the domestic industry.

(c) In determining whether a *threat of serious injury* exists, the ITC may consider a decline in sales or market share; higher and growing inventories; a downward trend in production, profits, wages, or employment (or increasing underemployment); the extent to which affected domestic firms are able to generate adequate capital to modernize and to maintain current levels of research and development; and the extent to which the U.S. "is the focal point for diversion of exports" because of export requirements in the home country or import restraints in another country.

(d) The *substantial cause* element is among the most controversial in application to actual cases. The Trade Act defines the term as "a cause which is important and not less than any other cause." As a result, increased imports must be both "an important cause" and one that is "equal to or greater than any other cause."

The Act directs the ITC to consider all relevant economic factors, including "an increase in imports (either actual or relative to domestic production) and a decline in the proportion of the domestic market supplied by domestic producers." The difficulty with the "substantial cause" element comes in determining whether increased imports are "equal to or greater than" the myriad of other competing factors that may cause harm to an industry, including inept management, negative general economic or market trends, and technological innovations.

As a foundation for all of these analyses, the ITC must identify the specific domestic "industry" that is affected by the increased imports. The Act identifies the relevant industry as "the domestic industry producing an article that is like or directly competitive with the imported article." In turn, the Act defines a "domestic industry" as the "the producers as a whole" of the competitive goods or those producers "whose collective production . . . constitutes a major proportion" of total production of the competitive goods.

Protective Relief

The statute requires the ITC to report its findings to the President within four months after the petition is filed. If the ITC finds that imports have increased, and that this increase has been a "substantial cause" of actual or threatened serious injury to the industry, it will make recommendations to the President on appropriate protective relief. In doing so, the Trade Act requires the ITC to consider what relief measures would prevent or remedy the injury; any "adjustment plans" submitted by the petitioner as well as any "individual commitment" it has made; available information concerning domestic and global competition; and whether international negotiations may address the domestic injury or facilitate adjustment by the industry.

The Act authorizes the President to grant escape clause relief only if the ITC has made an affirmative finding that the increased imports have caused or threaten to cause serious injury. But if the ITC makes an affirmative finding, the President "shall" take all appropriate and feasible action to facilitate efforts by the industry to make "a positive adjustment to import competition."

The President need not, however, follow the ITC's relief recommendations. Thus, even though the word "shall" is used, the Act leaves substantial discretion to the President in defining the appropriate protective action. In other words, unlike antidumping and countervailing duty proceedings, the President has effective control over both whether any relief will be given in a Section 201 proceeding, and what form of relief will be granted. The Act generally sets a four year limit on any such relief.

One reason why protective escape clause relief is difficult to obtain is that the Safeguards Agreement entitles most trading partners to seek compensation for the adverse effects of any relief granted by another member state. Formal retaliation through a return suspension of concessions on exports generally is prohibited for three years.

Because escape clause proceedings do not concern any unfair trade practice, protective relief measures typically are a source of substantial friction in world trade. This perspective helps explain why the President frequently decides that it is not in the economic interest of the United States to impose escape clause relief or, if granted, decides to terminate the relief before three years have expired.

If nonetheless granted by the President, escape clause measures for an affected industry and its workers may be in the form of either protective relief or trade adjustment assistance (see below). The former is directed toward the imported goods and can include increased tariffs, tariff rate quotas (tariffs which increase after reaching a certain quota), import quotas, or—at least according to the statute's text—orderly marketing agreements (OMAs).

In the past, the threat of such protective relief prompted some countries to agree to such OMAs "voluntarily" and thus to limit the volume of their exports or otherwise limit competition. Prominent examples included the agreements by Japan to restrain auto exports to the United States and to Europe. As explained above, however, the 1994 Safeguards Agreement now expressly prohibits such agreements.

Special Safeguard Rules for Chinese Imports

In addition to the general rule in Section 201, U.S. law has a special provision—which arose in connection with China's accession to the WTO in 2000—for safeguard measures relating to imports from China. Because of worries over a flood of inexpensive Chinese imports, these "Section 421" safeguard measures require only that increased imports be a "significant cause" of a "material" injury to a domestic industry. These standards are significantly lower than for regular safeguard measures, which (as noted above) require a cause that is "equal to or greater than any other cause" and a real or threatened "serious" injury to a domestic industry.

In recent years, the special Section 421 safeguards rule has played a much more significant role than the traditional Section 201 rule. Between 2003 and 2012, the ITC initiated six investigations under Section 421, but none under Section 201. A prominent example is President Obama's imposition in June 2009 of protective tariffs of 35% on vehicle tires from China. These special safeguards rules for Chinese imports expired in 2013.

U.S. SAFEGUARD ACTIONS REVIEWED BY THE WTO

The rulings of the WTO's Appellate Body concerning the Safeguards Agreement have strictly limited the use of escape clause remedies. Indeed, the United States has lost a number of related disputes before the WTO, including in complaints brought by Australia and New Zealand on lamb; by the European Union on wheat gluten; by India and Pakistan on wool shirts and blouses; by South Korea on line pipe; and by Japan and numerous others on steel.

In 2001 alone, the Appellate Body (AB) ruled against the United States in three separate safeguard cases. In *U.S.-Wheat Gluten from the EC*, the AB emphasized the critical issue of causation. The AB found that the ITC's causation analysis lacked clarity and inadequately addressed factors other than imports that may have caused domestic industry injury. It also criticized the U.S. for a failure to give timely notice and to allow for a "meaningful exchange" in the required consultations.

In *U.S.-Lamb Meat from New Zealand*, the AB reiterated that all causation factors must be isolated and examined. Further, it rejected the "domestic industry" definition adopted by the ITC because growers were included. Both of these decisions also emphasized the need for the ITC to find "unforeseen developments" in its injury determinations. The third 2001 AB ruling against U.S. safeguard measures concerned cotton yarn from India and Pakistan. In this decision, the AB rejected an exclusion of vertically integrated yarn producers from the definition of "domestic industry."

In its 2002 decision on U.S. safeguards on line pipe from Korea, the WTO similarly criticized the ITC for a "mere assertion" that challenged imports were "an important cause of serious injury and . . . not less than any other cause." More generally, the AB has repeatedly emphasized that the U.S. may not exclude consideration of imports from NAFTA countries (Canada and Mexico) in making safeguard determinations (the concept of parallelism).

The U.S. Steel Safeguards Dispute

Perhaps the most controversial recent escape clause action by the United States was the imposition of tariffs on steel by President Bush in 2002. The ITC found, following an extensive investigation and numerous hearings, that certain categories of steel imports caused, or threatened to cause, serious injury to the domestic steel industry. President Bush then imposed tariffs of up to 30 percent on imported steel for three years. This escape clause relief was tempered by exclusions for selected steel from selected countries. Most Australian and Japanese steel products, for example, were not subject to the extra U.S. tariffs. About half of all EU steel imports were exempt. Canada and Mexico, as members of NAFTA, were fully exempt.

Numerous WTO member states promptly challenged the imposition of this safeguard relief before the WTO's Dispute Settlement Body (as well as in U.S. federal court). In 2003, the Appellate Body (AB) ultimately ruled that the special U.S. tariffs on steel were illegal under the WTO Safeguards Agreement.

The AB held that the U.S. erred in utilizing the protective tariffs some four years after the surge of steel imports during the Asian economic meltdown, and in excluding NAFTA partners Canada and Mexico. It also found that the ITC failed properly to address the requirement of "unforeseen developments." Although the AB acknowledged that the term does not appear in the Safeguards Agreement, it reiterated its earlier holdings that the Agreement must be understood against the backdrop of GATT Article XIX, which conspicuously includes such a requirement.

The European Union then threatened over $2 billion annually in retaliatory tariffs on U.S. exports of clothing, citrus, and boats, products thought to be politically damaging to the Bush Administration. But before the WTO could authorize such sanctions, President Bush rescinded the duties in December, 2003 pursuant to corresponding authority in the

Trade Act. Interestingly, in the meantime domestic interests separately petitioned the ITA and ITC to impose CVDs or ADs on many of the same products. Reasoning that the temporary safeguard measures effectively mitigated the damaging effects of imports, the ITC concluded that there was no material injury to justify responsive duties on either basis. *See Nucor Corp. v. U.S.*, 414 F.3d 1331 (Fed.Cir.2005).

U.S. TRADE ADJUSTMENT ASSISTANCE

Escape clause proceedings often lead to separate "trade adjustment assistance" for affected workers (and sometimes firms). This assistance is designed to provide financial relief for the effects of the increased imports, not to prevent, reduce, or restrict the imports. Escape clause relief is always considered temporary, but adversely affected workers may be provided with "adjustment assistance" payments and other displacement benefits for a longer period. For example, automobile workers have received such assistance because foreign automobile manufacturers enjoyed great marketing success in the United States.

Trade adjustment assistance decisions for workers are made by the U.S. Department of Labor, for firms by the Department of Commerce. Such assistance does not require an affirmative determination by the ITC on import injuries (as is required for protective relief, see above). Adjustment assistance is also available to workers whose plants relocate to U.S. free trade partners, or GSP, CBI, Andean or African trade preference countries. Since 2015, workers affected by trade with any country, say China or India, are eligible. During the past 40 years, trade adjustment assistance has benefitted over 2 million U.S. workers.

U.S. law permits petitions for trade adjustment assistance by a "group of workers," union, or "employers of such workers." Generally, three groups of workers may be eligible for adjustment assistance: (1) those who have lost their jobs because increased imports caused significant harm to production by their former employer; (2) those who lost their jobs because increased imports caused their former employer to shift production to a foreign country; and (3) "adversely affected secondary workers"—those who lost their jobs with a supplier of a primary firm harmed by increased imports.

Congress expanded the trade adjustment assistance (TAA) programs significantly in 2002, 2009, 2011 and 2015. Among the variety of benefits and services available for eligible workers are employment counseling and job referrals; job search allowances for travel and related costs; "relocation allowances" to cover moving expenses; retraining assistance; and, perhaps most important, income support after state unemployment benefits have run out.

Recent expansions of the TAA programs also now allow financial assistance for health insurance as well as special wage subsidies for workers over fifty. Congress also has authorized a separate, but more limited, program of Trade Adjustment Assistance for

Firms (TAAF) which is administered by the Department of Commerce.

Such expansions and extensions of trade adjustment assistance often are closely connected with the granting of Trade Promotion Authority ("fast track") by Congress to the President for free trade agreements, as well as to actual congressional approval of such agreements once concluded by the President. An example is the extension of the enhanced TAA programs in 2011 in connection with the approval of the free trade agreements with South Korea, Colombia, and Panama. The 2015 expansion was coordinated with the President's new fast track trade promotion authority.

PROTECTION FROM PIRATED AND IP INFRINGING IMPORTS

The Basics of TRIPs

The Uruguay Round accords of late 1993 include an agreement on trade-related intellectual property rights (TRIPs). This agreement is binding upon the roughly 160 nations that are members of the World Trade Organization. In the United States, the TRIPs agreement has been ratified and implemented by Congress under the Uruguay Round Agreements Act. There is a general requirement of national and most-favored-nation treatment among the parties.

Many developed nations had been trying unsuccessfully to promote expanded intellectual property rights through the U.N.-created World Intellectual Property Rights Organization (WIPO).

WIPO agreements are not mandatory, and much of the developing world had declined to opt into their terms. Much to the benefit of private parties in the developed world, the TRIPs Code covers the gamut of intellectual property. It has de facto become a near-global IP Code.

On copyrights, there is protection for computer programs and databases, rental authorization controls for owners of computer software and sound recordings, a 50-year motion picture and sound recording copyright term, and a general obligation to comply with the Berne Convention (1971 version)(except for its provisions on moral rights).

On patents, the Paris Convention (1967 version) prevails, 20-year product and process patents are available "in all fields of technology", including pharmaceuticals and agricultural chemicals. However, patents can be denied when necessary to protect public morals or order, to protect human, animal or plant life or health, and to avoid serious environmental prejudice. The TRIPs provisions did not stop the Indian Supreme Court in 2013 from denying Novartis a patent on its cancer drug, Gleevac. The court took the view that Novartis was engaged in "evergreening", i.e., making small, inconsequential changes to existing patents and that Indian law could require proof of "improved therapeutic efficacy" before a patent grant.

Article 31 of the TRIPs permits compulsory licensing of patents in national emergencies or other circumstances of extreme urgency, subject to a duty to reasonably compensate the patent owner.

Thailand, for example, has issued compulsory licenses on a range of cancer, heart disease and AIDS drugs. There is considerable controversy over pharmaceutical patents based on traditional medicines of indigenous peoples, which some see as bio-piracy. Proposals have been made to amend TRIPs to require disclosure of the origins of bio-patents, obtain informed consent from the indigenous communities involved, and share the benefits of such patents.

Note that by incorporating the Berne and Paris conventions, TRIPs and the WTO DSU become an enforcement mechanism for those longstanding treaties. For trademarks, the Paris Convention also rules, service marks become registrable, internationally prominent marks receive enhanced protection, the linking of local marks with foreign trademarks is prohibited, and compulsory licensing is banned. But gray market trading and related IP issues are explicitly not covered by TRIPs, allowing each WTO member state to differ on such law.

In addition, trade secret protection is assisted by TRIPs rules enabling owners to prevent unauthorized use or disclosure. These rules closely parallel those of NAFTA. Integrated circuits are covered by rules intended to improve upon the Washington Treaty. Lastly, protection of industrial designs and geographic indicators of product origin (e.g., Canadian Whiskey) are also part of the TRIPs regime.

Remedies Against Counterfeiting and IP Infringement

Theft of intellectual property and use of counterfeit goods are rapidly increasing in developing and developed countries. Such theft is not limited to consumer goods (Pierre Cardin clothing, Rolex watches). Industrial products and parts (e.g., automotive brake pads) are now being counterfeited. Some developing countries see illegal technology transfers as part of their economic development. They encourage piracy or choose not to oppose it. Since unlicensed producers pay no royalties, they often have lower production costs than the original source.

This practice fuels the fires of intellectual property piracy. Unlicensed low cost reproduction of entire copyrighted books (may it not happen to this book) is said to be rampant in such diverse areas as Nigeria, Saudi Arabia, and China. Apple computers have been inexpensively counterfeited in Hong Kong. General Motors estimates that about 40 percent of its auto parts are counterfeited in the Middle East. Recordings and software are duplicated almost everywhere without license or fee. And the list goes on.

Mandatory IP infringement and anti-counterfeiting remedies are included in the TRIPs, for both domestic and international trade protection. There are specific provisions governing injunctions, damages, judicial and customs seizures, and discovery of evidence. Willful trademark counterfeiting and copyright piracy on a commercial scale must be criminalized. Counterfeit goods may not be re-exported by customs authorities in an unaltered state.

U.S. Section 337 Proceedings

Legal protection against intellectual property theft and counterfeit goods is not very effective. In the United States, trademark and copyright holders may register with the Customs Service and seek the blockade of pirated items made abroad. Such exclusions are authorized in the Lanham Trademark Act of 1946 and the Copyright Act of 1976. Patent piracy is most often challenged in proceedings against unfair import practices under Section 337 of the Tariff Act of 1930.

Section 337 proceedings traditionally involve some rather complicated provisions in Section 1337 of the Tariff Act of 1930. Prior to 1988, the basic prohibition was against: (1) unfair methods of competition and unfair acts in the importation of goods, (2) the effect or tendency of which is to destroy or substantially injure (3) an industry efficiently and economically operated in the United States Such importation was also prohibited when it prevented the establishment of an industry, or restrained or monopolized trade and commerce in the United States.

The Omnibus Trade and Competitiveness Act of 1988 revised Section 337. The requirement that the U.S. industry be efficiently and economically operated was dropped. The importation of articles infringing U.S. patents, copyrights, trademarks or semi-conductor chip mask works is specifically prohibited provided a U.S. industry relating to such articles exists or is in the process of being established. Proof of injury to a domestic industry is not required in intellectual property infringement cases. Such an industry exists if there is significant plant and equipment investment, significant employment of labor or capital, or substantial investment in exploitation (including research and development or licensing).

Determination of violations and the recommendation of remedies to the President under Section 337 is the exclusive province of the International Trade Commission (ITC). Most of the case law under Section 337 concerns the infringement of patents. While not quite a per se rule, it is nearly axiomatic that any infringement, even after lawful entry as a result of how imported goods are used, of U.S. patent rights amounts to an unfair import practice for purposes of Section 337.

Section 337 proceedings result in general exclusion orders permitting seizure of patent counterfeits at any U.S. point of entry. However, the Customs Service finds it extremely difficult when inspecting invoices and occasionally opening boxes to ascertain which goods are counterfeit or infringing. Many counterfeits do look like "the real thing."

For most seizure remedies to work, the holder must notify the customs service of an incoming shipment of offending goods. Use of private detectives can help and is increasing, but such advance notice is hard to obtain. Nevertheless, the Customs Service seizes millions of counterfeit goods each year. In 2009, U.S. officials seized about $260 million in counterfeit goods.

Chinese gangs accounted for the bulk of these goods, which were most often footwear, consumer electronics, luxury goods and pharmaceuticals. U.S. military and civilian procurement agencies have begun actively targeting counterfeit suppliers.

Patent-based Section 337 proceedings are multiplying. For example, in a major 2007 decision, the ITC excluded the importation of cell phones containing Qualcomm microchips found to infringe Broadcom patents. In 2012, Samsung succeeded before the ITC in alleging patent infringement by imported Apple cellphones, but the President denied a general exclusion order because the patents in question were part of an industry standard and thus he determined it was against the public interest to exclude the imports on the basis of such patent infringement.

This was the first denial of ITC-recommended Section 337 relief since President Reagan. Apple's subsequent attempt to bar Samsung cellphones on patent infringement grounds were upheld by the ITC. Absent involvement of industry standards, no Presidential veto was forthcoming.

ITC decisions take about 12 to 15 months, versus three to five years for federal court lawsuits. General exclusion orders are typically sought. Hearings are held before one of four administrative law judges specializing in patent law, with final decisions taken by the ITC. Infringing products are excluded from importation during the appeals process. About one-fourth of all 337 proceedings find infringements. An increasing number of foreign owners of U.S. patents are invoking 337 procedures. About half of all such complaints are settled, often using cross-licensing among the parties.

Other U.S. Trade Remedies Against Counterfeit and IP Infringing Imports

Infringement and treble damages actions may be commenced in U.S. courts against importers and distributors of counterfeit goods, but service of process and jurisdictional barriers often preclude effective relief against foreign pirates. Even if such relief is obtained, counterfeiters and the sellers of counterfeit goods have proven adept at the "shell game," moving across the road or to another country to resume operations. Moreover, the mobility and economic incentives of counterfeiters have rendered the criminal sanctions of the Trademark Counterfeiting Act of 1984 largely a Pyrrhic victory.

Ex parte seizure orders are also available under the 1984 Act and the Lanham Trademark Act when counterfeit goods can be located in the United States. Goods so seized can be destroyed upon court order.

International solutions have been no less elusive. The WTO agreement on TRIPs addresses these problems by mandating certain national remedies, but their effectiveness remains to be tested. Various U.S. statutes authorize the President to withhold trade benefits from or apply trade sanctions to nations inadequately protecting the intellectual property rights of U.S. citizens. This is true of the Caribbean Basin Economic Recovery Act of 1983, the Generalized System of Preferences Renewal Act of 1984, the Trade and Tariff Act of 1984 (amending Section 301 of the 1974 Trade Act), and Title IV of the 1974 Trade Act as it applies to most favored nation tariffs.

Slowly this carrot and stick approach has borne fruit. Under these pressures for example, Singapore drafted a new copyright law, South Korea new patent and copyright laws, and Taiwan a new copyright, patent, fair trade and an amended trademark law. Brazil introduced legislation intended to allow copyrights on computer programs. Though these changes have been made, there is some doubt as to the rigor with which the new laws will be enforced when local jobs and national revenues are lost.

France and Italy have made it illegal to knowingly purchase counterfeit goods. For example, if a student buys a "Louis Vuitton" bag for $15 in a Paris or Florence flea market, he or she may be arrested, fined and imprisoned. France has gone a step further. A new agency monitors Internet piracy. French offenders are subject to a "three strikes" rule: Two warnings are issued before Net accesses can be terminated and fines imposed by court order. South Korea and Taiwan also employ warnings and penalties against illegal downloading.

TRADE IN GRAY MARKET GOODS

One of the most controversial areas of customs law concerns "gray market goods," goods produced abroad *with authorization* and payment but which are imported into *unauthorized* markets. Trade in gray market goods has dramatically increased in recent years, in part because fluctuating currency exchange rates create opportunities to import and sell such goods at a discount from local price levels. Licensors and their distributors suddenly find themselves competing in their home or other "reserved" markets with products made abroad by their own licensees. Or, in the reverse, startled licensees find their licensor's products intruding on their local market shares.

In either case, third party importers and exporters are often the immediate source of the gray market goods, and they have little respect for who agreed to what in the licensing agreement. When pressed, such third parties will undoubtedly argue that any attempt through licensing at allocating markets or customers is an antitrust or competition law violation.

In the early part of the century, gray market litigation provoked a U.S. Supreme Court decision, *A. Bourjois & Co. v. Katzel*, 260 U.S. 689 (1923), blocking French cosmetics from entering the United States. A U.S. firm was assigned the U.S. trademark rights for French cosmetics as part of the sale of the American business interests of the French producer. The assignee successfully obtained infringement relief against Katzel, an importer of the French product benefitting from exchange rate fluctuations. The Supreme Court reversed a Second Circuit holding which followed a line of cases allowing "genuine goods" to enter the American market in competition with established sources. The Supreme Court emphasized the trademark ownership (not license) and independent public good will of the assignee as reasons for its reversal.

U.S. Genuine Goods Exclusion Act

Congress, before the Supreme Court reversal, passed the Genuine Goods Exclusion Act, now appearing as Section 526 of the Tariff Act of 1930. This Act bars *unauthorized importation* of goods bearing trademarks of U.S. citizens. Registration of such marks with the Customs Service can result in the seizure of unauthorized imports. Persons dealing in such imports may be enjoined, required to export the goods, destroy them or obliterate the offending mark, as well as pay damages.

The Act has had a checkered history in the courts and Customs Service. The Customs Service view (influenced by antitrust policy) was that genuine (gray market) goods may be excluded only when the foreign and U.S. trademark rights are not under common ownership, or those rights have been used without authorization. The practical effect of this position was to admit most gray market goods into the United States, thereby providing substantial price competition, but uncertain coverage under manufacturers' warranty, service and rebate programs. Some firms excel at gray market importing and may provide independent warranty and repair service contracts. Since 1986, New York and California require disclosure by sellers of gray market goods that manufacturers' programs may not apply.

A split in the federal courts of appeal as to the legitimacy in light of the Genuine Goods Exclusion Act of the Customs Service position on gray market imports resulted in a U.S. Supreme Court ruling. In an extremely technical, not very policy oriented decision, the Supreme Court in *K Mart Corp. v. Cartier, Inc.*, 486 U.S. 281 (1988) arrived at a compromise. The Customs Service can continue to permit entry of genuine goods when common ownership of the trademarks exists. The Service must seize such goods only when they were authorized (licensed), but the marks are not subject to common ownership. Many believe that the bulk of U.S. imports of gray market goods have continued under this ruling.

Other U.S. Gray Market Import Barriers

An attempt in 1985 by Duracell to exclude gray market batteries under Section 337 of the Tariff Act of 1930 as an unfair import practice was upheld by the U.S. International Trade Commission, but denied relief by President Reagan in deference to the Customs Service position.

Injunctive relief under trademark or copyright law is sometimes available against gray market importers and distributors. When available, injunctive relief applies only to the parties and does not prohibit gray market imports or sales by others. This remedy is thus useful, but normally insufficient.

In *Quality King Distributors, Inc. v. L'anza Research Intern., Inc.*, 523 U.S. 135 (1998), however, the U.S. Supreme Court held that the "first sale doctrine" bars injunctive relief under the Copyright Act against gray market re-importation of U.S. exports. More recently, the Supreme Court went further and denied copyright injunctive relief against foreign-made gray market goods in *Kirtsaeng v. John*

Wiley & Sons, 133 S.Ct. 1351 (2013). This decision allowed an entrepreneurial student to import gray market textbooks from Asia. In *Lever Bros. v. United States,* 877 F.2d 101 (D.C.Cir.1989), the D.C. Circuit allowed Trademark Act injunctive relief against materially different gray market goods where those differences had not been disclosed in labeling.

Gray Market Trading Outside the USA

An excellent review of the treatment of gray market goods in other jurisdictions is presented in an article by Takamatsu at 57 Wash. L. Rev. 433 (1982). This review is of particular interest to U.S. *exporters* of gray market goods. For the most part, his review indicates that other jurisdictions permit gray market goods to enter. This is true of the *Parker Pen* cases under Japanese law, the *Maja* case under German law and the *Agfa-Gevaert* case in Austria, all of which are reviewed by Takamatsu. Canadian Supreme Court law strongly supports free trade in gray market goods. *See Consumers Distributing Co., Ltd. v. Seiko Time Canada Ltd.,* 1 Can. Sup. Ct. 583 (1984).

The legal analysis contained in these opinions has been very influential in European Union law. EU law basically posits that once goods subject to intellectual property rights of common origin have been sold on the market with authorization, the holders can no longer block importation of those goods ("parallel imports") through the use of national property rights. Such use is not thought to have been intended as part of the original grant of rights and is said to have been "exhausted" upon sale.

An extensive body of EU law permits parallel imports (even of qualitatively different goods) as part of the promotion of the Common Market and rejects attempts to divide the market territorially along the lines of national property rights. Product labeling as to source and contents is thought sufficient notice to consumers that qualitatively different goods are involved.

In a major decision, the European Court of Justice ruled that trademark rights can be used to block gray market imports into the Common Market. These rights are not exhausted once the goods are voluntarily put into the stream of international commerce. An Austrian maker of high-quality sunglasses was therefore entitled to bar imports from Bulgaria. *See Silhouette International v. Hartlauer,* 1998 Eur. Comm. Rep. I–4799. In other words, the exhaustion doctrine does not apply externally. Levi Strauss, for example, seized upon this distinction to actively pursue EU importers of its blue jeans from non-EU sources. The jeans were being sold cheaply at a British supermarket.

CHAPTER 5

EXPORTS

Export Controls   **Boycotts**   **Anti-Boycotts**
Foreign Corrupt Practices   **U.S. Section 301**

A merchant in the United States wishing to export goods must consider all limitations imposed by the *importing* nation which affect the proposed transaction. Foreign import controls may or may not be comparable to the U.S. import controls discussed in Chapter 3. For nations which are members of the WTO, the controls are likely to be relatively similar.

A merchant in the United States must also consider that the U.S. may have *export* controls which affect goods or technology. Additionally, if there are any third party nation components in the goods to be exported, the export controls of that third nation must also be reviewed. For example, if a U.S. manufacturer of shirts made of materials from India wishes to export the finished shirts to Pakistan, it must consider whether India prohibits or regulates that trade.

Control of the re-export (including trans-shipment or diversion) of goods from a foreign nation is difficult to police and creates ill feeling on the part of the re-exporting nation. Assume that India is engaged in a trade embargo of Pakistan and attempts to halt the export of the shirts mentioned above from the United States, Sri Lanka or Bangladesh. All three

governments might ignore the Indian demand.
Canada and Argentina, for example, ignored
demands by the United States to halt shipping to
Cuba automobiles made in GM and Ford subsidiary
plants in Canada and Argentina, respectively.

Why does a nation control exports? Exports earn
revenue and create jobs. This suggests that export
controls are imposed more for political or foreign
policy reasons than for economic reasons. But
sometimes the controls have a mixture of these goals.
For example, exports may be limited to protect
national security (military weapons and technology,
regulated in the U.S. by the Arms Export Control Act
of 1976), to limit the spread of nuclear components
(partly controlled by the Nuclear Nonproliferation
Act), to preserve natural resources (endangered
species, subject to an international convention—
CITES), to reserve resources for domestic use
(certain hardwoods for making furniture), or to hold
resources for sale at expected higher prices in the
future (oil).

Apart from the law of export subsidies and
countervailing duties and to a degree the law of
export quotas, the WTO package of agreements
marginally touches upon export issues. See Chapter
2. Why does the World Trade Organization fail to
have extensive legal disciplines regarding exports?

The answer is less than clear. National export
controls have certainly been less numerous, and
therefore less on the international trade radar
screen. Restricting exports is often counterintuitive
to trade policy. Exports represent local production,

employment and earnings, whereas imports may disrupt domestic companies, jobs and economic growth. Governments are therefore inclined to promote exports, not inhibit them. In the developing world, there has been a major policy shift away from import substitution in favor of export enhancement.

In the absence of WTO rules on export controls, member states have pursued different policies. The United States, one of the world's top exporters, shipping trillions of dollars of exports each year, has nevertheless maintained an extensive system of export controls. This system is the focus of this Chapter.

U.S. EXPORT POLICY

To understand the U.S. regulation of *imports*, one must understand a complex matrix of trade acts and agreements. To understand the regulation of *exports* as opposed to imports, the path is somewhat less cluttered. There is no comparable extensive matrix of laws regulating U.S. exports. There is one major U.S. export law which is especially important to those engaging in international trade. It is the Export Administration Act of 1979 (EAA).

This Act makes a number of Congressional policy statements that suggest an intent to restrict export controls only to the extent necessary to achieve certain political goals. It outlines the licensing procedure for exports, requiring a license only in a limited number of specific export situations. It includes the concept of "foreign availability", that export controls should not be placed on goods which are readily available from other sources. Additionally, it is within the EAA that Congress has placed the foreign anti-boycott provisions prohibiting U.S. persons from taking part in boycotts against countries friendly to the United States.

U.S. export policy primarily involves questions of *what* goods may be exported, and to *which* countries they may not be exported. There is usually less immediacy about controlling the nature of the goods as opposed to their destination. Restrictions are often introduced to punish nations for actions so distasteful that limits on U.S. exports to that country are thought justified, despite economic losses caused by the diminished exports.

The President is thought to be in a better position than Congress to respond quickly to foreign acts which may justify immediate export controls. For example, President Reagan took action after the Soviets imposed martial law in Poland, prohibiting the export of component parts for the Siberian oil pipeline. The President's decision generated substantial adverse reaction from several European nations which were the location of U.S. owned subsidiaries affected by the order.

The provisions of the EEA, as in the case of several trade laws, are followed-up by extensive administrative regulations. Finally, the EAA contains very severe penalties for violating U.S. export controls, including loss of all export rights. This leads to preventative lawyering under ongoing, proactive compliance programs.

U.S. EXPORT GOVERNANCE

United States export controls involve three primary laws and government agencies. The U.S. Dept. of Commerce, Bureau of Industry and Security (BIS), administers the Export Administration Act Regulations (EAR, 22 C.F.R. Parts 730–774), and the U.S. anti-boycott laws. The U.S. Dept. of the Treasury, Office of Foreign Asset Controls (OFAC), administers U.S. boycott laws. Lastly, the U.S. Dept. of State administers the International Traffic in Arms Regulations (ITAR, 22 C.F.R. Parts 120–130).

The United States also supports various non-proliferation treaties, and U.N. Security Council Resolution 1540 calling on all nations to enforce effective laws against non-state actors' possession and use of weapons of mass destruction, particularly for terrorist purposes.

THE EXPORT ADMINISTRATION ACT (EAA)

U.S. exports are principally regulated by the Export Administration Act (EAA), and several hundred pages of associated regulations. Congress' power to regulate exports as expressed in these laws originates in the *foreign commerce* clause. It is the same provision establishing Congressional authority to regulate imports. This power often conflicts with the President's conception of *foreign affairs* powers, and can lead to disagreements with the executive branch over the extent to which Congress may restrict Presidential discretion in limiting exports to achieve foreign policy goals.

The Export Administration Act is of limited duration. The last one was enacted in 1979 and amended (extended) in 1985. It expired in 1994. Since that time the executive and legislative branches have not been able to agree on the substance of a new act. President George H. P. Bush vetoed one attempt in 1990 to adopt a new EAA because he believed that his powers were unduly restricted by Congress. In order to continue controls over exports, every President since 1994 has extended the duration of the EAA by declaring a state of emergency under the International Emergency Economic Powers Act (IEEPA).

The policy of the United States toward export controls is set forth in Section 3 of the Export Administration Act of 1979, which provides:

It is the policy of the United States to use export controls only after full consideration of the impact on the economy of the United States and only to the extent necessary—

(A) to restrict the export of goods and technology which would make a significant contribution to the military potential of any other country or combination of countries which would prove detrimental to the national security of the United States;

(B) to restrict the export of goods and technology where necessary to further significantly the foreign policy of the United States or to fulfill its declared international obligations; and

(C) to restrict the export of goods where necessary to protect the domestic economy from the excessive drain of scarce materials and to reduce the serious inflationary impact of foreign demand . . .

* * *

It is the policy of the United States . . . to oppose restrictive trade practices or boycotts fostered or imposed by foreign countries against other countries friendly to the United States or against any United States person.

EAA REGULATIONS

The EAA does not contain many substantive provisions regulating exports. They are contained in the Export Administration Regulations (EAR). These regulations constitute an extensive set of provisions detailing the governance of U.S. exports, and re-exports. Following the "nationality of the goods", the EAR are primarily focused on the "end-use" or "end-user" of U.S. exports, including technology. The EAR rely heavily on "know your customer" determinations by exporters.

Important questions to which the exporter must give thought include:

What is the item?

Where is it going?

Who will actually receive and use it?

What will the item be used for?

Answers to these questions will help the exporter determine whether the EAR are applicable. The BIS maintains a list of "Red Flags" to assist with compliance and signal the need for further inquiries by exporter.

Control of U.S. exports is principally done by The Department of Commerce's Bureau of Industry and Security (BIS). But other departments also have some regulatory authority, especially the Department of State where the goods are "dual-use" items, meaning that they have both commercial and military application. Application for a license may be done electronically under the Simplified Network Application Process Redesign (SNAP-R), but only if the exporter has a BIS Company Identification Number (CIN).

A party who wishes to know whether a license is required may obtain an Advisory Opinion from the BIS. Receipt of an opinion does not mean the subsequent application will be granted, opinions are not binding. But the BIS is likely to help the applicant in the preparation of an application which will meet the Advisory Opinion's requirements. Certainly, obtaining an unfavorable opinion and then exporting without a license creates a rather clear case of intent to disregard the law. But the Advisory Opinion is a good route to follow. If an unfavorable opinion is received, the BIS may explain what is required to obtain permission, unless the case is a clear one where no exports are permitted.

The BIS processes tens of thousands of export licenses annually, affecting hundreds of billions of dollars of U.S. exports. In recent years, for example, high-tech goods involving encryption software and advance semiconductor chips with military applications have been a focus of these licenses.

THE PROCESS OF LICENSING U.S. EXPORTS

U.S. merchants contemplating exports of their products or technology must understand the licensing regulations. Prior to 1996 essentially *all* commercial exports had to be licensed. But that was deceptive. Most exports required only a *general* license (i.e., one which did not require individual application and approval), which the exporter acquired by use of the Department of Commerce form "Shipper's Export Declaration." The exporter actually issued its own general license.

But in some cases the exporter needed to obtain a *validated* license (i.e., one authorizing a specific export, issued after approval of an application). Time and changing attitudes generated many variations of licenses, such as a general license GLV allowing shipments of limited value which otherwise would have required a validated license, or a validated license authorizing multiple exports to approved distributors or users in non-controlled countries, or sales to foreign subsidiaries, or sales to an entire activity or project, or sales of replacement or spare parts for goods previously sold.

The current regulations eliminate the terms "general license" and "validated license". "License" refers to an authorization to export granted by the Department of Commerce. The change is to some degree a matter of semantics. General licenses, which were in a sense "self-granted", are abolished in favor of referring to such exports as exports permitted without any license. The new export "license" replaces the old "validated license."

Much more was accomplished in the 1996 rearrangement of the EAA regulations. The myriad of "special" licenses has been redone. There are now ten general prohibitions making up Part 736 of the C.F.R., rather than the previous scattering of the prohibitions throughout the regulations. These prohibitions indicate the circumstances where a license must be obtained.

Note particularly that under the EAR disclosure of controlled technology to a foreign national located *in the United States* constitutes a "deemed export". Transfers to foreign affiliates or subsidiaries within a corporate family are also treated as exports, as are electronic transmissions, donations and hand-carried items.

Although delay is attendant to many export applications, there is a timetable which governs processing license applications. Within 10 days after proper submission, the Secretary of Commerce must acknowledge receipt of the application and provide advice about any other applicable procedures. Unless referral to another government department is necessary, the license should be granted formally or denied within 90 days. Even if referral is necessary, the statutory timetable requires issuance or denial within 180 days of the application. If the exports are to certain countries designated terrorist supporting nations, Congress may have to be advised and the approval period is further extended.

The statutory timetable of the EAA is not always met, despite Congressional attempts to mandate administrative conduct. Delay has been used by the government, especially by the Department of Defense, as a means of discouraging exports which might be permissible, but to which the Department objects. The *Daedalus Enterprises, Inc. v. Baldrige,* 563 F.Supp. 1345 (D.D.C. 1983) case is an example. Twenty-nine months after the filing of an application, the Department of Commerce had not reached a decision. The company had to seek a court order that the Secretary comply with the statutory timetable.

When delay occurs, there is little a company can do. It may not export the goods when the time period has expired if no response has been made by the government. It must go to court at each stage when the government fails to comply with the statute. Fortunately, the *Daedalus* case is an exception, and this kind of delay has been much diminished. The filing process is considerably improved.

Commerce Control and Country Lists

Whether or not a license is required depends primarily on two issues; the type of goods or technology to be exported, and the destination country. The Bureau of Industry and Security (BIS) maintains the Commerce Control List (CCL). This includes all items subject to export controls, except for those under the control of another branch of the government, such as the control of defense articles and services by the Department of State. The transfer by Executive Order of control over encryption devices from State to Commerce in 1996 was particularly contentious.

The CCL is divided into ten general categories (e.g., "Category 3—Electronics"). Within each category are five different groups of products, identified by letters A through E (e.g., "Group C—Material"). Three further numbers identify the reasons for control (001 for national security, for example). Together this makes a four digit and one letter Export Control Classification Number (ECCN, i.e., 3C001).

The Commerce Control List Supplement No. 1 includes the many variations of ECCNs. For each ECCN, this Supplement includes the License Requirements, the License Exceptions, and the List of Items Controlled. Gradually this list has been relaxed, notably to allow exports of high performance computers in 2002. The 1996 revisions provide a fairly easily understood path through the maze of regulations by means of a 29 step process to determine whether a license is needed, and if needed whether there are applicable exceptions.

Use of the process involves reference to the Commerce Country Chart, which helps identify countries subject to controls for such reasons as national security, missile technology, U.N. or U.S. embargo, etc. For example, Country Group A includes several dozen nations with which the U.S. generally has good political and trade relations.

Country Group E, contrastingly, includes the few nations currently subject to either a U.N. or U.S. trade embargo, such as North Korea.

Licensed Exports

When a license is required, a critical decision usually made by counsel to the exporter, application is made to the BIS in the Department of Commerce. The application must be approved and the license issued before the goods or technology may be exported. In many cases, a license will only be issued upon certain conditions, such as limiting the capability of the export product, restricting it to civilian use and prohibiting its use for any military or intelligence gathering purposes, or prohibiting resale to another controlled country.

There is often a considerable negotiating process between the exporter and the BIS. When a license is issued, the exporter is responsible for the performance of all terms and conditions of the license, both by the foreign licensee and by foreign buyers or subsequent buyers. It is important for the exporter to know what conditions might be imposed on the license at the time the original contract is signed, so that such conditions may also be imposed in the contract on the foreign parties.

Speed may be important in processing an application for a license. But the administration of the EAA often has been characterized by delay, uncertainty and lack of accountability, as conflicts arise between national defense and export promotion policies. Many sensitive items have nevertheless evaded export controls, demonstrated in the 1980s sale to the USSR by Toshiba of Japan and Kongsberg of Norway of propeller milling machines and numerical controllers, respectively, which allowed the manufacture of submarine propellers which would function as quietly as U.S. submarines. The companies were subjected to sanctions prohibiting some trade to the United States.

Before its demise, a multilateral review by COCOM might extend the review period to 240 days. COCOM was the Coordinating Committee of the Consultative Group on Export Controls. It was an informal multilateral organization of the U.S. and its military allies (NATO countries less Iceland, plus Japan) established to regulate certain strategic materials exports to communist countries. The U.S. rules were often more restrictive than were those of COCOM, and COCOM review was sometimes used as leverage to grant rather than to deny an application.

COCOM members continually tried to convince the United States to relax some of its export rules. But the United States often acted alone in regulating sensitive exports, as it did in 1990, when President George H. P. Bush announced the "Enhanced Proliferation Control Initiative," which expanded controls on items used in chemical and biological weapons. Following changes in Eastern Europe and the breakup of the USSR, COCOM was abolished in 1994, with promises by many of its members to create a new organization for multilateral export review. The successor organization, established in 1995 and composed of about 28 nations, is the Wassenaar

Arrangement on Export Controls for Conventional Arms and Dual-Use Goods and Technologies. Its purpose is similar to that of COCOM.

Sanctions for EAA Violations

Violation of laws and regulations governing U.S. exports brings into play both the basic law and the regulations. The EAA contains provisions governing violations of both the EAA and EAR. The Export Administrative Regulations contain supplementary provisions, applying strict liability standards. The general sanction for violations of the export laws, where the conduct was entered into *knowingly,* is a fine of the higher of $250,000 or twice the value of the exports. This can obviously be *very* substantial.

Willful violations, with knowledge that the commodities or technology will be used to benefit, or are destined for, a controlled country, may result in a fine for business entities of the higher of $1 million per violation. For individuals who engage in such willful violations the fine is $1,000,000 and/or 20 years imprisonment. This provision covers misuse of licenses.

Cases involving violations of the licensing requirements tend to be quite complex. If the party exported to a controlled country commodities or technology under a license with knowledge that the commodities or technology were being used for military or intelligence gathering purposes, and willfully fails to report this use, the business entity fine is the same as above, the higher of $1 million or five times the value of the exports, but for the individual the imprisonment drops to five years, with the fine remaining the same, $250,000. Even possession of goods or technology either with the intent to export in violation of the law, or knowing that the goods might be so exported, can result in a fine.

Perhaps the most severe statutory penalty in the EAA is in the civil penalty section. The Department of Commerce (DOC) may impose a fine of $10,000 for violations (in certain cases up to $100,000), and they may *suspend or revoke the authority to export.* The "debarment" sanction is used only in extreme cases. It was used in the Toshiba dispute, where Toshiba (Japan) and Königsberg (Norway) enterprises sold to the Soviet Union technology allegedly useful for developing submarine propellers which would be sufficiently silent to avoid detection.

DOC debarment Lists can effectively "blacklist" foreign violators, barring U.S. firms from dealing with named parties, such as Dresser France in the Reagan-era Russian pipeline dispute. Temporary Denial Orders can also be employed against "related parties", as they were against Delft Instruments concerning the illegal export of munitions and night-vision devices. At one point, the Denial Order was extended to all 47 Delft companies located in 13 countries! Subsequently, the Multilateral Export Control Enhancements Act in 1988 amended the EAA stipulating trade prohibition sanctions for two to five years. These sanctions are applied whether or not the other nations take action against their companies.

The EAR repeat and expand upon these statutory sanctions. They further add provisions dealing with actions including "causing, aiding, or abetting" a violation, and "solicitation and attempt", and "conspiracy." More details are provided addressing misrepresentation and concealment of facts, or evasion, failing to comply with reporting and record keeping requirements', alterations of documents, and acting contrary to the terms of a denial order.

The high profile nature of export controls is emphasized by judicial refusal to agree to a settlement negotiated between a company accused of violations of the export laws and the Justice Department. In one instance a bargained $1 million fine was rejected by the court, which imposed a $3 million fine.

In addition, the practice of "designating" foreign nationals merits separate consideration because it is so potentially restrictive. The Office of Foreign Assets Control (OFAC) in the Department of the Treasury may designate individuals and companies owned or controlled by, or acting for or on behalf of, targeted companies. They become so-called "specially designated nationals" or "SDNs." Their assets are blocked and U.S. persons are for the most part prohibited from dealing with them. The list of such designated nationals exceeds 550 pages. It can be a devastating designation and effectively end trade with the United States.

U.S. BOYCOTTS

Boycotts affect both exports and imports. Most nations, including the United States, use trade boycotts as a means to achieve political goals, although there is considerable debate regarding their effectiveness. A boycott by many nations, such as that imposed under U.N. auspices against South Africa in the 1970s and 1980s, was only questionably effective, and certainly caused a loss of jobs for those it was intended to benefit. But formal apartheid ended and the boycott deserves partial credit.

When a boycott is by only one nation against another, contrastingly, such as the U.S. boycott of trade with Cuba, the likelihood of success in achieving a political goal is considerably diminished. The intention of the Cuban boycott has been to remove the Castro brothers from leadership. Some sixty years later Raul Castro continues in office, frequently invoking the U.S. boycott as justification for harsh domestic Cuban policies. Such invocations have been tempered by improving "normalized" Cuba-U.S. relations in the final years of the Obama administration. At this writing, however, a milder version the U.S. boycott continues.

U.S. boycotts tend to be the subject of specific legislation directed towards identified countries. Enforcement is shifted from the Department of Commerce to the Department of the Treasury. The Office of Foreign Assets Control (OFAC) within Treasury is the responsible agency for controlling these specific boycotts.

The pattern of governance is a broad assets control law with additional laws directed to specific countries, such as the Cuban Assets Control Regulations. The various country specific regulations prohibit specific transactions and transfers. By controlling the flow of currency, whether to pay for imports or be paid for exports, trade is thereby restricted. Terminating the flow of currency is intended to terminate trade. It works, but not completely, because considerable trade may take place through third nations. Many U.S. goods are sold in Cuba, transferred first to middle-men in such nations as Mexico or Panama. Unilateral boycotts which are unpopular in other nations are difficult to enforce.

U.S. boycott policy, as expressed in such laws as the Cuban Democracy Act of 1992, the Iran and Libya Sanctions Act of 1996, the Cuban Liberty and Democratic Solidarity (Libertad) Act of 1996 ("Helms-Burton"), and the Burmese Freedom and Democracy Act of 2003, may attempt to reach the conduct of third party nations toward the boycotted country. Such devices seek to exert extraterritorial power over entities located in third nations. The United States thus attempts to draw these third nations into the boycott. It is not surprising that third nations have often responded with extremely strong criticism about interference with their sovereignty by the United States.

Iran, for example, protested long and hard against U.S. boycott sanctions commenced in 1995. These sanctions embraced arms, missiles, nuclear technology, oil and gas, banking, insurance, shipping, goods (save food and medicines) as well as the freezing of Iranian assets, coverage of elite Revolutionary Guard Corps military officials and companies, and blockage of international bank transfers (payments). The EU and to a lesser extent the UN joined the United States in this boycott effort. The combined impact of these sanctions was powerful, sufficient to drive Iran into a 2015 nuclear accord in return for their gradual removal.

Curiously, and perhaps hypocritically, the United States is attempting to mandate conduct by third party nations which it expressly rejects in U.S. anti-boycott laws, most notably concerning the Arab boycott of Israel.

U.S. ANTI-BOYCOTT PROVISIONS

While boycotts are governed as outlined above by regulations enforced by the Department of the Treasury, the Export Administration Act addresses a special problem relating to exports—anti-boycotts. The provisions are a direct consequence of the Arab League economic boycott against Israel commenced initially in 1954, and erratically enforced since then.

When the Arab boycott was extended beyond the primary level (no trading with Israel), to the secondary level (no trading with any nation's enterprise which trades with Israel), and to the tertiary level (no trading with any third party nation's enterprise trading with Israel if it obtained components from a nation trading with Israel), Congress began to debate whether U.S. companies ought to be allowed to assist the boycott of a nation friendly to the United States.

After several years of debate and the failure of voluntary controls to have any effect, the EAA was amended in 1977. The purpose of the anti-boycott provisions is to prohibit any U.S. person "from taking or knowingly agreeing to take [certain actions] with intent to comply with, further, or support any boycott" against a country friendly to the United States. It specifically exempts boycotts pursuant to U.S. law. The requirement of intent is essential, but what constitutes intent may seem marginal.

In *United States v. Meyer,* 864 F.2d 214 (1st Cir.1988), the defendant Meyer was held to have knowledge that a form required by Saudi Arabia to have a trademark registered in that country was not used to obtain information needed for the registration, but to further the boycott of Israel. Meyer claimed that his actions were inadvertent and not intentional. But Meyer's knowledge and intention were rather clearly illustrated by his receipt of information from the Department of State that it could not notarize the form because of the boycott, and his subsequent acquisition of a notarization through the U.S.-Arab Chamber of Commerce. The *Meyer* decision involves a clear attempt to find a way past the law. It is thus not very helpful for a case where the intent is based on less apparent criteria.

Focus on the Arab Boycott of Israel

The U.S. anti-boycott rules are intended to achieve a political end, to assist Israel, although the language of the law never refers to any country by name. Nevertheless, of 376 boycott requests notified to the Office of Anti-Boycott Compliance in 2011, 369 involved an Arab League member.

The EAA provisions include broad language which directs the President to issue regulations prohibiting any U.S. person from doing business in a boycotting country; refusing to hire or discriminating against any U.S. person; furnishing a broad range of information; or paying, honoring or confirming letters of credit, where such action would comply with, further or support the boycott of a country friendly to the United States.

Refusals to Deal

The first prohibition in the EAA is against directly refusing to do business with or in the boycotted country (i.e. Israel), or with a national or resident of that country. Also prohibited is any refusal to do business with the boycotted country by agreement with or response to requests from any other person. This means a U.S. company may not refuse to do business with Israel at the request of the central boycott office of the Arab nations in Damascus. Intent to refuse to do business is not established by the absence of any business relationship with the boycotted country.

Discrimination

The second statutorily prohibited conduct is refusing to employ or otherwise discriminating against any U.S. person on the basis of race, religion, sex or national origin, where such conduct is intentional and in furtherance of an unlawful boycott.

This section addresses the Arab nations' attempts to injure Jewish people wherever they may live, rather than to harm Israel as a nation. Thus, a company may not refuse to employ Jewish persons so that it may gain favor with Arab clients. In one of the few court decisions involving the anti-boycott provisions, Baylor College of Medicine was found to have persistently appointed non-Jewish persons for a project with Saudi Arabia. *See Abrams v. Baylor College of Medicine,* 581 F.Supp. 1570 (S.D.Tex.1984), *aff'd,* 805 F.2d 528 (5th Cir.1986).

The antidiscrimination section of the EAA includes both refusals to employ and *other discrimination.* For example, a requirement that a U.S. company not use a six-pointed star on its packaging of products to be sent to the Arab nation would be a violation because it is part of the enforcement effort of the boycott. But it is not a violation if the demand is that no symbol of Israel be included on the packaging. The former is a religious symbol generally, the latter an acceptable request which does not include reference to any person's religion.

This example can be found in the EEA anti-boycott regulations. It illustrates a general attempt to acknowledge that the boycotting nations are entitled to have *some* control over what comes into their nation. They are entitled to say no imports may be stamped "Products of Israel", but they may not attack the Jewish religion more broadly by requiring certification that no religious symbols appear on any packages. The United States is attempting to say that Arab nations may have a right to engage in a primary boycott against Israel, but they may not draw U.S. persons into supporting that boycott.

Furnishing Information

The third specific prohibition relates to the refusal to hire for reasons of race, religion, sex or national origin, discussed immediately above. This provision prohibits furnishing information with respect to race, religion, sex or national origin. It is supplemented by regulations that make it applicable whether the information is specifically requested or offered voluntarily and whether stated in the affirmative or negative. Furthermore, prohibited information includes place of birth or nationality of the parents, and information in code words or symbols that would identify a person's race, religion, sex or national origin. The regulations also reaffirm the element of intent.

The examples in the regulations illustrate the difficulty of clearly defining "prohibited information". If the boycotting nation requests a U.S. company to give all employees who will work in the boycotting nation visa forms, and these visa forms request otherwise prohibited information, the company is not in violation for giving the forms to its employees or for sending the forms back to the boycotting country party. This is considered a ministerial function and not support of the boycott. But the company may not itself provide the information on race, religion, sex or nationality of its employees, if it meets the intent requirement. The company might certify that none of its employees to be sent to the boycotting nation are women, where the laws of the boycotting country prohibit women from working. The reason for the submission has nothing to do with the boycott.

Blacklists

The fourth prohibition is one that is often at issue. It involves the use of blacklists. The Arab nations maintain a blacklist of persons and companies with whom they will not do business. Arab nations often ask a prospective commercial agreement party to certify that none of the goods will include components obtained from any companies on the blacklist.

Persons are prohibited from furnishing information about an extensive list of business activities ("including a relationship by way of sale, purchase, legal or commercial representation, shipping or other transport, insurance, investment, or supply"), with an equally extensive list of business relationships ("with or in the boycotted country, with any business concern organized under the laws of the boycotted country, with any national or resident of the boycotted country, or with any other person which is known or believed to be restricted from having any business relationship with or in the boycotting country"). At the end is a statement that the section does not prohibit furnishing "normal business information in a commercial context as defined by the Secretary." Thus, U.S. businesses are very extensively governed with regard to the flow of information between the company and the boycotting country.

The most publicized blacklist case involved Baxter International Inc., a large U.S. medical supply company. As a result of an informant's disclosure, Baxter was investigated and charged with violating the EAA because of the way in which it attempted to have its name removed from the Arab blacklist. Commerce was prepared to charge Baxter and a senior officer with providing over 300 items of prohibited information to Syrian authorities and a Saudi Arabian firm. The company and the officer admitted civil and criminal violations and were assessed total civil penalties of $6,060,600—the highest at the time. The case would not have succeeded without the informant providing substantial documentation of the violations.

Anti-Boycott Sanctions

Since the 1977 amendments to the EAA which introduced the anti-boycott provisions, relatively few cases have reached the courts. There have been many challenges by the Department of Commerce's Office of Anti-Boycott Compliance, but most have ended in a consent decree. The same severe sanctions as outlined above for violations of the U.S. export laws apply to violations of the anti-boycott provisions, but consent decrees often have resulted in negotiating the minimum fines under the EAA, substantially less than the costs and adverse publicity of litigation.

For example, in 1995 U.S. subsidiaries (and a corporation counsel) of the French L'Oréal S.A. agreed to pay fines of $1.4 million for allegedly furnishing or agreeing to furnish information by the subsidiaries to the French parent about business relationships with Israel. The penalties were among the highest negotiated under the laws.

There is no clear indication whether the EAA includes a private right of action. A Texas federal district court, in *Abrams v. Baylor College of Medicine,* 581 F.Supp. 1570 (S.D.Tex.1984), *aff'd* 805 F.2d 528 (5th Cir.1986) addressed a claim by two Jewish medical students that Baylor University denied them opportunities when it excluded Jews from medical teams it sent to Saudi Arabia. The Fifth Circuit upheld the decision.

But in *Bulk Oil (ZUG) A.G. v. Sun Co.,* 583 F.Supp. 1134 (S.D.N.Y.1983), *aff'd* 742 F.2d 1431 (2d Cir.1984), the Second Circuit rejected the existence of a private right of action, affirming a New York federal district court decision involving an accusation of violation of the anti-boycott provisions by failing to deliver oil to Israel. The Seventh Circuit has also rejected private causes of action under U.S. anti-boycott law (*Israel Aircraft Ind. v Sanwa Business Credit Corp.,* 583 F.Supp. 1134 (S.D.N.Y.1983), *aff'd* 742 F.2d 1431 (2d Cir.1984).

U.S. FOREIGN CORRUPT PRACTICES ACT

One further export and foreign investment issue involves the practice of U.S. companies making payments to foreign government officials or agents to encourage purchasing the company's products or services (or accept or extend its direct foreign investment). During the Watergate investigations of payments to U.S. political candidates, it was discovered that many U.S. companies had been making payments to foreign officials, notably to obtain sales of Lockheed airplanes to Japan and The Netherlands. The response was swift.

The Foreign Corrupt Practices Act was passed in 1977. The original law included three substantive sections, one establishing stringent accounting and disclosure standards requiring that a bribe must be labeled a bribe. Two sections govern "corruptly" made payments or gifts of value to foreign officials or *state instrumentalities* to obtain, retain or influence business, and payments to "other" persons (think well-connected consultants), where those persons "knew or had reason to know" payments would be passed on to a foreign official.

Payments made to state-owned or state-controlled companies have been deemed to fall within the scope of the FCPA. You might ponder whether extorted payments or gifts involve acting "corruptly." Whether hiring relatives of senior officials in China constitutes making corrupt payments is currently in dispute.

The law included no definitions and only a brief exclusion for payments which were "ministerial" in nature, such as minor "grease" payments often necessary to pass goods through customs.

The law was ambiguous, and from the beginning U.S. businesses requested that the Department of Justice issue guidelines. None were forthcoming until 2012. Like the anti-boycott laws discussed above, few cases reach the courts, most being settled with consent decrees and fines, thus avoiding the label "corrupt payor".

1988 Amendments

Business interests continued to press for changes, which were finally forthcoming in the 1988 trade law. The most significant change was replacing the "reason to know" language with a requirement that any payment to a third person be made "knowing that" it would be passed on to a foreign official. But new definition provisions state that "knowing" may well include reason to know. Having "a firm belief" or being "aware of a high probability" is sufficient to constitute "knowing."

Another important amendment was the further clarification of permissible "grease" payments. Payments are allowed for a "routine government action," which includes obtaining permits to do business, processing papers, providing certain routine services such as police protection or telephone or power, and "actions of a similar nature." But it specifically does not include any decision by a foreign official regarding new business or retaining old business, decisions which are more than merely routine government actions.

The 1988 amendments law also included an affirmative defense section which stipulates several payments which are not prohibited. They include payments permissible under the *written* laws of the other nation, and reasonable and bona fide expenditures such as travel and lodging if related to the promotion or performance of contracts. Other changes to the FCPA in 1988 include some clarification of the accounting provisions.

One difficulty with the FCPA is defining what constitutes a wrongful payment. Because the payment is made to a foreign official, cultural standards of that official's nation may affect the payment. Conflicts of interest by government officials may be governed by very different notions. While apparently no foreign country has written laws permitting foreign officials to accept bribes to influence their conduct, the "operational code" or unwritten law of many countries makes such conduct reasonably commonplace.

A final change in 1988 removed what was known as the Eckhardt provision, which prohibited bringing a suit directly against an employee without first having received a judgment finding the employer in violation of the Act. With the removal of the Eckhardt provision, corporate officers may find themselves scapegoats, and required to defend charges while the company remains free of any litigation.

1998 Amendments

The FCPA was amended in 1998 to comply with U.S. obligations under the 1997 OECD Convention on Combating Bribery of Foreign Officials in International Business Transactions, discussed below. The Convention included language, added to the FCPA, making it unlawful to make payments directly or indirectly to gain "any improper advantage". The OECD concept of improper advantages is broad. For example, procurement contracts, tax benefits and customs preferences, and foreign investment privileges fall within its scope.

The FCPA was further amended to expand its scope to cover prohibited acts by "any person." Domestic concerns other than issuers and "other" persons are now covered. This makes the FCPA cover all *foreign* natural and legal persons who commit acts, however minor, while in the United States.

The amendments also reach extraterritorial payments by business entities and persons taking place wholly outside the United States, and payments to officials of international agencies as well as political parties. In 2015, for example, Hitachi of Japan agreed to pay $19 million to settle FCPA charges concerning payments made to South Africa's ruling party regarding power station construction contracts.

Finally, penalties for non-U.S. citizen employees and agents of U.S. employers and principals, previously limited to civil sanctions, now include the

same criminal sanctions as for U.S. citizen employees
and agents.

FCPA Sanctions

FCPA violations for making illegal payments are
governed by two different provisions, for issuers and
domestic concerns, respectively, and their officers,
directors, agents and shareholders acting on behalf of
the entity. Each section leads to the same levels of
penalties.

The entities are subject to fines of not more than
$2 million or double the intended benefit. The
officers, directors, employees, agents, and
shareholders acting on behalf of the concerns are
subject to fines up to $250,000, or five years'
imprisonment, or both, if the violation was willful.
Only willful violations are subject to criminal
penalties. *See Trane Co. v. O'Connor Securities*, 718
F.2d 26 (2d Cir.1983). Any criminal fine imposed on
a person under the FCPA may not be paid or
indemnified by the company directly or indirectly.

Individual and corporate civil penalties may also
be assessed, along with disgorgement of corruptly
obtained proceeds. These penalties illustrate that the
U.S. government is serious about violations of the
FCPA. For example, two units of Litton Industries
pleaded guilty in 1999 to fraud and conspiracy in
making payments to obtain defense business in
Greece and Taiwan. Litton agreed to pay $18.5
million to settle the matter (including an amount to
reimburse the Department of Justice for the costs of
the investigation).

Violations of the record-keeping and internal accounting-control FCPA standards, may lead, where there is a willful violation, or a willful and knowing making of a false or misleading statement in filed applications, statements or reports, to a criminal penalty for individuals of not more than $5,000,000 and not more than 20 years imprisonment, or both. Corporate criminal violations can result in up to $25 million fines or double the intended benefit. Individual and corporate civil penalties may also be assessed, along with disgorgement of corruptly obtained proceeds.

Other "sanctions" are less formal, but potentially no less severe. Reputational damage, procurement exclusion, shareholder lawsuits and higher capital costs may follow. FCPA settlements typically also impose ongoing compliance costs. For example, in 2015 a small Florida company (IAP) paid over $7 million to settle criminal charges regarding procurement payments to Kuwaiti officials made via a consultant. In addition, IAP promised high-level commitment against corruption, a clear corporate policy against corruption and regular corruption risk reviews, assignment of compliance responsibilities to a senior executive reporting to independent monitoring bodies, extensive training, reporting and investigation systems, disciplinary procedures, and corruption due diligence in mergers and acquisitions.

Enforcement of the FCPA

Particularly in the last decade, the FCPA has been strongly enforced. Some 150 U.S. investigations are pending at this writing, encouraged by Dodd-Frank whistleblower rewards. While the FCPA has mostly concerned foreign investment practices, it has also been applied where corrupt practices favor U.S. exports. Anyone dealing with the FCPA should read the 2012 Department of Justice Resource Guide to the U.S. Foreign Corrupt Practices Act.

The severity of penalties for violations of the FCPA mandates close consideration of its provisions by all persons doing business abroad. Subsidiaries owned or controlled by U.S. companies fall within its jurisdictional scope. Violations of the FCPA are dealt with principally by the SEC (which monitors the record keeping) and the Department of Justice (which enforces the anti-bribery provisions). Over 400 companies have been investigated since 1977, with at least 50 firms charged with FCPA violations in numerous countries around the world, most notably of late China.

It is not only the largest corporations which have been the subject of FCPA actions. One action, for example, involved an individual who owned a postage stamp concession for a Caribbean island and who paid for flights for citizens to return to the island to vote for the reelection of the president, allegedly to influence the government to renew the concession.

Investigations are often reported in the news. For example, some allegations involved IBM and Mexico in 1993, during the sensitive negotiations for the North American Free Trade Agreement. An Iranian-born British businessman was retained by IBM to be its agent in a tender bid for a new air-control system in Mexico City. The agent alleged that soon after a meeting with several Mexican officials at which they tried to obtain a $1 million bribe, IBM's bid was rejected and the contract given to the French Thomson Company.

The agents' subsequent public disclosure and numerous newspaper articles led nowhere, but caused a sensation in Mexico. The Minister of Communications was ousted in a cabinet reorganization. The agent alleged that the Mexican government later tried to buy him off. IBM did not support the agent in his claims, and settled with the agent out of court.

The whole episode illustrates many problems. The U.S. government showed no inclination to become involved or investigate the matter. There were foreign policy problems, NAFTA priorities, perhaps a sense that the story was not implausible, but a realization that this is how things work. Aliases or no names, secret meetings, finger pointing, and leaks to the press were all part of the game. No one seems to have asked how the French Thomson Company got the bid so quickly after IBM was rejected.

IBM was subsequently again in the news regarding an investigation of bribes in Argentina to obtain a $250 million contract to modernize the computer system for the Banco de la Nación. IBM allegedly paid bribes to CCR, a computer systems company, in connection with obtaining a contract with Nación, money which soon found its way into Swiss accounts.

Comparatively few actions brought by the Department of Justice have reached the appellate courts. One example, involving the International Harvester Company, alleged participation in a series of charges relating to dealings with officials of Petroleos Mexicanos (PEMEX), the national oil company. The company pleaded guilty to conspiracy to violate the FCPA. *See McLean v. International Harvester Co.*, 902 F.2d 372 (5th Cir.1990).

Nearly all FCPA enforcement proceedings are settled, often under deferred prosecution agreements. This explains the relative absence of case law, and reinforces the power of the SEC and DOJ to interpret the FCPA as they see fit. In 2010, the DOJ and SEC collected over $1.8 billion in FCPA fines and penalties. Other significant recent prosecutions and settlements include Lucent Technologies, involving payments to Chinese officials and resulting in penalties of $137 million. KBR/Halliburton settled for $579 million in 2009, BAE for $400 million in 2010, Daimler for $185 million also in 2010, and Johnson & Johnson for $70 million in 2011.

The FCPA can apply to extraterritorial activities of foreign as well as U.S. firms. For example, Siemens AG of Germany paid bribes in numerous countries and an agreed to fine of $800 million in 2008. The Siemens' FCPA settlement remains the largest to date, though a 2015 settlement with the French firm, Alstom, came close at $772 million. German and 20 other anti-bribery law enforcement authorities also pursued Siemans, which is reported to have spent over $1 billion in legal and accounting fees. The Siemens cases involved the Oil-for-Food program, which resulted in four other settlements against Akzo Nobel of the Netherlands for $3 million in penalties, against Flowserve Corporation for $10.55 million, against AB Volvo for $12.6 million, and against Fiat for $17.8 million in civil and criminal penalties.

There have also been individual prosecutions, including some high profile persons. Albert Stanley, CEO of KBR, a subsidiary of Halliburton, agreed to serve seven years in prison and pay $10.8 million in restitution. In 2010, the FBI conducted its first FCPA sting operation ("Shot Show"), resulting in the arrest of 22 executives from military and law enforcement products companies. The government has also seized personal assets (pensions, cars and homes) of violators as forfeited proceeds of bribery. Corporate compliance personnel may need prior DOJ/SEC approval, and government monitors be given unfettered access to records and compliance processes.

A New York Times article in December 2012 covered more than three full pages describing bribes allegedly made by Wal-Mart in Mexico. The article triggered a Department of Justice investigation, an expensive global in-house review of payments' practices by Wal-Mart (still ongoing and said to be costing $1 million a week), and a dramatic drop in the value of Wal-Mart stock.

FCPA Compliance Programs

The severity of FCPA sanctions and dramatic increase in FCPA proceedings during recent years, combined with minimal jurisdictional requirements and major reputational and corrective action costs (not to mention share price declines), have caused widespread adoption of company compliance policies and programs. Online and in person training of all employees who might have contact with foreign officials has become routine. Such training is repeated regularly, and recorded in personnel files.

Vendors, customs brokers, transport carriers, construction and other service providers of U.S. corporations engaged are being required to undergo FCPA training. Such third parties must also complete FCPA audits, and sign contract clauses and affidavits as to compliance and awareness of FCPA risks. Some firms decline absolutely to make any grease payments.

Dealing with agents and consultants creates special problems. They should be asked for details about the existence of any relatives or business associates who are in the government. The company should contact various persons in the U.S. government, Chambers of Commerce, local counsel, and the like to check on their reputation, and conduct a Google search. All this "due diligence" might help to later establish that the company did not act "while knowing" (the FCPA standard) that payments to third parties would end up going corruptly to officials. Finally, the agreement with the agent or consultant should contain a clause that none of the funds paid to the agent will be used in any manner which might violate the FCPA.

Corporate policies and compliance programs cannot assure that illegal payments will not be made. But even if illegal payments are later found to have been made, a written policy, acknowledged by employees' signatures, will to establish the company's good intentions and should help in minimizing penalties. Morgan Stanley is thought to have avoided penalties completely when one of their Chinese employees "went rogue" despite major repeated training and compliance efforts.

FCPA due diligence in connection with international mergers and acquisitions has become the norm. The resulting business assumes FCPA liabilities, though it may seek indemnification. Record keeping and internal control compliance programs are critical to adhering to the strict FCPA accounting and disclosure rules, which require a bribe to be labeled a bribe.

OECD and U.N. Codes

The FCPA imposed a U.S. ethic on conduct in the United States and abroad by U.S. persons, and to conduct within the United States by foreign persons. For 20 years, the United States stood almost alone in the global community on foreign corrupt practices law.

A few nations attempted to prohibit payments by their nations' entities, but some encouraged such payments by allowing them to constitute deductions against taxes as ordinary business expenses. Attempts within the United Nations to govern payments to foreign officials on the international level initially failed. The U.S. Trade Representative began an intense effort in 1996 to gain agreement by other nations to prohibit such deductions. The influential NGO organization, Transparency International, urged adoption of laws prohibiting such payments, and has published annually maps of the world reflecting levels of perceived official corruption. Every country is rated from very clean (e.g., Denmark) to highly corrupt (e.g., Somalia). Perhaps the most difficult "corruption" to address is that which is culturally ingrained, for example "ttokkap" (rice cake expenses) in Korea.

Finally, efforts of the Organization for Economic Cooperation and Development (OECD) led to the 1997 OECD Convention on Combating Bribery of Foreign Officials, which obligates signatories to criminalize bribery of foreign officials and sanction inaccurate accounts. Some 35 major nations participate, including China, Russia, Nigeria, Brazil, France, Britain, Germany, India and Japan. Particularly because the OECD Convention contains an extraterritorial element, multinational enterprises can simultaneously be exposed to criminal bribery sanctions in multiple jurisdictions.

In 2004, the United Nations promulgated a widely ratified Convention against Corruption. The United States ratified this Convention in 2006, which did not require amendments to the FCPA. Some 170 nations have subscribed to the U.N. Convention. It notably includes cooperative provisions facilitating the recovery of corrupt payment "assets" hidden abroad by officials.

British Bribery Act

Years after the OECD and U.N. Conventions, the British Bribery Act of 2010 (BBA) may have been late in arriving, but is now widely perceived to be one of the most rigorous in the world. It extends not just to payments to foreign officials, but also to private parties. Its coverage is broad in scope (for example, "grease payments" are not exempted) and its criminal and civil liability is strict, extending to essentially all firms doing business in the U.K. Hypothetically, therefore, the BBA reaches U.S. firms with U.K. stock listings or sales offices, and those processing illegal payments via British banks.

Administered by Britain Serious Fraud Office (SFO), the BBA governs the activities of such firms around the world, say bribes in India. Alstom of France, already having paid the DOJ $772 million for FCPA violations, stands charged under the BBA for making $75 million in payments to secure $4 billion in Egyptian, Saudi Arabian, Bahamian and Indonesian projects. The SFO need not take into account the FCPA fines Alstom has already paid.

The BBA applies to solicitation as well as receipt of bribes, and has no statute of limitations! Furthermore, a violator can be disbarred from competing for EU public contracts. The Act is tempered by an undefined "adequate procedures" compliance defense not found in the FCPA.

In sum, neither the OECD or U.N. Convention, nor the British Bribery Act, is a clone of the FCPA, but the lonely U.S. position on foreign corrupt practices law now has allies.

U.S. SECTION 301 AND
SUPER 301 PROCEEDINGS

Section 301 of the Trade Act of 1974 is one of the most politically motivated provisions of U.S. trade laws. Basically, this section applies when U.S. rights or benefits under international trade agreements are at risk or when foreign nations engage in unjustifiable, unreasonable or discriminatory conduct. Thus, Section 301 primarily focuses on the activities of foreign governments. Although it has been used to protect U.S. markets from foreign imports, Section 301 has been most notably applied to open up foreign markets to U.S. exports, investments and intellectual property rights. The focus has been on foreign market access for U.S. goods and services, including food, tobacco, technology and insurance.

Section 301 of the Trade Act of 1974 authorizes and in some cases mandates *unilateral* U.S. retaliation if another nation is in breach of a trade agreement or engaging in unjustifiable, unreasonable or discriminatory conduct. Amendments contained in the Trade and Tariff Act of 1984 broadened the scope of Section 301 to include retaliatory action against foreign country practices in connection with *services*. Special remedies are allowed, including denial of "service sector access authorizations." Presumably, for example, the U.S. Trade Representative (subject to presidential directives) could deny access to foreign banks by withholding licenses from federal authorities.

Section 301 Procedures

Private sector petitions for action under Section 301 are filed with the U.S. Trade Representative, who undertakes appropriate relief after investigation, consultation with the relevant foreign country and other interested parties, and an affirmative determination of a Section 301 "offense." The USTR may self-initiate Section 301 proceedings, a practice increasingly undertaken since 1988. Remedies are mandatory (subject to various exceptions) when U.S. trade agreement rights are being denied or an unjustifiable foreign country practice is found. Remedies are discretionary when unreasonable or discriminatory practices are involved.

The remedies available include suspending trade agreement concessions, various import restraints, and bilateral agreements with the offending country. The USTR chooses the remedy subject to presidential "direction." The remedy chosen need not have any connection with the complaints.

Perhaps the most critical difference between the Section 301 offenses concerns "international legal rights," which is part of the definition of unjustifiable practices. Discriminatory practices are those which deny national or MFN treatment, but there is no reference to doing so inconsistently with U.S. legal rights. Unreasonable practices are expressly not premised on international legal rights, and only need to be "unfair and inequitable." There is a long list of examples of unreasonable practices in Section 301(d) (3)(B).

The statutory definitions of unreasonableness were expanded in 1988. They include inequitable treatment in connection with market opportunities, investment and protection of intellectual property rights. There is no requirement that such behavior violate an international agreement to which the United States is a party. This has the advantage of not linking relief to international dispute settlement procedures. Thus, Section 301 is a statutory provision of remarkable breadth.

Most Section 301 proceedings have been resolved through negotiations leading to alteration of foreign country practices. Ultimately, if the President or the USTR is not satisfied with any negotiated result in connection with a Section 301 complaint, the United States may undertake unilateral retaliatory trade measures. Unlike subsidy, dumping, escape clause and market disruption proceedings, Section 301 of the Trade Act of 1974 has no origins in or other imprimatur of legitimacy from the GATT or World Trade Organization. Indeed, the unilateral nature of Section 301 is thought by many to run counter to the multilateral approach to trade relations embodied in the GATT and WTO.

Nevertheless, in 1999 the WTO Appellate Body affirmed the legality of Section 301, provided the President does not employ it in a manner inconsistent with the WTO agreements, particularly the Dispute Resolution Understanding. See Chapter 2. The Appellate Body relied heavily on President Clinton's congressionally approved administrative statement that the U.S. would refrain from Section 301 retaliation until the WTO has ruled on disputes falling within its domain. Should some future administration fail to adhere to this policy, the Appellate Body indicated that Section 301 would violate the WTO Dispute Settlement Understanding.

Super 301

Section 301 received hostile responses from U.S. trade partners, especially after the amendments to Section 301 implemented in 1988 through the Omnibus Trade and Competitiveness Act. These amendments include the so-called "Super 301 procedures" which required the USTR to initiate Section 301 proceedings against "priority practices" in "priority countries" identified by the USTR as most significant to U.S. exports. In May of 1989, the USTR initiated Super 301 procedures against the following:

(a) Japanese procurement restraints on purchases of United States supercomputers and space satellites, and Japanese technical barriers to trade in wood products;

(b) Brazilian import bans and licensing controls; and

(c) Indian barriers to foreign investment and foreign insurance.

Super 301 was timed to dovetail with the Uruguay Round of GATT negotiations scheduled to end in late 1990. Some saw it as a clever U.S. bargaining chip. It was anticipated that intergovernmental negotiations concerning alleged unfair trading practices would be undertaken in the 12 to 18 months that followed. This proved to be true for Japan and Brazil, but not India, which refused to even discuss its Super 301 listing. Settlements were negotiated with Japan and Brazil which significantly opened these markets to U.S. exporters.

The Super 301 procedures and designations created in Section 301 of the Trade Act of 1974 were limited in application to 1989 and 1990. They expired in 1991. Super 301 was perceived to be an acceptable alternative to the "Gephardt Amendment" which would have required 10 percent annual reductions in U.S. trade deficits with countries having excessive and unwarranted trade surpluses. Either way, Japan was clearly the main target of the Gephardt Amendment, Super 301 and continuing efforts to renew Super 301.

These efforts, a notable rise in Japan's 1993 trade surplus with the United States and the failure of a trade summit early in 1994, all contributed to the revival of Super 301 in 1994 by President Clinton. This revival was undertaken for two years by executive order and (once again) may have forestalled more severe trade sanctions by Congress. The Uruguay Round Agreements Implementation Act in 1995 codified President Clinton's executive order.

Since then, on a few occasions executive orders have continued to give life to Super 301. As long as Super 301 is an option, it may be used by a U.S. president.

Effect of WTO Dispute Settlement

U.S. adherence to the WTO package of Covered Agreements, including the Dispute Settlement Understanding (DSU), has reduced the frequency with which it unilaterally invokes Section 301. The DSU obligates its signatories to follow streamlined dispute settlement procedures under which unilateral retaliation is restrained until the offending nation has failed to conform to a WTO ruling. See Chapter 2. However, disputes falling outside the scope of the WTO agreements, and disputes with nations that are not WTO members, remain vulnerable under Section 301.

CHAPTER 6

PREFERENTIAL TRADE: FREE TRADE AREAS AND CUSTOMS UNIONS

GATT Article 24   GATS Article 5
Africa   Latin America   ASEAN   East Asia

There is a massive movement towards free trade agreements and customs unions throughout the world, though not often of the consequence of that occurring in the European Union (Chapter 7) and NAFTA (Chapter 8). Some of these developments are a competitive by-product of European and North American integration. Others simply reflect the desire (but not always the political will) to capture the economic gains and international negotiating strength that such economic relations can bring. This is particularly true of attempts at free trade and customs unions in the developing world.

The explosion of such agreements creates systemic risks for the World Trade Organization, covered in Chapter 2. The WTO reports that nearly all of its members are partners in one or more regional or bilateral trade agreements.

One reason for this proliferation may be doubts about the prospects of success for the Doha Round of WTO negotiations. GATT/WTO regulatory failures have also fueled this reality. Yet these "negatives" do not fully explain the FTA and CU feeding frenzy. A range of attractions are also at work. For example, FTAs and CUs often extend to subject matters beyond WTO competence. Foreign investment law is a prime example, and many such agreements serve as investment magnets. Government procurement, optional at the WTO level, is often included in free trade and customs union agreements. Competition policy and labor and environmental matters absent from the WTO are sometimes covered.

In addition, FTAs and CUs can reach beyond the scope of existing WTO agreements. Services are one "WTO-plus" area where this is clearly true. Intellectual property rights are also being "WTO-plussed" in free trade and customs union agreements. Whether this amounts to competitive trade liberalization or competitive trade imperialism is a provocative question.

FTAs and CUs are politically and economically selective. In other words they avoid not only global most-favored-nation principles, but also domestically "sensitive" national politics and economics. For example, Singapore's absence of farm exports helped make it an ideal U.S. and Japanese free trade partner. The micro-sized economy of Chile contributed to its attraction as a free trade partner with Mexico, China, the European Union, the United States and others. U.S. free trade deals with Jordan, Bahrain and Oman fit economically in a similar fashion, not to mention national security objectives.

The United States has roughly 20 free trade agreements, most of them negotiated under "fast track" authority (discussed in Chapter 3), all available at www.ustr.gov. See Chapter 3. Here is a sampling of agreements around the globe: Hong Kong-China, Japan-Singapore, Russia-CIS states, New Zealand-China, Mexico-Israel, Canada-Peru, EU-South Africa, Chile-South Korea, the South Asian Free Trade Area (India, Pakistan, Bangladesh, Nepal, Bhutan, Sri Lanka) . . . and the list goes on. At this point the only nation without a bilateral free trade deal is Mongolia.

Like it or not, the "spaghetti-bowl" maze of FTAs and CUs is driven by powerful negative and positive forces. It is not only the preferred trade medium of today, but very likely the future. Already more than half of world trade is conducted under them. While international trade lawyers may celebrate full employment, it bears remembering that FTAs and CUs *are* discriminatory. They could render MFN the least favored status in world trade. Such an outcome would be especially harmful to the world's poorest nations, those with whom few WTO partners seek a preferential trade agreement.

Preferential Trade Options and Impacts

There is a continuum of sorts, a range of options to be considered when nations contemplate economic integration. In "free trade areas," tariffs, quotas, and other barriers to trade among participating states are reduced or removed while individual national trade barriers vis-á-vis third party states are retained. "Customs unions" not only remove trade barriers among participating states, but they also create common trade barriers for all participating states as regards third-party nations. "Common markets" go further than customs unions by providing for the free movement of factors of production (capital, labor, enterprise, technology) among participating states.

"Economic communities" build on common markets by introducing some harmonization of basic national policies related to the economy of the community, e.g. transport, taxation, corporate behavior and structure, monetary matters and regional growth. Finally, "economic unions" embrace a more or less complete harmonization of national policies related to the economy of the union, e.g. company laws, commercial treaties, social welfare, currencies, and government subsidies. The difference between an economic community and an economic union relates only to the number and importance of harmonized national policies.

All such agreements are inherently discriminatory in their trade impact. As non-universalized trade preferences, they tend to simultaneously *create trade* among participating states and *divert trade* between those states and the rest of the world. Thus, while trade creation may represent an improvement in the allocation of scarce world resources, trade diversion may generate an opposite result.

With free trade agreements, diversionary trade effects are usually not distinct because of the absence of a common trade wall against outsiders. Trade diversion nonetheless occurs. "Rules of origin" in free trade area agreements keep third-party imports from seeking the lowest tariff or highest quota state and then exploiting the trade advantages within a free trade area. Under rules of origin, free trade areas are "free" only for goods substantially originating therein. This causes member state goods to be preferred over goods from other states. Rules of origin under a free trade agreement can be as trade diversionary as common external tariffs in customs unions.

GATT ARTICLE 24

Article 24 of the GATT (1947 and 1994) attempts to manage these internal trade-creating and external trade-diverting effects. Free trade area and custom union proposals must run the gauntlet of a formal GATT/WTO review procedure during which "binding" recommendations are possible to bring the proposals into conformity. Such recommendations might deal with Article 24 requirements for the elimination of internal tariffs and other restrictive regulations of commerce on "substantially all" products originating in a customs union or free trade area. Or they might deal with Article 24 requirements that common external tariffs not be "on the whole higher or more restrictive" in effect than the general incidence of prior existing national tariffs. The broad purpose of Article 24, acknowledged therein, is to facilitate trade among the GATT contracting parties and not to raise trade barriers.

It is through this review mechanism that most free trade and customs union agreements have passed *without* substantial modification. The GATT, not economic agreements, most often has given way.

Early Regulatory Failure

During GATT review of the 1957 Treaty of Rome creating what we now call the European Union, many "violations" of the letter and spirit of Article 24 were cited. The derivation of the common external tariff by arithmetically averaging existing national tariffs was challenged as more restrictive of trade than previous arrangements. Such averaging on a given product fails to take account of differing national import volumes. If a product was faced originally with a lower than average national tariff and a larger than average national demand, the new average tariff is clearly more "restrictive" of imports than before. Averaging in high tariffs of countries of low demand quite plausibly created more restrictions on third-party trade. If so, the letter and spirit of Article 24 were breached.

Despite these and other arguments, the Treaty of Rome passed through GATT study and review committees without final resolution of its legal status under Article 24. Postponement of these issues became permanent. GATT attempts—through the lawyer-like conditions of Article 24 to maximize trade creation and minimize trade diversion—must be seen as generally inadequate. Treaty terms became negotiable demands that were not accepted.

Attempts at Regulatory Reform

The Uruguay Round, which created the World Trade Organization, presented an opportunity to come to grips with the regulatory failure of Article 24 and the implications of the Enabling Clause. Agreement was reached in 1994 on an "Understanding on the Interpretation of Article 24," which presently binds the roughly 150 member nations of the WTO. This Interpretation reaffirms that free trade area and customs union agreements *must* satisfy the provisions of Article 24, clarifies the manner in which before and after evaluations of common external tariffs are to be undertaken, limits in most cases interim agreements to 10 years, and details Article 24 notification, report and recommendation duties and processes.

Most importantly, the 1994 Understanding on Interpretation expressly permits invocation of standard WTO dispute settlement procedures (DSU) regarding any Article 24 matters. All that said, the 1994 Understanding did not come to grips with the systemic ambiguities that led to Article 24's early and ongoing regulatory failure.

The failure to launch a new round of WTO negotiations in Seattle (1999), followed by delays and perceptions of possible failure in the Doha Round that commenced in 2001, has contributed to the feeding frenzy of CU and FTA agreements. Supported by provisional application of a Doha Round WTO Transparency Mechanism, hundreds of agreements have been notified to the WTO. A large additional number are believed *not* to have been

notified. In general, most of the notified agreements
are bilateral, not regional in character.

Meanwhile, the WTO Regional Trade Agreements
Committee, working by consensus, has been unable
since 1995 to complete even one assessment of a
bilateral agreement's conformity to GATT Article 24
or GATS Article 5 (below). The same is true for WTO
Committee on Trade and Development "review" of
Enabling Clause arrangements (also below).

It has been suggested that this record can be
explained by the ambiguous relationship between
Committee reports and WTO dispute settlement
proceedings. For example, can such reports be used
in evidence in WTO dispute proceedings? Can fact-
finding by WTO Secretariat and information
gathered for WTO regulatory purposes be similarly
used? This "dispute settlement awareness" makes
WTO members reluctant to provide information or
agree on conclusions that could later be used or
interpreted in DSU proceedings.

Decades later, the ineffectiveness of GATT/WTO
supervision of free trade and customs union
agreements continues. At best Article 24 exerts a
marginal influence over their contents. Whether the
extraordinary   proliferation   of   preferential
agreements undermines or supports WTO trade
policies is hotly debated.

GATS INTEGRATED
SERVICES AGREEMENTS

Since 1995 "economic integration agreements" (EIAs) covering services are permitted under Article 5 of the General Agreement on Trade in Services (GATS). Such agreements, which can be staged, must have "substantial sectoral coverage," eliminate "substantially" all discrimination in sectors subject to multilateral commitments, and not raise the "overall" level of barriers to trade in GATS services compared to before the EIA. EIAs involving developing nations are to be accorded "flexibility". As with GATT Article 24 customs unions (but not free trade area agreements), there is an Article 5 duty to compensate EIA nonparticipants.

Review of GATS Article 5 notifications is undertaken, when requested by the WTO Council for Trade in Services, by the Committee on Regional Trade Agreements (CRTA). Thus, whereas CRTA examinations of GATT Article 24 agreements are required, such examinations are optional under GATS. Nevertheless, numerous Article 5 examinations have been conducted, including notably the services components of NAFTA, the EEC Treaty (1957) and EU Enlargement (2004), Japan's FTAs with Singapore, Mexico and Malaysia, China's FTAs with Hong Kong and Macau, and various U.S. bilaterals.

None of these examinations have resulted in a final report on consistency with GATS Article 5. This pattern continues the GATT/WTO record of regulatory failure regarding economic integration agreements.

DEVELOPING WORLD INTEGRATION

Developing nations in Africa, the Caribbean, Central America, South America and Southeast Asia (among others) had free trade and customs union agreements in place as early as the 1960s. In 1979, under what is commonly called the Enabling Clause, the GATT parties decided to permit developing nations to enter into differential and more favorable bilateral, regional or global arrangements among themselves to reduce or eliminate tariffs and nontariff barriers applicable to trade in goods.

Like Article 24, the Enabling Clause constitutes an exception to MFN trade principles. It has generally been construed to authorize third world free trade area and customs union agreements. Whether the Enabling Clause was intended to take such agreements out of Article 24 and its requirements, or be construed in conjunction therewith, is unclear. However, the creation of alternative notification and review procedures for Enabling Clause arrangements suggests Article 24 is inapplicable.

Notification to GATT of Enabling Clause arrangements is mandatory. Since 1995, the WTO Committee on Trade and Development (CTD) is the forum where such notifications are reviewed, but in practice not examined in depth. Enabling Clause arrangements should be designed to promote the trade of developing countries and not raise external trade barriers or undue trade difficulties.

Consultations with individual GATT members experiencing such difficulties must be undertaken, and these consultations may be expanded to all GATT members if requested.

Unlike GATT Article 24 and GATS Article 5, neither compensation to nonparticipants nor formal reporting on the consistency with the Enabling Clause of developing nation arrangements is anticipated. The ASEAN-China (2004), India-Sri Lanka (2002), and "revived" Economic Community of West African States (ECOWAS 2005) agreements illustrate notified but unexamined preferential arrangements sheltered by the Enabling Clause.

Africa

Several groups have been formed in Africa. In 1966 the central African countries of Cameroon, Central African Republic, Chad, Congo (Brazzaville) and Gabon formed the Economic and Customs Union of Central Africa (Union Douaniere et Économique de l'Afrique Centrale: UDEAC) to establish a common customs and tariff approach toward the rest of the world and to formulate a common foreign investment code. Implementation has proceeded very slowly.

In 1967 Kenya, Tanzania and Uganda created the East African Community (EAC) in an attempt to harmonize customs and tariff practices among themselves and in relation to other countries. The practical effect of that Community has frequently been negated by political strife, but efforts are underway to revive it with Rwanda and Burundi included. In 1974 six French speaking West African nations formed the West African Economic Community (known by its French initials CEAO). This Community is a sub-group within and pacesetter for ECOWAS, the Economic Community of West African States (now the West African Economic and Monetary Union, WAEMU).

ECOWAS was created in 1975 by Dahomey, Gambia, Ghana, Guinea, Guinea-Bissau, Ivory Coast, Liberia, Mali, Mauritania, Niger, Nigeria, Senegal, Sierra Leone, Togo and Upper Volta to coordinate economic development and cooperation. Some progress on liberalized industrial trade has been made and a Cooperation, Compensation and Development Fund established. During the 1980s the pace of regionalization quickened. ECOWAS countries agreed upon formulative policies for the Community, especially regarding air transport, communications, agriculture, freedom of movement between Member States, currency convertibility, and a common currency.

ECOWAS and CARICOM have agreed upon policies and programs for mutual promotion of inter-Community trade. In June of 1991, the Organization of African Unity (OAU) member states agreed to a Treaty Establishing the African Economic Community. This wide-ranging Treaty embraces 51 African nations, and includes a regional Court of Justice. In September of 1995, 15 southern African countries, with South Africa under Mandela participating for the first time, targeted free trade under the Southern African Development Community (SADC). A 20-member Common Market for Eastern and Southern Africa (COMESA) has also been created.

In 2015, COMESA, SADC and the EAC agreed to work toward a 26-member free trade area.

Islamic World

Bahrain, Kuwait, Oman, Qatar, Saudi Arabia, and United Arab Emirates have formed the Gulf Cooperation Council (GCC) with objectives to establish freedom of movement, a regional armaments industry, common banking and financial systems, a unified currency policy, a customs union, a common foreign aid program, and a joint, international investment company, the Gulf Investment Corporation (capitalized in 1984 at two and one-half billion dollars). The Council has implemented trade and investment rules concerning tariffs on regional and imported goods, government contracts, communications, transportation, real estate investment, and freedom of movement of professionals.

Progress has been made on a GCC Uniform Commercial Code and a Commission for Commercial Arbitration. In 1987, the GCC entered into negotiations with the EU which resulted in a major 1990 trade and cooperation agreement. In 2003, the non-Arab states of Iran, Pakistan, Turkey, Afghanistan and five Central Asian nations joined together in an Economic Cooperation Organization Trade Agreement (ECOTA). In 2004, Jordan, Egypt, Tunisia and Morocco concluded their Agadir free trade agreement.

Latin America and Caribbean

Other regional groups have been established in Latin America and the Caribbean. Since 1973, the Caribbean countries of Barbados, Belize, Dominica, Jamaica, Trinidad-Tobago, Grenada, St. Kitts-Nevis-Anguilla, St. Lucia, and St. Vincent have participated in the Caribbean Community (CARICOM), an outgrowth of the earlier Caribbean Free Trade Association. In 1958 Costa Rica, El Salvador, Guatemala, Honduras and Nicaragua formed the Central American Common Market (CACM), another victim of political strife, but still functioning in a limited way.

Numerous countries in Latin America were members of the Latin American Free Trade Association (LAFTA) (1961) which had small success in reducing tariffs and developing the region through cooperative industrial sector programs. These programs allocated industrial production among the participating states.

The Grand Anse Declaration commits CARICOM to establishment of its own common market. The Latin American Integration Association (LAIA) (1981), the eleven member successor to LAFTA, is continuing arrangements for intra-community tariff concessions. They agreed to a 50 percent tariff cut on LAIA goods. Antigua, Dominica, Grenada, Montserrat, St. Kitts-Nevis, St. Lucia, St. Vincent and the Grenadines have formed the Organization of Eastern Caribbean States (OECS) in part "to establish common institutions which could serve to increase their bargaining power as regards third countries or groupings of countries." Some 37 nations signed the Association of Caribbean States agreement in 1994 with long-term economic integration goals.

Latin America became a central focus in the 1990s of economic integration. Mexico not only signed a free trade agreement with the United States and Canada, it also agreed to free trade with Colombia, Venezuela, Chile, Bolivia, Costa Rica, Nicaragua, Guatemala, Honduras, El Salvador, Peru and Uruguay. Furthermore, Mexico has negotiated free trade agreements with Japan, the European Union, EFTA (European Free Trade Assn) and entered in 2013 into The Pacific alliance with Peru, Chile and Colombia.

Argentina, Brazil, Paraguay and Uruguay signed a treaty establishing the MERCOSUR (Southern Cone) common market in March of 1991 and Chile and Bolivia joined them as Associates in 1996. Venezuela under Chavez created the Peoples' Trade Treaty in 2007 aligned with Cuba, Bolivia, Nicaragua, Ecuador and others. Venezuela finally obtained membership in MERCOSUR in 2012.

The longstanding United States economic boycott of Cuba under Fidel Castro has isolated that nation from FTAA negotiations. U.S. policy has not stopped Canada and Mexico from actively trading and investing (tourism especially) in Cuba. And it certainly propelled post-Soviet Cuba into a close relationship with Venezuela under Chavez and Maduro, including a well-known "doctors for oil" agreement. Cuba's larger problem is its regime's isolationist tendencies, fear of "capitalist pollution" and dogmatic ideology. But the winds of change are blowing in Havana, and a dollarized-economy is emerging from the underground. In 2015, the U.S. and Cuba commenced "normalization" of their relations, but a softer embargo remains in place.

ANCOM ("The Cartagena Agreement") was founded by Bolivia, Chile, Colombia, Ecuador, and Peru in 1969 primarily to counter the economic power of Argentina, Brazil and Mexico and to reduce dependency upon foreign capital and technology. Its Decision No. 24 regulating foreign investment and technology transfers was widely copied during the 1970s. A major boost came in 1973 with the addition of Venezuela, but some of the fragile dynamics of the regional grouping are illustrated by Chile's withdrawal in 1977, Bolivia's withdrawal in 1981 and resumption of membership barely four months later, and Peru's economic (but not political) withdrawal in 1991 and return in 1996.

All of this activity occurs against the background of the Free Trade Area of the Americas (FTAA) initiative of the United States (below). In 2003 the ANCOM and MERCOSUR groups nominally agreed upon free trade, at least partly to counterbalance United States power in the FTAA negotiations (below). The United States, pursuing in turn a divide and conquer strategy, has attempted bilateral free trade agreements with all ANCOM members save Venezuela.

The FTAA

The U.S. "Enterprise for the Americas Initiative" (EAI) under elder President Bush raised hopes of economic integration throughout the Americas against a background of competitive regionalism in trade relations, especially between the European Union and North America. At the Americas Summit in Miami, President Clinton and 33 Latin American heads of state (only Fidel Castro was absent) renewed this hope by agreeing to commence negotiations on a Free Trade Area of the Americas (FTAA). The year 2005 was targeted at the Summit for creation of the FTAA.

Preparatory working groups have regularly met since 1995 to discuss the following topics: (1) Market Access; (2) Customs Procedures and Rules of Origin; (3) Investment; (4) Standards and Technical Barriers to Trade; (5) Sanitary and Phytosanitary Measures; (6) Subsidies, Antidumping and Countervailing Duties; (7) Smaller Economies; (8) Government Procurement; (9) Intellectual Property Rights; (10) Services; (11) Competition Policy; and (12) Dispute Settlement. It is expected that each of these areas would be covered in any FTAA agreement. Formal FTAA negotiations were delayed several times, particularly because of differences between Brazil-led MERCOSUR and U.S.-led NAFTA.

Divisions were particularly evident during the November 2003 FTAA ministerial meeting in Miami. Lowered expectations, known as FTAA-Lite, reflect U.S. refusal to budge on agricultural protection and trade remedies, and Brazilian refusal to fully embrace investment, intellectual property, services and procurement "free trade." Absent successful resolution of these issues in the WTO Doha Round negotiations, an unlikely prospect at this writing, FTAA-Lite, even with different levels of country commitments, seems unlikely.

The absence of U.S. fast track authority (see Chapter 3) and the general perception that political support for free trade in the United States is weak has clearly slowed FTAA developments. MERCOSUR and Brazil in particular seized the opportunity to move towards South American free trade. At this point, MERCOSUR's trade associates include every South American nation. This puts it in a much better position to negotiate terms and conditions with the NAFTA/CAFTA bloc than individual countries or sub-groups within South America.

A CASE STUDY: THE ASSOCIATION OF SOUTHEAST ASIAN NATIONS (ASEAN)

Some interesting moves toward third world free trade and rule-making have been taken by the Association of Southeast Asian Nations (ASEAN). Its problems, failures and successes are representative of third world attempts at legal and economic integration. ASEAN has its genesis in the 1967 Bangkok Declaration, with common trade rules in various states of growth, implementation and retrenchment. ASEAN has internal tariff preferences, industrial development projects, "complementation schemes," and regional joint ventures, all discussed below.

An important juncture in the integration process is the point in time at which member countries of a regional group accept a supranational mechanism for enforcing the regime's law irrespective of national feelings and domestic law within a member country. The 1957 Treaty of Rome provided for a supranational European Court of Justice, which decided quickly upon a mandatory enforcement stance regarding national (Member State) compliance with regional law. ASEAN does not have a comparable enforcement mechanism.

A vigorous administrator can also make regional law a reality. In Europe, the Commission frequently issues regulations and decisions which are binding within the territories of Member States. These rules are enforced through fines and penalties, and ultimately by the Court of Justice and General Court. Violations are investigated and, if necessary, prosecuted by the Commission. See Chapter 7. In contrast, the ASEAN Secretary-General once remarked that ASEAN's Secretariat was "a postman collecting and distributing letters." The surrender of national sovereignty to ASEAN institutions has been a painfully slow process. That said, NAFTA provides an alternative example of achieving free trade without significantly surrendering national sovereignty to regional institutions. See Chapter 8.

Declarations and Summits

ASEAN was formed in 1967 by Indonesia, Malaysia, the Philippines, Singapore and Thailand. Brunei joined in 1984, Vietnam in 1995. Laos and Myanmar (Burma) joined in 1997, and more recently Kampuchea (Cambodia) became a member. Rarely have such culturally, linguistically and geographically diverse nations attempted integration. The Bangkok Declaration establishing ASEAN as a cooperative association is a broadly worded document. Later proposals were made for a formal ASEAN treaty or convention, but were rejected as unnecessary. The Bangkok Declaration sets forth numerous regional, economic, cultural and social goals, including acceleration of economic growth, trade expansion and industrial collaboration.

The Bangkok Declaration establishes several mechanisms, but little supranational legal machinery, to implement its stated goals. An annual ASEAN Meeting of Foreign Ministers is scheduled on a rotational basis among the Member States. Special meetings are held "as required". The Declaration provides for a Standing Committee composed of the Foreign Minister of the State in which the next annual Ministerial Meeting is to be held, and includes the ambassadors of other ASEAN States accredited to that State. The Declaration also provides for "Ad Hoc Committees and Permanent Committees of specialists and officials on specific subjects". Each Member State is charged to set up a National Secretariat to administer ASEAN affairs within that Member State and to work with the Ministerial Meeting and the Standing Committee.

There have been relatively infrequent meetings of the ASEAN heads of government. This contrasts with the semiannual European "summits" that have kept that group moving forward along the path of integration. The third ASEAN summit was held in Manila in 1987. This summit produced an agreement for the promotion and protection of investments by ASEAN investors (national and most-favored-nation treatment rights are created), made revisions to the basic ASEAN joint venture agreement, and continued the gradual extension of regional tariff and nontariff trade preferences. Goods already covered by the ASEAN tariff scheme were given a 50 percent margin of preference. New items received a 25 percent preferential margin. The nontariff preferences generally co-opt GATT rules, e.g. regarding technical standards and customs valuation.

The fourth ASEAN summit in 1992 committed the parties to the creation of a free trade area within 15 years. Five years were cut from this schedule by agreement in 1994, but operational reality has eluded ASEAN free trade. In 2003, a "watershed" date for complete integration in an ASEAN Economic Community targeted 2020. In 2007, this target date was changed to 2016, a reflection of the fear that ASEAN risks being overwhelmed by the powerhouse economies of China, India and Japan. At least on paper, this deadline was met. Malaysia, Brunei, Singapore and Vietnam are partnered with the

United States through the Trans-Pacific Partnership (TPP) agreement, now awaiting ratification. Most of the remainder ASEAN states have expressed interest in joining the TPP. See Chapter 8.

ASEAN Trade Rules and Industrial Projects

Between 1967 and 1976, few steps were taken to further the economic cooperation called for in the Declaration. As with most third world regional groups, ASEAN required a period in which its members got to know and trust each other. The annual Ministerial Meetings did facilitate, however, the formation of committees to study economic development projects and economic cooperation, to establish a working relationship with the EU, and to develop close ties with private sector industries within ASEAN Member States.

Early ASEAN economic cooperation focused upon showcase "industrial projects." A "Basic Agreement" and a set of general "Guidelines" govern their creation and operation. ASEAN industrial projects were modeled on the ANCOM "sectoral programs of industrial development" (SPIDs). They are largely government owned industrial development projects. Several of these projects are now in place with the assistance of Japanese financing, notably the ammonia-urea plants in Indonesia and Malaysia. SPIDs are supported by certain monopoly production rights and tariff preferences. Foreign investors may participate in ASEAN industrial development projects through finance, supply, managerial, technical or limited equity relationships.

ASEAN Freer Trade

ASEAN cooperation has accelerated. Rather than focusing upon the creation of common, protective external tariffs, ASEAN has fostered freer trade by instituting preferential tariffs for goods originating in other Member States. Tariff reductions have been negotiated pursuant to the Agreement on ASEAN Preferential Trading Arrangements. The "Manila Agreement" is aimed primarily at encouraging the establishment of preferential tariffs with respect to basic commodities, particularly rice and crude oil, products of ASEAN industrial projects, and products expanding intra-ASEAN trade. Some of the tariff preferences are negotiated on a bilateral basis; others are negotiated multilaterally by the ASEAN states.

By late 1982, tariff reductions had been agreed for approximately 9,000 products, and the scope of the preferences extended well beyond foodstuffs and textiles. Since then, the ASEAN preferential tariff arrangements have been extended to approximately 2,000 additional items each year. Across the board tariff cuts on items of lesser import value have also increased intra-ASEAN trade opportunities. Progress notwithstanding, these efforts stop short of the automatic tariff elimination schedules of the European Union and NAFTA. As ASEAN moves toward freer trade within the bloc, overhead costs for investors, practical sources of supply materials, and product marketing opportunities may undergo substantial change.

The "Framework Agreement on Enhancing ASEAN Economic Cooperation" (1993) as accelerated in 1994 envisions an ASEAN free trade area (AFTA) that will cover goods but not services or unprocessed agricultural products. The ASEAN countries also signed an agreement on Common Effective Preferential Tariffs (CEPT). Under this agreement, internal tariffs on manufactured products were reduced to 20 percent by 1998. To qualify, at least 40 percent of the content of the goods must originate within ASEAN, a relatively "liberal" rule of origin. Vegetable oils, cement, chemicals, pharmaceuticals, fertilizer, plastics, rubber and leather products, pulp, textiles, ceramic and glass products, gems and jewelry, cooper cathodes, electronics and wooden furniture are included in this first round of tariff cuts.

The goal was to have all tariffs on manufactured goods fall to no less than five percent by 2000. Once again this goal proved elusive. Only five percent of ASEAN trade takes advantage of the CEPT. One reason for such a low percentage is unilateral tariff cuts below MFN commitments: Thailand from 41% to 18%, Indonesia from 25% to 8%. Such preference erosion makes it less likely that ASEAN traders will document origin to achieve free trade. There are ongoing efforts to reduce the number of goods excluded from the CEPT.

In common with global trade, as ASEAN tariffs have been eased, nontariff trade barriers (NTBs) have become the chief internal trade problem. These NTBs principally involve safety, health and environmental regulatory rules that keep ASEAN goods from crossing borders, and are often vigorously supported by local interests.

ASEAN's International Impact

ASEAN has entered into negotiations with all of its major world trading partners, dealing with them as ASEAN rather than as individual states. For example, ASEAN negotiated a limited number of preferences for its products entering the EU, and annually negotiates with its biggest trading partners, including the United States. ASEAN has free trade agreements with China, Japan, India, and Australia-New Zealand.

These negotiations exemplify ASEAN seeking bargaining strength through unity. However, unlike the EU, where virtually all major trade relations are determined by the Union, ASEAN states also pursue individual commercial negotiations with trade partners. Singapore and Thailand, for example, have negotiated or are seeking bilateral free trade agreements with the United States, Japan and others. This less than completely united regional approach to trade relations is indicative of the gradual development of ASEAN supra-nationalism and more in tune with NAFTA than the European Union.

Likewise, there is no ASEAN legislature and no ASEAN court. There is a voluntary ASEAN Law Association and an "emerging law" within ASEAN as evidenced by the various rules, agreements and guidelines supporting economic cooperation in the region. For example, ASEAN has established certain rules covering the "origin" of products subject to its tariff preferences. Under these rules, products not wholly produced or obtained within ASEAN cannot qualify for preferential tariff treatment unless they are processed so that the total value of the materials originating from non-ASEAN countries or from an undetermined origin does not exceed 50 percent of the FOB value of the products.

However, if the final process of manufacture is performed within ASEAN, the goods will qualify for ASEAN tariff preferences. The value of the non-originating materials is determined CIF at importation. In the case of goods entering another ASEAN nation from Indonesia (the least developed ASEAN nation prior to Vietnam), the non-ASEAN component cannot exceed 40 percent. Reductions in these local content requirements were adopted in 1987. An investor producing goods in an ASEAN country might need to work with these rules so as to qualify for regional tariff reductions.

ASEAN Complementation Schemes

ASEAN has encouraged development in the private business sector by urging the formation of numerous regional "Federations" or "Clubs" in various areas of industry and commerce. Sponsored by the ASEAN Chambers of Commerce and Industry, the Clubs are ASEAN-wide and have been formed to assist with "Complementation Schemes." Complementation involves the reduction, as needed, of trade barriers between Member States so that entire manufacturing processes, such as automobile assembly, make maximal use of ASEAN products. Moreover, each participating country produces a component which can be traded within ASEAN as parts for assembly into a more finished manufacture. Each Club, such as the ASEAN Federation of Cement Manufacturers, plays an initiating role in proposing tariff reductions for products which are of concern to that industry.

Formation of the Clubs, while not envisioned in principal ASEAN Agreements, has been encouraged at the Ministerial Meetings. Club recommendations are approved tentatively by the Committee on Industry, Minerals and Energy of the ASEAN Governments. Recommendations are forwarded from that Committee to the Economic Ministers and Foreign Ministers for final approval.

General Guidelines and a Basic Agreement for ASEAN industrial complementation schemes were completed in 1980 and 1981. The Guidelines have been approved by the Economic Ministers of ASEAN and include "exclusivity" provisions guaranteeing (with limited exceptions) that no similar public or private projects to manufacture a product covered by a complementation scheme will be approved by any Member State of ASEAN. The Guidelines also provide that complemented products will be given priority in other ASEAN countries having foreign exchange controls.

Additional Guidelines deal with the percentage of equity ownership by non-ASEAN nationals, tax incentives, remittances, repatriation of profits and expropriation. In 1983, the ASEAN Foreign

Ministers approved an ASEAN auto parts complementation scheme involving local content requirements, exclusivity rights and tariff preferences. Many foreign investors or licensors are potential beneficiaries of this scheme (e.g., a Ford Motor Co. subsidiary has an auto body plant in the Philippines). Despite its origins in the private sector, the success of ASEAN automotive complementation is problematic. The desire to produce "national cars" not "ASEAN cars" is strong and supported by local subsidies. Malaysia, for example, now produces the Proton Saga in cooperation with Mitsubishi Motors.

ASEAN Joint Ventures

Since 1982, ASEAN has focused on creating rules for ASEAN Industrial Joint Ventures which involve participation by only two ASEAN Member States, permit foreign equity participation up to forty nine percent, contain limited monopoly rights and grant extensive tariff preferences. A set of general Guidelines and a Basic Agreement on ASEAN joint ventures have been promulgated. ASEAN joint ventures may be proposed through the private sector initiative of industry clubs, few of which seem to have taken up the opportunity as yet. A 1987 revision of the Basic Agreement on joint ventures permits exclusivity privileges and protection against unfair trade practices. ASEAN joint ventures are a unique contribution to regional development and represent an investment alternative holding out the possibility of significant economies of scale.

Eight joint ventures were approved in 1991, including enamel and heavy equipment production by Indonesia and Malaysia, aluminum hydroxide by Indonesia and Thailand and four food products' joint ventures with the Nestlé Co. In general, the ASEAN trade and investment programs have been hard to implement because of tariff exemptions and nontariff trade barriers. The need to solve such problems is heightened by China's rapidly growing economy and foreign investment magnetism.

ASEAN complementation schemes and joint ventures present potential antitrust law problems for U.S. participants insofar as American foreign commerce is affected. For example, if Ford Motor Co.'s participation in the automotive complementation scheme reduces U.S. export or import opportunities, the scheme could fall within the extraterritorial reach of the Sherman Act. If so, United States prosecutors and plaintiffs will surely claim that ASEAN "clubs" amount to government sponsored cartels.

There may also be U.S. customs law problems when and if complemented "ASEAN cars" are exported to the American market. Such cars could, for example, be subject to countervailing tariff duties if it is determined that ASEAN has subsidized their production and the U.S. auto industry is threatened with injury. These potential legal problems may deter involvement in ASEAN joint ventures and complementation schemes by U.S. firms and their business affiliates within the region.

The Asian financial crisis of the late 1990s led to a broad ASEAN Investment Area agreement built around national treatment and MFN treatment principles. The objective is the free flow of investment within ASEAN by 2020.

EAST ASIAN INTEGRATION

East Asia, ranging from Japan in the North to Indonesia in the South, enjoyed truly remarkable economic growth during the 1980s and 1990s. When the Asian financial crisis hit in 1997–98, the region took it on the chin economically, but bounced back quickly. United States and other foreign investors participated in this growth largely on a country-by-country basis. All signs are that rapid growth, especially in China, will continue.

East Asia, unlike Europe or NAFTA, has not developed a formal agreement with uniform trade, licensing and investment rules. Only recently has the APEC (Asia-Pacific Economic Cooperation) group even begun to address this idea. The APEC group is comprised of Asia-Pacific nations including the United States. Late in 1994 the APEC nations targeted free trade and investment for industrial countries first and developing countries second. Nine industries have been selected for initial trade liberalization efforts.

With the European Union and the North American Free Trade Area maturing rapidly, one provocative question is the future of Japan. It is not in the interests of any nation that Japan should feel economically isolated or threatened. Yet it is hard to imagine incorporating Japan into the NAFTA, though some have suggested this. To some degree, what appears to be happening is that regional integration in East Asia is growing along lines that follow Japanese investment and economic aid decisions. Japan now has "economic cooperation" agreements with ASEAN, Thailand, Malaysia, the Philippines, Indonesia, Vietnam, Switzerland, India and Brunei.

Japan has also joined in the negotiation of a Transpacific Partnership Agreement (TPP) spearheaded by the United States and including Vietnam, Malaysia, Brunei, Singapore, Australia, New Zealand, Chile, Peru, Colombia, Mexico, and Canada. Some have seen in these well-advanced negotiations a "containment" of China strategy. Japan and China have commenced negotiating a Regional Comprehensive Economic Partnership (RCEP) with the 10 ASEAN states, Australia, India, New Zealand and South Korea participating, but not the United States.

The role of China in all of this is critical. China and Japan are clearly rivals for economic leadership of the region. China is pushing for influence in the East Asian economic sphere. Hong Kong's return in 1997 and Macau in 1999 moved in this direction. ASEAN and China have a free trade agreement, achieved before that of Japan. China also has free trade agreements with Chile, Pakistan, Costa Rica, Peru, New Zealand and Singapore. Some commentators foresee, as a practical matter, the emergence of a powerful Southern China coastal economic zone embracing Hong Kong, Taiwan, Guangdong and Fujian.

CHAPTER 7

THE EUROPEAN UNION

Internal and External Trade Law

The European Union (EU), often called the Common Market, is a supranational legal regime with its own legislative, administrative, treaty-making and judicial procedures and powers. To create this regime, 28 European nations have surrendered substantial sovereignty to the EU. European Union law has replaced national law in many areas and the EU legal system operates as an umbrella over the legal systems of the member states.

The European Union has an aggregate population exceeding 500 million and a gross "national" (Union) product exceeding $8000 billion. It is the largest market for exports from the United States. No other regional legal regime rivals Europe in detail of rulemaking and the extent to which its member states have achieved integration. Anyone doing business with Common Market nations will have contact with EU law, which is vast and intricate. There are law school courses devoted entirely to a study of the European Union.

The European Court of Justice is the "supreme court" for EU legal issues. There was no supremacy clause in the founding Treaty of Rome. But the Court ruled that supremacy of European law is absolutely necessary to make the Common Market work and is implied by the very existence and structure of its treaty foundations. National courts have generally adhered to this supremacy doctrine, which invalidates conflicting national law. Since 2009, supremacy principles have been incorporated into the now governing EU treaty, the Treaty on the Functioning of the European Union.

Full coverage of the remarkably complex EU legal system is portrayed in my *European Union Law Nutshell*. After a brief survey of the internal customs union trade rules of the EU, the focus in this chapter is on EU international trade and economic relations law.

The Members

The original six 1957 member states of Belgium, France, Italy, Luxembourg, the Netherlands, and West Germany, were joined by Denmark, Ireland and the United Kingdom in 1973, Greece in 1981, Portugal and Spain in 1986, and Austria, Finland and Sweden in 1995. Norway failed to join as planned in 1973 and again in 1995 after national referenda. Switzerland is not a member, though closely linked via bilateral agreements with the EU.

Greenland (admitted with Denmark) withdrew in 1983. The Norwegians and Greenlanders strongly disliked the Union's Common Fisheries Policy. This Policy regulates the type and number of fish that can be caught in European waters, significantly subsidizes the fishing industry, and protects it from foreign competition. Its most controversial feature requires common access to all fishing grounds beyond six (sometimes twelve) miles.

Turkey, an Associate for many years, formally applied for membership in 1987. It may be unable to join because of Greek hostility and the requirement of a unanimous Council vote on new members. There are also questions as to Turkey's commitment to democracy and its "European" status. Turkey's candidacy as an EU member state has also been diluted by the rush of Central European applicants after the fall of the Soviet Union. Estonia, Poland, the Czech Republic, Hungary, Slovenia, Malta, Lithuania, Latvia, Slovakia, and Cyprus joined in 2004. Bulgaria and Romania became members in 2007, and Croatia in 2013. Thereafter, Serbia, Bosnia, Montenegro, Macedonia and Albania appear next in line, with or without Turkey, and conceivably with Moldova, Georgia, Kosovo, and Ukraine.

CHRONOLOGY OF EUROPEAN UNION MEMBERSHIP

1957—France, Germany, Italy, Belgium, Netherlands, and Luxembourg create EEC (6)

1973—United Kingdom, Eire and Denmark (9)

1981—Greece (10)

1986—Spain and Portugal (12)

1995—Austria, Finland, and Sweden (15)

2005—Cyprus, Estonia, Slovenia, Poland, Hungary, Czech Republic, Slovakia, Latvia, Lithuania, and Malta (25)

2007—Bulgaria and Romania (27)

2013—Croatia (28)

EUROPE WITHOUT INTERNAL FRONTIERS

Development of the EU customs union has taken
decades. National interests and laws have often
frustrated treaty rules and regional policies. This
"hardening of the arteries" of trade and growth
caused major 1987 revisions to the founding Treaty
of Rome. These revisions were undertaken through
the Single European Act of 1987. Their principal
focus was on nontariff trade barriers to internal trade
and free movement. The goal was, by the end of 1992,
to establish a Europe "without internal frontiers",
leaving customs, immigration and other controls to
points of entry into the Union. Hundreds of new
legislative acts were adopted in pursuit of this goal.

In 1993, the Treaty of Rome was again amended
substantially, this time by the Maastricht Treaty on
European Union (TEU). The tasks of the Union
thereafter included creation of an economic and
monetary union with emphasis upon price stability.
The listing of activities in pursuit of that goal was
expanded to include environmental, social, research
and development, trans-European network, health,
education, development aid, consumer protection,
energy, civil protection, internal market, visas and
other policy endeavors. On the other hand, the TEU
sought to limit regional activities to those areas
where the results are best achieved at the European
(versus national) level. This is known as the

"subsidiary principle" and is the subject of intense controversy.

EU Customs Law

EU law eliminates customs duties and all other charges having "equivalent effect" amongst its 28 member-states. This elimination applies both to goods having their origin within EU, *and* to those emanating elsewhere provided appropriate EU tariffs have been paid and EU nontariff trade barriers cleared, Such non-EU goods are said to be in "free circulation." Thus, for example, potatoes from Canada in free circulation in Britain may not be subjected to Irish import tariffs, licenses or other controls.

A Common Customs Tariff (CCT) for trade with the outside world has been established. This means that exporters to the EU pay the same tariff regardless of the point of entry for their goods. These duties are established by regional law, but it is the member states that apply the rules and collect the tariffs. The revenues are forwarded by the national customs' services to the Commission less an administrative charge. The CCT was originally derived by arithmetically averaging the tariffs of the EU member states.

CCT customs duties are now negotiated by agreement with third countries, most often via the GATT/WTO as discussed in Chapter 2. The EU regularly negotiates as a bloc within the WTO and subscribes to various GATT Codes (e.g., the Dumping, Subsidies and Safeguard Codes, see

Chapter 4), as well as the Customs Valuation code, see Chapter 3). It also participates in GATT? WTO programs (e.g., the generalized system of tariff preferences for developing countries, see Chapter 3).

Hence most applicable EU tariffs for U.S. exports are WTO most-favored-nation (MFN) tariffs. After the Tokyo Round (1978), European tariffs on manufactured goods dropped on average to about 8 percent, and after the Uruguay Round (1995) to about 4 percent. Many imported goods from the developing world enjoy more preferential, even duty free, tariff status under various EU trade agreements and programs, such as the GSP, Lomé/Contonou Conventions, EU free trade agreements, and Mediterranean Policy noted below.

Unlike NAFTA, the EU members no longer apply antidumping or countervailing duties (see Chapter 4) to internal EU trade. Such special tariffs remain possible on imports from non-EU nations. Some of these proceedings involve goods from nonmarket economy states (NMEs). Apart from NMEs, Chinese, Japanese and United States exports have most frequently been involved in antidumping proceedings. Many of these proceedings are settled by promises of the exporters to raise prices and refrain from "dumping." The standing of most exporters and complainants to challenge Commission dumping decisions has been affirmed by the European Court. Such persons would otherwise lack any possible judicial remedy. Importers, on the other hand, have remedies in the national courts of the member states and are therefore generally unable to challenge

Commission dumping decisions directly before the Court.

Predictably, the combined effect of the removal of internal tariffs and the creation of the CCT has been to increase trade among member states and reduce trade with non-member states. For example, Britain's trade with Europe increased from 33 to 41 percent of its total trade volume in the first eight years of membership. This increase came largely at the expense of Britain's formerly extensive Commonwealth trade.

The European Union has established special tariff and commodity support preferences for third world nations (mostly former colonies) participating in the Lomé/Cotonou Conventions. These Conventions establish innovative commodity export earnings protection programs known as STABEX and MINEX. The Union also has negotiated preferential trade treaties with Mediterranean basin nations, much as the United States has done in the Caribbean basin. Europe's trade relations can create duty free import opportunities for goods originating in favored nations.

The Europeans have adopted a Common Customs Code. It took effect Jan. 1, 1994. The Code gathers together basic customs rules previously distributed among some 25 individual directives and regulations. The Code includes coverage of customs clearance procedures, customs warehouses and free trade zones, duty free entry for processing and re-export, duty free re-entry of components that have been processed abroad, classification, valuation, origin, payment and customs' bonds. Customs appeals must be allowed to a national court capable of referring questions of Customs Code law to the European Court of Justice. The EU follows the 1999 Kyoto Convention on modernized customs procedures.

Internal Trade Barriers and the Cassis Formula

Quantitative restrictions on imports between member states and measures having an equivalent effect are also prohibited. A number of Commission directives and Court rulings have stringently enforced this provision against trading rules even remotely capable of hindering regional trade. For example, the Court of Justice invalidated the Belgian Royal Decree mandating cubic package sales of margarine was a measure equivalent to a quantitative restriction upon imports because of its capacity to hinder trade.

In a famous case, the Court of Justice held that Belgium could not block the importation via France of Scotch whiskey lacking a British certificate of origin as required by Belgian customs law. *Procureur du Roi v. Dassonville,* 1974 Eur. Comm. Rep. 837 ("*Cassis* formula"). The Court of Justice decided that any national rule directly or indirectly, actually or potentially capable of hindering internal trade is generally forbidden as a measure of equivalent effect to a quota. However, *if* European law has not developed appropriate rules in the area concerned (here designations of origin), the member states may enact "reasonable" and "proportional" (no broader than necessary) regulations to ensure that the public is not harmed.

Products meeting reasonable national criteria may be freely traded elsewhere in the region. This *Cassis* formula is the origin of the innovative "mutual reciprocity" principle used in significant parts of the single market legislative campaign for a Europe without internal frontiers.

The Court has used a Rule of Reason analysis for national fiscal regulations, public health measures, laws governing the fairness of commercial transactions, and consumer protection. Environmental protection and occupational safety laws of the member states have been similarly treated. Under this approach, for example, a Danish "bottle bill" requiring returnable soft drink and beer containers was generally upheld. The Danes successfully argued that this law was environmentally necessary and reasonable.

The Court of Justice has made it clear that all of the Rule of Reason justifications for national laws are temporary. Adoption of Common Market legislation in any of these areas would eliminate national authority to regulate trading conditions. These judicial mandates vividly illustrate the powers of the Court of Justice to expansively interpret the Treaty and to rule on the validity under regional law of national legislation affecting internal trade in goods.

Under *Cassis,* national rules requiring country of origin or "foreign origin" labels have fallen as measures of effect equivalent to quotas. So have various restrictive national procurement laws, including a "voluntary" campaign to "Buy Irish." Minimum and maximum retail pricing controls can also run afoul of the Court's expansive interpretation of measures of equivalent effect. Compulsory patent licensing can amount to a measure of equivalent effect. Where demand for the patented product was satisfied by imports from another member state, the U.K. could not compulsorily require manufacturing within its jurisdiction.

Member states may not impose linguistic labeling requirements so as to block trade and competition in foodstuffs. In one instance, a Belgian law requiring Dutch labels in Flemish areas was nullified as in conflict with the Treaty. These cases vividly illustrate the extent to which litigants are invoking the TFEU and the *Cassis* formula in attempts at overcoming commercially restrictive national laws.

There are cases which suggest that "cultural interests" may justify national restrictions on European trade. For example, British, French and Belgian bans on Sunday retail trading survived scrutiny under the *Cassis* formula. And British prohibitions of sales of sex articles, except by licensed sex shops, are compatible.

However, national marketing laws (e.g., prohibiting sales below cost), when applied without discrimination (especially market access discrimination) as between imports and domestic products, are not considered to affect trade between the member states. In the remarkable *Keck and Mithouard* decision (1993 Eur. Comm. Rep. I–6097) signaling a jurisprudential retreat, the ECJ held that marketing rules may not be challenged under the traditional *Cassis* formula. As to what constitutes "marketing rules," deceptive trade practices laws ordinarily fall outside the scope of *Keck*, while national laws regulating sale outlets and advertising of goods may be embraced.

In recent years, member state regulations capable of being characterized as governing "marketing modalities" or "selling arrangements" have sought shelter under *Keck*. For example, the French prohibition of televised advertising (intended to favor printed media) of the distribution of goods escaped the rule of reason analysis of *Cassis* in this manner, but the Swedish ban on magazine ads for alcoholic beverages did not since it discriminated against market access by imports. Some commentators see in *Keck* and its progeny an unarticulated attempt by the Court to take subsidiarity seriously. Others are just baffled by its newly found tolerance for trade distorting national marketing laws. But the Court of Justice has poignantly refused to extend *Keck* to the marketing of services, and case law suggests *Keck* may be fading into obscurity.

Exceptions to Internal Free Trade

The EU treaty provisions dealing with the establishment of the customs union do not adequately address the problem of nontariff trade barriers (NTBs). As in the world community, the major trade barrier within Europe has become NTBs. To some extent, in the absence of a harmonizing directive completely occupying the field, this is authorized. The Treaty permits national restraints on imports and exports justified on the grounds of:

Public morality, public policy ("ordre public") or public security;

The protection of health and life of humans, animals or plants;

The protection of national treasures possessing artistic, historical or archeological value; and

The protection of industrial or commercial property.

These exceptions amount, within certain limits, to an authorization of nontariff trade barriers among the EU nations. This "public interest" authorization exists in addition to but somewhat overlaps with the Rule of Reason exception formulated under *Cassis* (above). However, in a sentence much construed by the European Court of Justice, the treaty continues with the following language: "Such prohibitions or restrictions shall not, however, constitute a means of arbitrary discrimination or a disguised restriction on trade between member states."

Case Law

In a wide range of decisions, the Court of Justice has interpreted these provisions in a manner which generally limits the ability of member states to impose NTB barriers to internal trade. Britain, for example, may use its criminal law under the public morality exception to seize pornographic goods made in Holland that it outlaws, but not inflatable sex dolls from Germany which could be lawfully produced in the United Kingdom.

Germany cannot stop the importation of beer (e.g., Heineken's from Holland) which fails to meet its "pure standards." This case makes wonderful reading as the Germans, seeking to invoke the public health exception arguing all manner of ills that may befall their populace if free trade in beer is allowed. Equally interesting have been the unsuccessful Italian health protection arguments against free trade in pasta made from common (not durum) wheat, and the similar failure of French standards' arguments against free trade in foie gras.

But a state may obtain whatever information it requires from importers to evaluate public health risks associated with food products containing additives that are freely traded elsewhere in the Common Market. This does not mean that an importer must prove the product healthful, rather that the member state seeking to bar the imports must have an objective reason for keeping them out of its market. Assuming such a reason exists, the trade restraint may not be disproportionate to the public health goal. A notable ECJ opinion invalidated a French public health ban on U.K. beef maintained after a Commission decision to return to free trade following the "mad cow" outbreak.

An unusual case under the public security exception involved Irish petroleum products' restraints. The Irish argued that oil is an exceptional product always triggering national security interests. Less expansively, the Court acknowledged that maintaining minimum oil supplies did fall within the ambit of Article 36. The public policy exception has been construed along French lines ("ordre public"). Only genuine threats to fundamental societal interests are covered. Consumer protection (though a legitimate rationale for trade restraints under *Cassis*), does not fall within the public policy exception.

NTBs and the Single Market

Nontariff trade barrier problems have been the principal focus of the campaign for a fully integrated Common Market. Many legislative acts have been adopted or are in progress which target NTB trade problems. There are basically two different methodologies being employed. When possible, a common European standard is adopted. For example, legislation on auto pollution requirements adopts this methodology. Products meeting these standards may be freely traded in the Common Market. Traditionally, this approach (called "harmonization") has required the formation of a consensus as to the appropriate level of protection.

Once adopted, harmonized standards must be followed. This approach can be deceptive, however. Some harmonization directives contain a list of options from which member states may choose when implementing those directives, particularly as regards remedies. In practice, this leads to differentiated national laws on the same so-called harmonized subject. Furthermore, in certain areas (notably the environment and occupational health and safety), the Treaty and certain directives expressly indicate that member states may adopt laws that are *more* demanding. The result is, again, less than complete harmonization.

Under the Single European Act of 1987, most single market legislation was adopted by qualified majority voting in the Council. Notable exceptions requiring a unanimous vote included new laws on taxation, employment and free movement of persons. However, if a measure is adopted by a qualified majority, the public interest exceptions to free internal trade noted above. This may provide an escape clause for member states that were outvoted in the Council on single market legislation.

Harmonization Principles

Many efforts at the harmonization of European environmental, health and safety, standards and certification, and related law have been undertaken. Nearly all of these are supposed to be based upon "high levels of protection." Some have criticized what they see as the "least common denominator" results of harmonization of national laws under the campaign for a Europe without internal frontiers.

One example involves the safety of toys. Directive 88/378 permits toys to be sold throughout the Common Market if they satisfy "essential requirements." These requirements are broadly worded in terms of flammability, toxicity, etc. There are two ways to meet these requirements: (1) produce a toy in accordance with private CEN standards (drawn up by experts); or (2) produce a toy that otherwise meets the essential safety requirements. Local language labeling requirements necessary for purchaser comprehension have generally, though not always, been upheld.

The least common denominator criticism is also raised regarding the second legislative methodology utilized in the internal market campaign. The second approach is based on the *Cassis* principle of mutual reciprocity. Under this "new" minimalist approach, European legislation generally requires member states to recognize the standards laws of other member states and deem them acceptable for purposes of the operation of the Common Market.

Product Standards

An important part of the battle against nontariff trade barriers (NTBs) in the European Union involves product testing and standards. More than half of the legislation involved in the single market campaign concerned such issues. Since 1969, there has been a standstill agreement among the EU states to avoid the introduction of new technical barriers to trade. A 1983 directive requires member states to notify the Commission of proposed new technical regulations and product standards. The Commission can enjoin the introduction of such national rules for up to one year if it believes that a Union standard should be developed, and failures to notify can invalidate national rules.

The goal is to move from different sets of regulatory approvals to one unified Union system embodying essential requirements on health, safety, the environment and consumer protection. Goods that meet these essential requirements will bear a "CE mark" and can be freely traded. Manufacturers will self-certify their compliance with relevant EU standards. Design and production process standards generally follow the ISO 9000 series on quality management and assurance. Firms must maintain a technical file documenting compliance and produce the file upon request by national authorities.

Under this approach, for example, directives on the safety of toys, construction products and electromagnetic compatibility have been issued. These directives adopt the so-called "new approach" of setting broad, exclusive standards at the Union level which if voluntarily met guarantee access to every member state market. Under the "old approach", which still applies to most standards for processed foods, motor vehicles, chemicals and pharmaceuticals, EU legislation on standards is binding law. The technical specifications and testing protocols of these directives must be followed and (unlike the new approach) the member states may add requirements to them. Under either approach, goods meeting Union standards bear a CE mark.

Standards Bodies

Private regional standards bodies have been playing a critical role in the development of this system. These include the European Committee for

Standardization (CEN), the European Committee for Electrotechnical Standardization (CENELEC), and the European Telecommunications Standards Institute (ETSI).

Groups like these have been officially delegated the responsibility for creating thousands of technical product standards, and are subject to EU law on free movement of goods lest market barriers be erected. They have been turning out some 150 common standards each year. North American producers have frequently complained that their ability to be heard by European standards' bodies is limited. They have had little influence on EU product standards to which they must conform in order to sell freely in the Common Market.

Product Testing and Certification

Testing and certification of products is another part of the EU campaign. The main concern of North American companies is that recognition of U.S., Canadian and Mexican tests be granted by the European Union. Many North American exporters have had to have their goods retested for Union purposes.

The EU is generally committed to a resolution of such issues under what it calls a "global approach" to product standards and testing. This involves creation of a regional system for authorizing certification and testing under common rules and procedures. In negotiations undertaken as part of the Uruguay Round on revising the Standards Code of the GATT, the EU gave its commitment to giving recognition to "equivalent technical regulations" of other nations, and to avoidance of unnecessary obstacles to trade.

In 1991, the United States and the European Union issued a nonbinding joint communiqué on product standards and certification procedures. Each side states its commitment to using international consensus standards in their legal régimes. This commitment extends to private sector standards.

Regarding certification, the EU indicates that testing facilities located outside its borders will be able to obtain "Notified Body" (official) status for purpose of applying the many new EU product standards. Such facilities may include subcontractors of official Notified Bodies. Relatively little progress has been made under this commitment. More recently, private European food standards set by Global Gap have spread to North American farmers and retailers, including Wal-Mart and McDonald's.

The Common Agricultural Policy (CAP) and Trade Barriers

EU law establishes the basic principles governing what is perhaps the most controversial of all regional policies, the Common Agricultural Program (CAP). The inclusion of agricultural trade in the Treaty was a critical political element. For many reasons, including the desire for self-sufficiency in food and the protection of farmers, free trade in agricultural products is an extremely sensitive issue. When the Common Market was established in 1957, France and Italy had substantial farming communities, many of which were family based and politically powerful. Both countries envisioned that free trade in agricultural products could threaten the livelihoods of these people. The solution was to set up a "common organization of agricultural markets."

The objectives of the CAP include the increase of productivity, the maintenance of a fair standard of living for the agricultural community, the stabilization of markets and the provision of consumer goods at reasonable prices. It has not proved possible to accommodate all of these objectives. Consumer interests have generally lost out to farmers' incomes and trading company profits. Target prices for some commodities (e.g., sugar, dairy products and grain) are established and supported through market purchases at "intervention levels". "Variable import levies" (tariffs) are periodically changed to ensure that cheaper imports do not disrupt CAP prices. External protection of this type is also extended to meat and eggs. Fruit, vegetables and wine are subject to quality controls which limit their flow into the market. Wine and agricultural products are subject to regulated designations of origin.

CAP Regulatory Controls

In recent years, perhaps the most controversial "common organization" has been for bananas. The Europeans import bananas under a complex quota system adopted in 1993 that favors former colonies and dependencies. Internally and externally those affected have gone bananas over this regulation.

Several challenges originating from Germany failed before the European Court of Justice, but in the end the United States, Mexico, Ecuador, Guatemala and Honduras prevailed in the World Trade Organization. After suffering "authorized retaliation" in the form of tariffs on EU exports, the Europeans have promised to adjust their "common organization" for bananas by replacing its quotas with non-preferential tariffs.

The European Agricultural Guidance and Guarantee Fund (better known by its French initials as FEOGA) channels the agricultural budget into export refunds, intervention purchases, storage, and structural adjustment. Agricultural policy regulations cannot discriminate against like or substitute products. But the bias towards producers, not consumers, in the CAP has been consistently upheld by the Court of Justice.

Agricultural goods, like industrial products, can trigger free movement litigation. In one case, for example, the Court of Justice suggested that British animal health regulations were a disguised restraint on trade in poultry and eggs. As with industrial goods, if the real aim is to block imports, such regulations are unlawful measures of equivalent effect to a quota. On the other hand, the United Kingdom could establish a Pear and Apple Development Council for purposes of technical advice, promotional campaigns (not intended to discourage competitive imports), and common quality standards for its members. But it could not impose a mandatory fee to finance such activities.

Apart from variable tariff protection, CAP quality control regulations can serve to keep foreign agricultural products from entering the European market. For example, the ban on beef hormones adopted by qualified majority vote in the late 1980s stirred opposition internally. In the United States, the beef hormones legislation was vehemently opposed by the White House, but accepted by the renegade Texas Department of Agriculture which offered as much hormone-free beef as Europe would buy. The Texas offer delighted the Commissioner on Agriculture who rarely has a U.S. ally and is said to have wired: "I accept."

A veritable maze of legislation and case law governs the CAP. For many years, special agricultural "monetary compensation amounts" (MCAs) were collected at national borders, greatly contributing to the failure to achieve a Europe without internal trade frontiers. It was not until 1987 that firm arrangements were realized to dismantle the MCA system. In most years, the net effect of the CAP is to raise food prices in Europe substantially above world price levels. The CAP has meant that agriculture is heavily subsidized. Indeed, it continues to consume the lion's share of the regional budget and at times seems like a spending policy that is out of control.

The Common Agricultural Policy does include a variety of "structural" programs intended to reduce the size of the farm population, increase the efficiency of its production and hold down prices. These programs have involved retirement incentives, land reallocations, and training for other occupations. There has been a gradual reduction in the number of farmers over the years. In 1988, the Council adopted rules designed ultimately to reduce agricultural expenditures by linking total expenditures to rates of economic growth, establishing automatic price cuts when production ceilings are reached, and creating land set-aside and early retirement programs for farmers.

France and Italy, in the early years, became major beneficiaries of CAP subsidies. West Germany, with a minimal agricultural sector, was the primary payor under the program. It, in turn, principally benefitted from the custom union provisions establishing free trade in industrial goods. Hence a basic tradeoff was established in 1957 by the Treaty of Rome. France and Italy would receive substantial agricultural subsidies out of the Common Market budget while West Germany gained access for its industrial goods to their markets.

Britain, like Germany, sees itself as a net payor under the CAP. It has repeatedly been able to negotiate special compensatory adjustments as a consequence. Greece, Spain, Portugal and Ireland, on the other hand, looked forward eagerly to membership as a means to CAP subsidies. So too the countries of Central Europe enjoy CAP subsidies with great relish. These countries, along with unified Germany, Austria, Sweden and Finland (whose agricultural subsidies were actually *reduced* upon joining the CAP), are often the least efficient producers of agricultural products. As such, they stand to lose the most if the CAP is substantially replaced by market forces.

Each enlargement of the Union plugs more farmers into the extraordinary CAP subsidy system. The ten members admitted in 2004 obtained full payments in 2013. The Amsterdam and Nice Treaties failed to resolve ongoing disputes over agricultural reform, but a last minute deal in 2002 capped costs at their 2006 level plus 1% a year starting in 2007. In theory this will force a gradual winding down of CAP subsidies. Significant efforts are being made to de-couple CAP subsidies from production levels, notably for cotton, tobacco and olive oil. Meanwhile, one wonders just how much longer European taxpayers will continue to pay for the CAP.

CAP's International Trade Ramifications

In the main, like the United States until recently, the Europeans seemed unable to stabilize the level of agricultural subsidies. This resulted in overproduction ("butter mountains" and "wine lakes") and frequent commodity trade wars. A significant amount of fraud to obtain CAP subsidy payments has occurred. Others legitimately farm marginal land with lots of fertilizer polluting this environment. The excess produce is stored, used in social welfare programs and frequently "dumped" in cheap sales abroad.

Despite its incredible cost, over half the EU budget, the CAP remains one of the political and economic cornerstones of European integration. In 1992 the Council of Agricultural Ministers agreed as an internal matter to cuts in support prices of 29 percent for cereals, 15 percent for beef and 5 percent for butter. Farmers received direct payments representing the income lost from the price cuts. Further price cuts and direct payments were agreed in 1999. It was hoped that these reductions would reduce export subsidies on agricultural goods and international trade tensions. They also supported the argument that the extraordinary level of European subsidization of agriculture was simply not sustainable.

European agricultural trade restraints are of enormous consequence to North American exporters. Equally significant are its "export refunds" on agricultural commodities, refunds that affect the opportunities of North American exporters in other parts of the world. The United States has argued (at times successfully) that these refunds violate the GATT/WTO rules on subsidies, while at the same time increasing its own export subsidies on agricultural goods. The result for many years was an agricultural "trade war" between the U.S. and Europe. Each side sought to outspend the other on agricultural export subsidies in a market that has been wonderful to buyers.

External protests from North America notwithstanding, the CAP is unlikely to disappear. Major attempts at a resolution or at least diminishment of the agricultural trade war were undertaken in the Uruguay Round of GATT negotiations during the late 1980s and early 1990s. Late in 1992, both sides announced the resolution of a number of longstanding subsidies' disputes (notably on oilseeds) and a compromise on contested agricultural trade issues. Agreement was reached on 20 percent mutual reduction in internal farm supports and a 21 percent mutual reduction on export subsidies measured on a volume basis over 6 years using a 1986–90 base period.

After a year of French protests and further negotiations, this agreement was formally incorporated into the WTO accords. Under it, the Union has been gradually switching from production and export subsidies to direct income support for farmers and rural businesses. This decoupling of agricultural subsidies from output has steadily progressed and is crucial to the long-term viability of the CAP.

Tensions between Europe and the United States on agricultural trade have of late diminished (though hardly disappeared), but U.S. Farm Bills threaten to reignite them. Agricultural trade will certainly be a major issue in the TTIP negotiations.

Intellectual Property Rights as Internal and External Trade Barriers

The Court of Justice has frequently issued significant opinions concerning national industrial and intellectual property rights. Traditionally, manufacturers typically hold a basket of national patent, copyright and trademark rights in the Common Market. The territoriality of IP rights threatens free trade within the Common Market because manufacturers can often sue for infringement and other relief in the national courts whenever goods to which those rights apply cross borders. Under its "exhaustion doctrine", the Court has in most cases eliminated this possibility.

Patented, copyrighted and trademarked goods, once sold in the Common Market with authorization, are said to "exhaust" the intellectual property rights with which they are associated. In the Court's view, blocking parallel imports through infringement actions was not intended to be part of the package of essential rights given by national laws. Even if so intended (as seems likely), the Court has ruled that the exercise of these rights would often amount to a means of arbitrary discrimination or disguised restrictions on EU trade. Thus, existing IP rights have been modified by the Court to promote the goal of Common Market integration.

A good example of this result can be found in *Centrafarm v. Sterling Drug*, 1974 Eur. Comm. Rep. 1147. A New York pharmaceutical company, Sterling Drug, held patent rights for several of its products throughout Europe. The products were produced under license by subsidiaries in Britain and Germany but not Holland. In Holland, an exclusive distributorship for Sterling Drug products was established. A Dutch importer (not the exclusive distributor) purchased certain of these drugs from UK and German third party suppliers at about half the price in the Netherlands.

Sterling Drug sued the importer for infringement of its Dutch patent and trademark rights. Employing the preliminary ruling procedure, the Dutch High

Court (Hoge Raad) sought the opinion of the European Court on the use of clearly existing legal rights to block trade in pharmaceuticals. The Court ruled that Sterling Drug's intellectual property rights had been exhausted upon sale of the goods in the UK and Germany. The rights existed as a matter of Dutch law, but they could not be exercised as a matter of European law. To allow them to be exercised would have the practical effect of giving to Sterling Drug the power to divide upon the Common Market.

While the goal of creation of the Common Market can override national intellectual property rights where internal trade is concerned, these rights apply fully to the importation of goods (including gray market goods) from outside the Common Market. In *Silhouette v. Hartlauer* (1998 Eur. Comm. Rep. I–4799), for example, an Austrian manufacturer's trademark rights blocked imports of its sunglasses from Bulgaria, not yet then a member of the European Union. North American exporters of goods subject to rights owned by Europeans may therefore find entry challenged by infringement actions in national courts. On the other hand, Levi Strauss successfully cited *Silhouette* to keep low-price Made in the USA Levi's out of the EU.

Internal Trade in Services

The freedom of nonresidents to provide services within other parts of Europe is another part of the foundations of EU law. The freedom to provide services (including tourism) implies a right to receive and pay for them by going to the country of their source. Industrial, commercial, health care, craft and professional services are included within this right, which is usually not dependent upon establishment or registration in the country where the service is rendered. In other words, the freedom to provide or receive services across borders entails a limited right of temporary entry into another member state.

The Council has adopted a general program for the abolition of national restrictions on the freedom to provide services across borders. This freedom is subject to the same public policy, public security and public health exceptions applied to workers and the self-employed. For example, Italian rules requiring that only pharmacists to operate pharmacies were justified as a matter of public health. The Council's program has been implemented by a series of legislative acts applicable to professional and nonprofessional services. As with the right of self-establishment, discrimination based upon the nationality or non-residence of the service provider is generally prohibited even if no implementing law has been adopted.

In parallel with law developed in connection with the free movement of goods, member state governments may require providers of services from other states to adhere to public interest rules under the *Cassis* formula. These rules must be applied equally to all service providers operating in the nation, and only if necessary to ensure that the out-of-state provider does not escape them by reason of establishment elsewhere. In other words, if the rules (e.g., ethics) of the country in which the service provider is established are equivalent, then application of the rules of the country where the service is provided does not follow.

Following *Cassis*, and notably not *Keck* (both discussed above), the Court of Justice has affirmed member state marketing controls over the sale of lottery tickets (social policy and fraud interests) and over "cold calling" solicitations for commodities futures. Telemarketing in most other areas is forbidden, except with prior consumer consent, under an EU directive.

Financial and Other Services

Bankers, investment advisors and insurance companies have long awaited the arrival of a truly common market. Their right of establishment in other member states has existed for some time. The right to provide services across borders without establishing local subsidiaries was forcefully reaffirmed by the Court of Justice in a decision largely rejecting a requirement that all insurers servicing the German market be located and established there.

EU legislative initiatives undertaken in connection with the single market campaign create genuinely competitive cross-border European markets for banking, investment and insurance services. Licensing of insurance, securities, investment service companies and banks is done on a "one-stop" or 'single passport" home country basis.

This represents a huge step forward from securing 28 member state banking, insurance etc. licenses.

To qualify for such treatment, banks must meet minimum capital, solvency ratio and other EU requirements (as implemented in member state laws). Banks, for example, cannot maintain individual equity positions in non-financial entities in excess of 15 percent of their capital funds and the total value of such holdings cannot exceed 60 percent of those funds. They can participate in and service securities transactions and issues, financial leasing and trade for their own accounts.

Member states must ordinarily recognize home country licenses and the principle of home country control. For example, the Second Banking Directive employs the home country single license procedure to liberalize banking services throughout Europe. However, host states retain the right to regulate a bank's liquidity and supervise it through monetary policy and in the name of the "general good." Similarly, no additional insurance permits or requirements may be imposed by host countries when large industrial risks (sophisticated purchasers) are involved. When the public at large is concerned (general risk), host country rules still apply.

Services' Reciprocity and the United States

Unless there is "effective market access" under United States law for European firms, U.S. companies entering Europe after 1992 may be unable to obtain the benefits of common service markets.

This problem is generally referred to as the "reciprocity requirement." It is this kind of requirement that gave the campaign for a Europe without internal frontiers the stigma of increasing the degree of external trade barriers. Many outsiders, in rhetoric which sometimes seems excessive, refer to the development of a "Fortress Europe" mentality and threat to world trading relations.

There was a rush by non-member state bankers, investment advisors and insurers to get established before January 1, 1993 in order to qualify for home country licenses. North Americans and others have been particularly concerned about the reciprocity requirement. Since state and federal laws governing banking, investment services and insurance are restrictive, and in no sense can it be said that one license permits a company to operate throughout the United States, one result of European integration has arguably been reform of U.S. regulatory legislation. Since 1994 the United States has noticeably relaxed its rules on interstate banking and largely repealed the Glass-Steagall Act limitations on universal banking.

Restrictions on the freedom to provide professional services across borders without local establishment are being abolished progressively. Removal of restrictions has been relatively simple where the subject activity is much the same in each member state. For example, the Council has adopted directives about freedom to supply services in the case of travel agents, tour operators, air brokers, freight forwarders, ship brokers, air cargo agents, shipping agents, and hairdressers. Similarly, it has been relatively easy to deal with those professions (e.g., medicine and accounting) in which diplomas and other evidence of formal qualifications relate to equivalent competence in the same skill. It did, however, take 17 years to negotiate the directive on free movement of veterinarians.

Litigation over the implementation of these directives continues. It took a Commission prosecution to remove the French requirement that doctors and dentists give up their home country professional registrations before being licensed in France.

Admission to the practice of law is still governed by the rules of the legal profession of each member state. However, several European Court judgments have upheld the right of lawyer applicants to be free from discrimination on grounds of nationality, residence or retention of the right to practice in home jurisdictions. By joining the bar in another country, lawyers acquire the right to establish themselves in more than one nation. This right is now generally secured by a directive providing for the mutual recognition of *all* professional diplomas after three years of study. Host country competence tests and additional training in the law of that country may still be required.

THE EURO

The EURO is of substantial interest to traders inside and outside the Common Market. Late in 1991 an historic agreement was reached at the Maastricht Summit to establish a common currency governed by a European central bank. To participate, member states were supposed to meet and maintain relatively strict economic criteria. The common currency took effect in 1999 for eleven nations.

All member states had to meet strict economic convergence criteria on inflation rates, government deficits, long-term interest rates and currency fluctuations. To join the third stage, a country was supposed to have an inflation rate not greater than 1.5 percent of the average of the three lowest member state rates, long-term interest rates no higher than 2 percent above the average of the three lowest, a budget deficit less than 3 percent of gross domestic product (GDP), a total public indebtedness of less than 60 percent of GDP, and no devaluation within the ERM during the prior two years. These criteria govern admission of the new member states into the EURO zone. One could argue they have been honored more in the breach than conformity.

Britain, Denmark and Sweden negotiated special rights to participate only when and if they wish. Greece, Malta, Slovakia, Estonia, Latvia, Lithuania, Slovenia and Cyprus subsequently joined the "EURO zone".

The arrival of the EURO has had important implications for the United States and the dollar. For decades, the U.S. dollar has been the world's leading currency, although its dominance in commercial and financial transactions, and in savings and reserves, has been declining since the 1980s. It was certainly the hope of many Europeans that they had successfully created a rival to the U.S. dollar.

European Central Bank, Financial Bailouts

The European Central Bank (ECB) and the European System of Central Banks (ECSB) govern the EURO Zone. The ECB and the ECSB are independent of other European institutions and in theory free from member state influence. Their primary responsibility is to maintain price stability, specifically keeping price inflation below two percent per year. In contrast, the U.S. Federal Reserve has two primary responsibilities: maximum employment and stable prices.

The ECB works closely with the Ecofin Council's broad guidelines for economic policy, such as keeping national budget deficits below 3 percent of GDP in all but exceptional circumstances (2 percent decline in annual GDP). If the Ecofin considers a national government's policy to be inconsistent with that of the region, it can recommend changes including budget cuts. If appropriate national action does not follow such a warning, the Ecofin can require a government to disclose the relevant information with its bond issues, block European Investment Bank credits, mandate punitive interest-free deposits, or levy fines and penalties.

Sanctions for failure to comply with the 3 percent budget deficit rule do not appear to be enforceable before the Court of Justice. Many Euro states have been under threat of sanctions for failure to comply with the 3 percent budget deficit rule, most notably

Greece, Portugal, Spain, Italy and Ireland after the global financial meltdown of 2008-09. No EURO Zone member state has ever been sanctioned, suggesting this system for controlling national deficits is toothless.

Furthermore, despite a specific Treaty prohibition against Union bailouts of member state governments, as the European financial crisis of 2010/11 demonstrated, bailouts of debt-ridden EURO zone members may occur. Joining with the IMF, a 110 billion EURO rescue package for Greece was organized by the IMF, ECB and European Commission (the "Troika") over German laments. Fearing a cascade of financial crises in Spain, Portugal, Italy and Ireland, a 1 trillion EURO liquidity safety net was devised using EU-backed bonds, special purpose EU-guaranteed investment loans, and more IMF funds. In addition, the ECB for the first time began buying EURO zone national government bonds in the open market.

All this caused Germany to publicly re-think its traditional role as paymaster and proponent of the European Union and EURO. Clearly the EURO was not as good as the fondly remembered Deutschmark. Sure enough, Ireland tapped into this safety net for over 100 billion EUROs late in 2010 followed by Portugal in 2011. In 2012, massive ECB loans to Spanish and Italian banks and their governments staved off bailouts and moderated interest rates, and Greece was bailed out a second time. These actions ran down the safety net and ECB resources. Most private holders of Greek debt have been pushed into a renegotiated deal with roughly a 50% "haircut" in the value of their holdings.

Fearing a meltdown, in July of 2012 the ECB President promised to "do whatever it takes" to save the EURO. This statement brought an immediate and surprisingly enduring calm to currency and financial markets. Nevertheless, in 2013, Cyprus was bailed out by the Troika under plan that for the first time "bailed in" bank bondholders and uninsured depositors who were obliged to take significant reductions in their assets. More positively, Ireland emerged from its bailout.

By 2014, the EURO Zone was back in crisis mode, primarily due to Greek debt problems. Greece under austere bailout conditions created by the Troika reduced public employment and spending, cut pension benefits, privatized state-owned enterprises, raised taxes and sought greater tax compliance. The net result was an increase the total Greek debt outstanding, and no reasonable prospect that Greece would ever be able to meet its debt obligations. With protests and violence in the streets, the Greeks elected an anti-austerity government committed to renegotiation of bailout conditions.

In 2015, Greek negotiations with the Troika failed to reduce and by July actually increased austerity requirements in the context of a third bailout. As always, these funds will be distributed in "slices" after measuring Greek compliance with the loan conditions. However, a split in the Troika emerged . . . the IMF arguing Greece's debt level needs to be cut to make repayment feasible, with Germany, the

ECB and the Commission rejecting this approach. Since a majority of Greek debt after three bailouts is held by the ECB and European central banks, these creditors are naturally wary of writing off portions of their debt holdings.

Treaty on Stability, Coordination and Governance (TSCG), ECB Bond Buying

In March of 2012, with market pressures and threats of a Greek default or exit from the EURO Zone escalating, 25 of the 27 EU members (minus Britain and the Czech Republic) adopted a Treaty on Stability, Coordination and Governance (TCSG) intended to provide a "permanent" solution to the EURO crisis. Only Ireland allowed its voters a referendum on this Treaty, which was negotiated outside the regular TFEU framework. The Irish, their bailout in progress, voted in favor of ratification by approximately a 60% margin. Importantly, ratification by the German Parliament was upheld by Germany's Constitutional Court under that country's "eternal democracy" clause. The TCSG has two principal components: The European Stability mechanism (ESM) and a "Fiscal Compact."

Effective in 2013, the ESM created a permanent 900 billion EURO loan fund, 27% of which is financed by Germany. Any increase in the ESM fund must be approved by the German Parliament. EURO Zone countries may apply for bailout loans conditioned upon fiscal and economic reforms. As a general rule, all EURO Zone national parliaments must approve of any ESM rescue package. Finland has indicated its approval may require loan collateral.

The "Fiscal Compact" incorporates a "balanced budget" rule. "Automatic corrective measures" apply if excessive budgets are reached. The EU Commission monitors national budget deficits under the "European Semester" economic indicators' system. Breach of the Compact can result in enforcement actions before the European Court of Justice with penalties payable to the ESM.

In addition, in 2012, the European Central Bank announced its willingness to buy unlimited, short-term national government bonds if an ESM rescue is secured by a EURO Zone member (Outright Monetary Transactions). Germany's revered Bundesbank openly opposed this announcement, which had the support of the Merkel government. Like ESM loans, such purchases will be conditioned upon fiscal and economic austerity commitments with the ECB serving as the regulator of Zone banks. The extent of the ECB's regulatory powers was much debated, though ECB licensing and penalty powers over banks represented a regulatory base line. Thanks principally to the ECB President's 2012 promise to do whatever it takes to save the EURO, no ESM rescues or Outright Monetary Transfers have been undertaken as yet.

Thus there is a three-part attempt at "permanently" solving the EURO crisis: The ESM, Fiscal Compact and ECB bond buying. This attempt once again seeks to come to grips with systemic flaws that have haunted the EURO since its creation . . .

can national spending policies be stabilized, coordinated and governed in support of a common currency? Since all EURO Zone countries are jointly liable for ESM and ECB monies, this amounts to a partial mutualization of national debt risk. It is not, however, as some have suggested is needed, EURO bonds backed by the EURO Zone. That said, the TGSG is certainly a step in that direction.

In sum, the EURO crisis has diminished its potential to rival the U.S. dollar as a global currency. Indeed, a noticeable flight to safety has occurred and the dollar is highly sought in the markets.

EXTERNAL EU TRADE LAW AND RELATIONS

EU law requires member states to coordinate and implement a *common commercial policy* toward non-member states. This policy is based upon uniform principles regarding tariff and trade agreements, fishing rights, export policy and other matters of external concern.

The Commission generally negotiates common external commercial policies, subject to a mandate from and ultimate control by the Council. Throughout 1986, for example, Europe and the United States vigorously disputed the amount of trade compensation that the U.S. was entitled to under the GATT as a result of the expansion of the Common Market to include Spain and Portugal. After a series of threats and counter-threats to increase tariffs, this dispute was finally resolved mainly by preserving substantial U.S. agricultural exports to Spain. Similar negotiations were replayed in 1995 when Austria, Finland and Sweden joined the Union, and again with the 12 member states acceding in 2004/2007.

EU Trade Treaties

Well establishes procedures are used in the negotiation of most international trade agreements. Basically, the Commission proposes and then receives authorization from the Council to open negotiations with third countries or within an international organization. When the Commission reaches tentative agreement, conclusion or ratification must take place in the Council. The Council votes by qualified majority on Common Commercial Policy agreements.

The Council must also vote unanimously on international agreements covering areas where a unanimous vote is required to adopt internal rules. Parliament's role in international agreements has been expanded. Its assent must now be obtained for virtually all EU trade and foreign investment agreements. The Council is also authorized to take emergency measures to cut off or reduce trading with other nations for common foreign or security policy reasons.

Trade agreements and other international treaties of the European Union are subject to judicial review by the Court of Justice as "acts" of its institutions. Moreover, such agreements are binding on the member states which must ensure their full implementation. When the European Court holds international agreements "directly effective" law, individuals may rely upon them in national litigation. The direct effects doctrine has led to cases where citizens end up enforcing trade agreements despite contrary law of their own or other member state governments.

WTO Agreements Case

The Court of Justice reviewed the Uruguay Round WTO trade agreements. The European Union had long represented the member states in the GATT and exclusively negotiated these agreements. But the General Agreement on Trade in Services (GATS) and the Agreement on Trade-Related Aspects of Intellectual Property (TRIPS) raised special concerns since EU law was ambiguous as to whether the Union or the member states or both had the power to conclude these agreements.

The Court of Justice, in the complex *WTO Agreements* opinion (1994 Eur. Comm. Rep. I–5267), ruled that the Union had exclusive power regarding trade in goods agreements (including agriculture) based on the Common Commercial Policy. While the cross-frontier supply of services not involving movement of persons also fell under that authority, all other aspects of the GATS did not. Regarding TRIPS, only the provisions dealing with counterfeit goods came under the Union's exclusive authority.

Noting that the effective surrender of national sovereignty over intellectual property is not (yet) total and that internal trade in services is not "inextricably linked" to external relations, the Court ruled the competence to conclude GATS and TRIPs was jointly shared by the Union and the member states. Likewise, they share a duty to cooperate within the WTO in the administration of these agreements and disputes relating to them.

Under Treaty reforms of 2009, trade in services, trade-related intellectual property rights, and notably foreign direct investment became exclusive EU competences.

Member State Involvement

As a rule, member states may not negotiate trade treaties in exclusively regional fields. They may do so on a transitional basis in areas where the Union lacks authority or (less clearly) has not effectively implemented its authority. For example, in the early 1970s there was no effective regional energy policy. Thus, the International Energy Agreement achieved through the Organization for Economic Cooperation and Development (OECD) after the first oil shocks is not a Union agreement. In contrast, the Union clearly had competence in the field of export credits for goods. OECD arrangements in this area are exclusively the province of the Union with no residual or parallel authority in the member states.

Likewise, in 2002 the ECJ ruled that bilateral "open skies" aviation agreements between eight individual member states and the United States were illegal incursions into an exclusively EU domain. A United States-European Union open skies agreement followed in 2008.

Recognizing the sensitivities involved, "mixed agreements" negotiated by the Commission (acting on a Council mandate) and representatives of the member states are frequently used. Both the Union and the member states are signatories to such accords. This has been done with the "association agreements" (see below), certain of the GATT/WTO Codes, the Ozone Layer Convention and the Law of the Sea Convention.

The Court of Justice has upheld the validity of mixed international agreements and procedures, but suggested that absent special circumstances their use should not occur when the Union's exclusive jurisdiction over external affairs is fully involved. In other words, mixed procedures should be followed only when the competence to enter into and implement international agreements is in fact shared between the Union and its member states. 1993 treaty amendments made it clear that trade agreements relating to cultural and audiovisual services, educational services, and social and human health services are shared competences. A lengthy list of shared competencies can now be found the 2009 Treaty on the Functioning of the EU (TFEU).

The TFEU also clarified that Common Commercial Policy matters are an exclusive EU competence, as are the customs union, business competition rules, EURO zone monetary policy, and marine biology conservation policies. The TFEU further indicates that the Union has exclusive competence to conclude international agreements provided for by EU legislative act, necessary to enable the EU to exercise its internal powers, or where concluding an international agreement may affect common rules or alter their scope. In all of these areas, therefore, trade agreements can only be concluded by the European Union.

Free Trade Agreements and Foreign Investment Treaties

Very significantly, Mexico and the European Union reached a *free trade* agreement in 2000. Mexico, with its NAFTA membership, thus becomes a production center with duty free access to the world's two largest consumer markets. The Union has been aggressively pursuing other free trade agreements. South Africa, Peru, Colombia, Central America (6 nations), Chile, Canada, South Korea and Vietnam have signed on. India, ASEAN, MERCOSUR and the Gulf Council may follow. One notable feature of these agreements is the inclusion of a Human Rights and Democracy Clause backed up by potential trade sanctions.

Foreign investment has traditionally been governed by the national laws of the member states. Hundreds of Bilateral Investment Treaties (BITs) have been negotiated between member states and other, largely developing nations. Germany, for example, has over 100 BITs, and France nearly as many. Since 2009, foreign investment law has become an exclusive competence of the European Union. It is expected that national BITs will in time be replaced by EU BITs, much as has already been done concerning international aviation agreements.

Association Agreements

EU law authorizes association agreements with other nations, regional groups and international organizations. The Council must act unanimously in adopting association agreements. Since the Single European Act of 1987, association agreements also require Parliamentary assent (which it threatened to withhold from renewal of the Israeli association agreement unless better treatment of Palestinian exports was achieved). The network of trade relations established by association agreements covers much of the globe. Those who are "associated" with Europe usually receive trade and aid preferences which, as a practical matter, discriminate against non-associates. Arguments about the illegality of such discrimination within the GATT/WTO and elsewhere have typically not prevailed.

According to EU law, association agreements should involve "*reciprocal* rights and obligations, common action and special procedures" (emphasis added). This reciprocity requirement mirrors GATT law on non-preferential trading and free trade area agreements. Nevertheless, European association agreements usually establish wide-ranging but not necessarily reciprocal trade and economic links. Greece for many years prior to membership was an associate. Turkey still is and has been since 1963.

These two agreements illustrate the use of association agreements to convey high levels of financial, technical and commercial aid preliminary to membership. Turkey now has a customs union agreement. Another type of association agreement links the EFTA nations with the European Union. These agreements originally provided for industrial free trade and symbolized an historic reconciliation of the EEC and EFTA trading alliances in 1973. A much broader European Economic Area agreement governs most remaining trade relations.

Mediterranean Policy

Still another type of association agreement involves pursuit of the "Mediterranean Policy." This policy acknowledges the geographic proximity and importance of Mediterranean basin nations to Europe. The Med is viewed as a European sphere of influence. Most of these association agreements grant trade preferences (including substantial duty free entry) and economic aid *without* requiring reciprocal, preferential access. Agreements of this type have been concluded with Algeria, Morocco, Tunisia, Egypt, Jordan, Lebanon, Syria, Israel, the former Yugoslavia, Malta, Cyprus and the Palestinian autonomous territories.

In 1995 Europe and these partners declared intentions to create a Mediterranean industrial free trade zone. Since then, EU trade agreements in the Mediterranean basin have moved significantly towards reciprocal trade preferences.

Central and Eastern Europe

Because the Soviet Union and its European satellites refused for many years to even recognize the European Union, some bilateral trade and cooperation agreements between those nations and the member states continued in place. It was not until 1988 that official relations between the Union and COMECON were initiated. As democracy took hold, first generation trade and aid agreements were concluded with nearly every Central and East European nation, including many nations formerly part of the Soviet Union.

The Union advanced to second generation "association agreements" with many of these countries. These are known as "Europe Agreements." They anticipate substantial adoption of EC law on product standards, the environment, competition, telecommunications, financial services, broadcasting and a host of other areas. Free movement of workers is not provided. Free trading is phased in over a ten-year period with special protocols on sensitive products like steel, textiles and agricultural goods. More fundamentally, Europe Agreements are clearly focused on the eventual incorporation of these countries into the Union, as many already have.

With respect to the former USSR, the basis of the relationship between the EU and the Commonwealth of Independent States initially was the Trade and Cooperation Agreement of 1989 concluded with the Soviet Union. This agreement has been replaced by bilateral Partnership and Cooperation Agreements. The negotiations with Ukraine were concluded in March 1994, with Kazakhstan and Kyrgyzstan in May 1994, with Russia in June 1994, and with Moldova in July 1994.

These new agreements laid down the framework for future commercial and economic cooperation and created a new legal basis for the development of trade and investment links. For example, the agreement with Russia on trade and trade-related issues removed all quotas and other quantitative restrictions on Russian exports to the European Union, with the exception of certain textile and steel products.

In 2005, responding to the admission of 10 new EU member states, Russia and the European Union concluded a Partnership agreement. Customs duties on cargo shipments between Russia its Kaliningrad enclave on the Baltic Sea are dropped, tariffs generally lowered, Russian steel quotas increased and EU antidumping duties relaxed. The European Union has also promised to guarantee language rights for the Russian-speaking minorities in Estonia and Latvia.

Russia has become increasingly concerned with the eastern drift of EU memberships. It is organizing its own Eurasian Economic Union to counterbalance EU expansion. Belarus, Kazakhstan and Armenia have signed on. Ukraine, Moldova and Georgia, on the other hand, are expected to become EU associates and eventually members.

U.S.-EU Trade Relations

Trade between the United States and the Common Market is voluminous, roughly in balance and yet fractious. While the focal point in recent years has been agricultural trade, especially the problems of export subsidies and nontariff trade barriers (notably Europe's banana quotas, beef hormone bans and freeze on GMO (genetically modified organism) approvals), there are many contentious issues. For example, Airbus subsidies are said to threaten Boeing and vice-versa, and the single market legislative campaign to erect a "Fortress Europe" in banking, insurance, broadcasting, data privacy and other areas. There is continuing concern in North America that Europe may turn inward and protective.

Europe, for its part, has begun imitating the United States' practice of issuing annual reports voicing *its* objections to U.S. trade barriers and unfair practices. Extraterritorial U.S. jurisdiction has been a constant complaint, including the Helms-Burton Cuban LIBERTAD and the Iran-Libya Sanctions Acts. These reports have also targeted Section 301 of the Trade Act of 1974 (see Chapter 4). The Europeans perceive Section 301 as a unilateral retaliatory mechanism that runs counter to multilateral resolution of trade disputes through the GATT/WTO. This perception has not stopped them from partially duplicating this mechanism in their law against foreign country trade barriers. Nevertheless, since the United States has been taking the bulk of its trade disputes to the WTO under its Dispute Settlement Understanding, the Europeans have less to complain about on this score.

Trade relations between the EU and the U.S. have improved in limited ways under the Transatlantic Economic Partnership Program. A 20-year dispute on wine production and labeling practices, for example, was finally resolved, and there is agreement on use of International Financial Reporting Standards, replacing U.S. Generally Accepted Accounting Principles. Common standards for electric vehicles have been agreed. In 2012, faced with recessionary economies and the rising economic tide of Asia, the EU and the United States started negotiations on a Transatlantic Trade and Investment Partnership Agreement (TTIP).

Nevertheless, deep underlying conflicts remain, especially regarding cultural goods (TV shows, films), agriculture, GMOs, airplane subsidies, and procurement. It is this author's view that NAFTA and the EU are competing with good reason for possession of the world's largest market. Larger markets bring greater leverage in intergovernmental trade negotiations, economies of scale, and improved "terms of trade" (pay less for imports, receive more for exports), as well as enhanced abilities to exercise global economic leadership. And so the struggle for market power is likely to continue.

Japan/China-EU Trade Relations

Europe's trade relations with Japan and China are less voluminous, less in balance and (at least superficially) less fractious than with the United States. Japan and China run growing surpluses, but the amounts are smaller than the huge surplus either accumulates in trading with the States. Many Europeans speak quietly and with determination about their intent to avoid the "United States example" in their trade relations with Japan and China. Less quietly, some national governments have imposed quotas on the importation of Japanese autos and instituted demanding local content requirements for Japanese cars assembled in Europe.

The Commission, for its part, has frequently invoked antidumping proceedings against Japanese and especially Chinese goods. It has also demonstrated a willingness to create arcane rules of origin that promote its interests at the expense of Japan and China. At the GATT/WTO level, however, Japan and the EU share common concerns about retaining their agricultural support systems. These concerns place them in opposition to the U.S. and others who seek to liberalize world trade in agricultural products.

CHAPTER 8

NAFTA

CUSFTA   NAFTA   Post-NAFTA   The TPP

The evolutionary character of the free trade agreements of the United States is readily apparent. The first with Israel in 1985 now seems seriously out of date. The second with Canada in 1989 was nothing less than path breaking; the most sophisticated free trade and foreign investment agreement in the world. This agreement provided the matrix for negotiating NAFTA Agreement of 1994.

In turn, NAFTA creates the bulk of the framework for negotiating the floundering Free Trade Area of the Americas (FTAA), U.S. NAFTA-Plus agreements, the imminent Trans-Pacific Partnership (TPP) and the potential Transatlantic Trade and Investment Partnership (TTIP).

For much more extensive coverage, see my Nutshell on *NAFTA, Free Trade and Foreign Investment in The Americas.* For full understanding, each agreement must be viewed in its own historical, geopolitical and economic context.

CANADA-U.S. FREE TRADE

The United States and Canada have the largest bilateral trading relationship in the world. As early as 1854, the Elgin-Marcy Treaty concluded a free trade agreement covering agriculture, resource and other primary products between the U.S. and Canadian provinces. Termination of this treaty in 1866 led to adoption of protectionist national trade policy in Canada. Canada made repeated (1891, 1896, 1911) unsuccessful attempts to negotiate bilateral trade agreements of various kinds with the United States. In the post-World War II era, Canada was an early participant in the GATT. The GATT proved successful in expanding U.S. and Canadian trade, but by the 1980s the pace of GATT had slowed and the significance of access to the U.S. market required attention.

Prior to the Canada-U.S. Free Trade Area Agreement (CUSFTA), about 70 percent of the trade between the two nations was already duty free. Tariffs on the remaining products averaged about five percent when entering the United States and about 10 percent when entering Canada. Annual trade between the two countries was valued at more than $200 billion U.S. dollars. This is more than three times U.S.-Japan trade.

Roughly one-third of all Canada-U.S. trading concerns automotive goods, an industry still largely dominated by U.S.-based (but not necessarily U.S.-owned) companies. Canada has continued to maintain a healthy trade surplus with the United States. Free trade between the United States and Canada is based upon reciprocity and can be terminated by either party with six months' notice.

THE CUSFTA AGREEMENT IN OUTLINE

Trade in Goods

The Canada-United States Free Trade Agreement covered manufactured and agricultural goods. It was generally oriented around the principle of national treatment and the Article III GATT rule to that effect was specifically incorporated in Chapter 1. Although the parties affirmed their existing trade agreements (including the GATT), if there was an inconsistency between CUSFTA and most of these agreements, it was agreed that the CUSFTA will prevail. The Provinces of Canada and the States of the U.S. must accord most-favored-treatment to goods that qualify under the CUSFTA.

The CUSFTA did not repeal or directly amend the longstanding U.S.-Canadian Automotive Agreement (1965) under which the large majority of trading in autos and original equipment auto parts is undertaken duty free. However, a tougher 50 percent CUSFTA content rule was established for autos entering the U.S. Canada agreed to phase out its embargo on used autos by 1994.

Government procurement contracts for $25,000 or more were opened to firms from both countries, but their goods must have at least a 50 percent U.S.-Canadian content. The CUSFTA expanded upon the GATT Procurement Code by creating common rules of origin, mandating an effective bid challenge system and improving the transparency of the bid process. Canada has created a Procurement Review Board before whom bid challenges based upon the

CUSFTA may be made. An analysis of the decisions of this Board suggests that it provides open and effective relief.

The CUSFTA tariff removals were phased in over ten years through 1998. The most sensitive tariff reductions occurred later in the decade and these included duties on plastics, rubber, wood products, most metals, precision instruments, textiles, alcoholic beverages, consumer appliances, and agricultural and fish products. There was a petitioning procedure which permits private parties on either side of the border to seek to accelerate duty free entry in advance of 1999. This petitioning procedure was invoked to a significant degree, resulting in increased duty free trade between the United States and Canada. The CUSFTA terminated customs user fees and duty drawback programs by 1994, and duty waivers linked to performance requirements by 1988 (excepting the Auto Agreement). All quotas on imports and exports were removed unless allowed by the GATT or grandfathered by the CUSFTA.

The GATT Code on Technical Standards (1979) was reaffirmed by mutual pledges not to use product standards (health, safety and environment) as trade barriers. National treatment and mutual recognition of testing laboratories and certification bodies was required, and general commitments to harmonize federal standards as much as possible were made. A mandatory 60-day notice and comment period on proposed standards' regulations operated at all levels of government. Canada challenged the 1991 upgrading of Puerto Rico's milk standards to existing federal requirements as a violation of CUSFTA. The practical effect of this upgrading was to end Puerto Rican imports of long-life milk from Canada.

On agriculture, the CUSFTA eventually eliminated most bilateral tariffs and export subsidies, and selectively limited or removed quotas (including quotas on sugar, poultry, eggs and meat imports). The Canadians agreed to terminate import licenses for wheat, oats and barley whenever U.S. price supports for those commodities were equal or less than those in Canada. Wine and distilled spirits (but not beer) were generally opened to free and nondiscriminatory trade. Import and export restraints on energy products, including minimum export prices, were prohibited. Petroleum, natural gas, coal, electricity, uranium and nuclear fuels were covered. In short supply conditions, export quotas must be applied so as to proportionately share energy resources. There was permission to export 50,000 barrels per day of Alaskan oil to Canada, and a lengthy list of specific regulatory changes by both sides.

Canada's Cultural Industries Exclusion

At Canadian insistence, "cultural industries" were specially treated, subject to a right in the other party to take measures of equivalent commercial effect in response to actions that would otherwise be inconsistent with the CUSFTA. Essentially, there was free trade in these goods, but ownership of them may be reserved to nationals and preservation of their Canadian character secured. Cultural industries are defined to include the publication, sale, distribution or exhibition of books, magazines, newspapers, films, videos, music recordings, and radio, television and cable dissemination. This exemption continues under NAFTA.

Cultural industry disputes have also been diverted from CUSFTA and NAFTA by using the World Trade Organization as an alternative forum. In March of 1997, a WTO Dispute Settlement Panel ruled that Canada's taxes, import regulations and postal subsidies concerning magazines (and advertising) violated the GATT 1994 agreement. This longstanding dispute centered on *Sports Illustrated*. Canada was seeking to protect and ensure "Canadian issues" of periodicals and prevent the export of its advertising revenues.

The United States overcame culturally-based Canadian policies by electing to pursue WTO remedies, although Canada's compliance was disputed. In May of 1999, a settlement was reached. United States publishers may now wholly-own Canadian magazines. In addition, Canada will permit U.S. split-run editions without Canadian editorial content. Such editions may contain Canadian advertisements not in excess of 12 percent by lineage (rising to 18 percent).

Professor Oliver Goodenough has thoughtfully analyzed Canada's preoccupation with culture. *See* 15 *Ariz. J. Int'l & Comp. Law* 203 (1998). He believes that the cultural industry exclusion reflects a weak national identity and that a principal purpose is to rally Canadians around their flag in a "recurring pageant of threat and defense." Professor Goodenough notes that the "war" against Hollywood is primarily protective of Anglophone Canada. Francophone Canada, with a healthy cultural identity, has already demonstrated resilience to U.S. and Anglophonic Canadian influences.

Reaching into the literature on "culture transmission theory," Professor Goodenough finds that most foreign influences will "bounce off" healthy cultures without government intervention or, at the very least, compartmentalize such influences in ways which separate them from hearth and home. He concludes that Canada is "defending the imaginary to death" and if it continues to press its cultural protection policies: "[I]t will indeed be to the death, a death brought about not by 'invasion' from the south, but by the incomparably better claims to culturally-based nationhood possessed by Francophone Quebec and by the First Nation Peoples. Rather than acting as a rallying cry for national preservation, cultural protection provides the intellectual basis for a break-up of Canada."

Rules of Origin

Either nation could invoke escape clause proceedings if there was a surge of imports resulting in injury to a domestic industry. Bilateral escape clause proceedings were eliminated after 1998. A "global" agreement altered traditional third party escape clause criteria to allow relief against CUSFTA goods only when these imports were substantial (over

10 percent of total) and contributed importantly to serious domestic injury or the threat thereof. Escape clause decisions were ultimately referred to binding arbitration if consultation between the United States and Canada did not result in a settlement.

The innovative rules of origin applicable under the Canadian-U.S. Agreement were established in Chapter 3. There were general and product-specific rules of origin. Ordinarily, goods must be either wholly-produced in the United States or Canada or (if they contain materials or components from other countries) must have undergone a transformation sufficient to result in a new designation under the Harmonized Tariff Classification System employed by both countries. This was treated as the equivalent of "substantial transformation."

In addition, regarding certain assembled products, at least 50 percent of the cost of manufacturing the goods must be attributable to U.S. or Canadian material or the direct cost of processing in the United States or Canada. Note that these rules focus on production costs. The costs of advertising, sales, profit and overhead were excluded for purposes of determining Canadian or U.S. origin. The 50 percent local content test also served as a residual rule of origin applicable whenever the required change in tariff classification was absent in certain cases (notably textiles).

The Canadian-U.S. rules of origin are found in Section 202 of the United States-Canada Free Trade Area Agreement Implementation Act. Special U.S.-Canada Free Trade Agreement Certificates of Origin must be completed by exporters seeking duty free entry. United States law requires the retention of records, including these certificates, supporting CUSFTA preferential treatment for five years.

Services and Investment

Apart from reductions in tariffs, one notable feature of the Canadian-U.S. Free Trade Area Agreement was its application to services and investment. Many provisions of the Agreement sought to liberalize trade in services and investment capital flows between the two nations. In Chapter 16, traditional Canadian controls over foreign investment were substantially reduced for United States investors.

In 1973 Canada enacted a restrictive investment law, the Foreign Investment Review Act (FIRA), and created a Foreign Investment Review Agency to pass upon new investment and acquisitions in Canada. The law was not as restrictive as those in the developing nations, but it did require substantial review. Joint ventures were not mandated, although the review agency often extracted local content promises before it approved new investment. That practice was condemned by the GATT after a request for review was submitted by the United States. The GATT based its decision on the Article III:4 national treatment requirements.

Canada replaced the FIRA with the Investment Canada Act in 1985. This Act continues the practice of reviewing proposed investment, but review is reserved for large investments. The Act is more investment encouraging and simplifies procedures. The CUSFTA changed the extensiveness of the restrictions that are placed on U.S. investment. Canada ended review of indirect acquisitions (U.S. firms buying U.S. firms with Canadian subsidiaries), but could still require divestiture of cultural subsidiaries to Canadian owners.

For direct acquisitions, thresholds were increased, time for review shortened and procedures made easier. A general rule of national treatment in establishing, acquiring, selling and conducting businesses within CUSFTA was created. Transportation investments were notably excluded from this general rule. Most investment performance requirements were banned, and profits and earnings are freely transferable.

Not all services could be freely provided across the Canadian-U.S. border under the CUSFTA. A lengthy listing of covered services is found in Annex 1408 to Chapter 14 of the Agreement. These include agriculture and forestry, mining, construction, distribution, insurance, real estate, and various commercial and professional services. Engineering and accounting services were included but transportation, legal and most medical services were not.

Covered services had to be accorded national treatment and a right of establishment, except as differences were required for prudential, fiduciary, health and safety and consumer protection reasons. State, provincial and local governments must grant most favored treatment to service providers. In addition, the U.S. and Canada agreed that their licensing and certification procedures not be applied on a discriminatory basis and be based upon assessments of competence.

A general "standstill" on trade restraints applicable to services was agreed. This had the effect of grandfathering most existing restraints or discrimination. Special rules permitting temporary entry for business persons in either country supported free movement in services. Individual rules for architecture, tourism, computer services and telecommunications network services were detailed in separate annexes to the CUSFTA. Professionals, investors, traders, business visitors and executives also benefitted from a newly created temporary entry CUSFTA visa agreement.

Financial services were covered in Chapter 17 of the CUSFTA. Each side made specific commitment to alter or apply its regulatory regimes for the benefit of the other's financial services' companies. For example, the U.S. promised not to apply less favorable treatment to Canadian banks than that in effect on Oct. 4, 1987 and to grant them the same treatment accorded U.S. banks if and when the Glass-Steagall Act was amended. The continuation of multi-state branches of Canadian banks was guaranteed.

Canada, for its part, removed various statutory restraints on foreign ownership of financial institutions (including insurance and trust companies) and assets' controls over foreign bank subsidiaries. Applications for entry into the

Canadian financial market were treated on the same basis as Canadian applications, and U.S. banks could underwrite and deal in Canadian debt securities. All of these commitments were continued under NAFTA. Financial services' disputes are subject to formal consultation between the U.S. Treasury Department and the Canadian Department of Finance.

DISPUTE SETTLEMENT UNDER CUSFTA

Disputes under CUSFTA were handled in one of two ways. Disputes of a general nature were taken up under the GATT (now WTO) or addressed under Chapter 18, first by consultation and then by a binding arbitration panel of five independent experts. Each side chose two experts and those experts chose a fifth. Panels were formed in 1989 on salmon and herring and in 1990 on lobsters.

Other trade disputes of special note focused on the allegedly low level of Canada's "stumpage fees" for timber (treated as a subsidy by the U.S.), mutual recriminations about trade restraints in beer and a ruling of the U.S. Customs Service regarding the Canadian-U.S. content of Hondas manufactured in Canada. This ruling had the effect of disqualifying these automobiles from CUSFTA tariff treatment.

Antidumping and Subsidy Disputes

Special, unique dispute settlement rules applied to antidumping and countervailing duty tariffs under Chapter 19. Basically, both nations agree to allow a binational panel to solve disputes of this kind, the governing law changing according to which is the importing country. The panels were drawn from a roster of 50 Canadian and United States citizens, a majority of whom were lawyers. Any final determination at the national level could be appealed by private or governmental parties to this panel using pleadings similar to those used in judicial proceedings. Binational panels replaced traditional judicial review of antidumping and countervailing duty orders.

The only appeal from a binational panel decision in countervailing duty and antidumping cases was to the so-called "Extraordinary Challenge Committee." This Committee was composed of ten judges or former judges from the United States and Canada. Three of these judges were chosen to hear extraordinary challenges. These could be raised only if the panel was guilty of gross misconduct, made errors in procedure, or exceeded its authority. Numerous antidumping or countervailing duty determinations had been reviewed under Chapter 19 by the end of 1994 and the arrival of NAFTA. Most of these panel decisions were unanimous.

Extraordinary Challenges

The first Extraordinary Challenge Committee decision involved U.S. countervailing duties on Canadian exports of pork. These duties and the underlying subsidy law decisions by United States agencies were challenged before a binational panel. The panel's first decision found that the International Trade Commission's domestic injury determination was based upon questionable

evidence. The panel remanded the matter to the ITC
for reconsideration. Upon reconsideration, the ITC
again found a threat of material injury to the U.S.
domestic pork industry.

A second binational panel decision held that the
ITC had exceeded its own notice of remand
proceedings. The second panel gave a number of
specific evidentiary instructions to the ITC and again
remanded the proceeding. In its second remand
proceeding, the ITC found no threat of material
injury expressly and only because of the binding
nature of the Canadian-U.S. Free Trade Area
Agreement. The ITC's second remand decision
bitterly denounced the binational panel's second
review decision. The ITC asserted that the panel's
decision violated fundamental principles of the
Agreement and contained egregious errors of U.S.
law.

The USTR sought review by an Extraordinary
Challenge Committee. The Committee ultimately
ruled that the panel's decisions did not contain gross
error. The Committee therefore declared itself
jurisdictionally ineligible to hear the dispute.
Specifically, there was no gross error even if some of
the panel's rulings might not follow U.S. rules of
evidence, but cautioned the panel not to rely on extra-
record evidence. There were two additional
extraordinary challenges to CUSFTA Chapter 19
panel decisions. Both were raised by the United
States, and in both Canada prevailed. One challenge
concerned Canadian live swine exports, and the other
Canadian softwood lumber exports. In the latter

case, a blistering dissent by a U.S. judge serving on the ECC asserted panelist conflicts of interest and egregious errors in applying U.S. law.

NORTH AMERICAN FREE TRADE

The economic integration of Canada and the United States was a certainty. The blueprint was already there. For most Canadians and Americans, revising the design to include Mexico required considerably more effort and discomfort. The discomfort came from years of observing protectionist Mexican trade policies, uncontrolled national debt, corruption, and the sense, somehow, that Mexico just did not "fit." In the end, these perspectives were overcome.

Mexico since the 1980s has been breaking down its trade barriers and reducing the role of government in its economy. Over half of the enterprises owned by the Mexican government a decade ago have been sold to private investors, and more are on the auction block. Tariffs have been slashed below WTO bindings and import licensing requirements widely removed. Export promotion, not import substitution, has become the highest priority. Like the U.S. and Canada, Mexico (since 1986) participates in the General Agreement on Tariffs and Trade (GATT) and World Trade Organization (WTO). This brought it into the mainstream of the world trading community on a wide range of fronts, including participation in nearly the full range of the WTO agreements.

Mexican debt, assisted by the Brady Plan with its emphasis on loan forgiveness, became a manageable problem, although the collapse of the peso in December of 1994 and Mexico's ensuing financial crisis brought back painful memories.

One party rule has ended, with signs of an increasingly pluralistic democracy on the horizon. Admittedly, political and economic corruption runs deep in Mexico, but the winds of change are blowing. Major prosecutions of leading police, union and business leaders have been undertaken. Perhaps most significantly, the rapid privatization of the state-owned sector of the economy combined with increasing tolerance of international competition has reduced not only the need for government subsidies, but also the opportunity for personal enrichment by public officials.

The United States is Mexico's largest trading partner, accounting for nearly 70 percent of all Mexican trade and more than 60 percent of its foreign direct investment. In contrast, trade with Mexico totaled only seven percent of all U.S. international trade. Those facts help explain why Mexico is the major beneficiary of the NAFTA accord.

Fast Track Negotiations

Presidents Bush and Salinas, and Prime Minister Mulroney, pushed hard in 1991 to open "fast track" negotiations (discussed in Chapter 3) for a free trade agreement. In 1992, these efforts reached fruition when a NAFTA agreement was signed by Canada, the United States and Mexico with a scheduled effective date of Jan. 1, 1994. President Bush submitted the agreement to Congress in December

1992. President Clinton supported NAFTA generally, but initiated negotiations upon taking office for supplemental agreements on the environment and labor. This delayed consideration of the NAFTA agreement in Congress until the Fall of 1993.

Ratification was considered under fast track procedures which essentially gave Congress 90 session days to either ratify or reject NAFTA without amendments. After a bruising national debate that fractured both Democrats and Republicans with each party doing its best to avoid Ross Perot's strident anti-NAFTA attacks, ratification was achieved in mid-November, just weeks before NAFTA's effective date. The North American "side agreements" on the environment and labor (see below) were adopted by Presidential executive orders.

During this same period, Canada's Conservative Party suffered a devastating defeat at the polls. This defeat was partly a rejection by the Canadian people of the earlier ratification of NAFTA under Prime Minister Mulroney. Mexico's President Salinas had no such problems implementing NAFTA.

THE NAFTA AGREEMENT IN OUTLINE

Although each partner affirms its rights and obligations under the General Agreement on Tariffs and Trade (GATT), NAFTA generally takes priority over other international agreements in the event of conflict. Certain exceptions to this general rule of supremacy apply; the trade provisions of the international agreements on endangered species, ozone-depletion and hazardous wastes notably take precedence over NAFTA (subject to a duty to minimize conflicts). Unlike the GATT, NAFTA makes a general duty of national treatment binding on all states, provinces and local governments of the three countries.

TRADE IN GOODS

Prior to NAFTA, Mexican tariffs on U.S. goods averaged about 10 percent; U.S. tariffs on Mexican imports averaged about five percent. Under NAFTA, Mexican tariffs were eliminated on all U.S. exports within 10 years except for corn and beans which were subject to a fifteen-year transition. United States tariffs on peanuts, sugar and orange juice from Mexico also lasted 15 years. Immediate Mexican tariff removals under the "A" list covered about half the industrial products exported from the United States. Further tariff eliminations occurred for the "B" list after five years and the "C" list when the treaty matured in 10 years. The existing Canada-U.S. tariff reduction schedule remained in place.

Import and export quotas, licenses and other restrictions have been eliminated under NAFTA subject to limited rights to restrain trade, e.g. to protect human, animal or plant health, or to protect the environment. Customs user fees on internal NAFTA trade were terminated in 1999 and tariff drawback refunds or waivers removed by 2001. These changes, it is thought, discourage the creation of "export platforms" in one NAFTA country to serve markets in the other member states by insuring that non-NAFTA components and materials are tariffed.

NAFTA essentially phased out maquiladora tariff preferences over seven years, notably disadvantaging producers who source heavily outside North America.

Export taxes and new waivers of customs duties are banned with few exceptions. Once goods are freely traded under NAFTA, they are subject to nondiscriminatory national treatment, including at the provincial and state levels of government. Goods sent to another NAFTA country for repair or alteration may return duty free.

Rules of Origin

NAFTA trade is subject to important "rules of origin" that determine which goods qualify for its tariff preferences. These include goods wholly originating in the free trade area. A general waiver of the NAFTA rules of origin requirements is granted if their non-regional value consists of no more than seven percent of the price or total cost of the goods. Goods containing non-regional materials are considered North American if those materials are sufficiently transformed so as to undergo a specific change in tariff classification.

Some goods, like autos and light trucks, must also have a specified North American content. For example, 62.50 percent of the value of such vehicles must be North American in origin. A 60 percent regional content rule applies to other vehicles and auto parts. Starting in 2004, U.S. auto producers no longer needed to manufacture in Mexico in order to sell there.

Regional value content may be calculated in most cases either by a "transaction value" or a "net cost" method. The former avoids costly accountings and requires 60% North American content for free trade access. The latter, a 50% NAFTA content rule, is based upon the total cost of the goods less royalties, sales promotion, packing and shipping, and allowable interest. Either requires manufacturers to trace the source of non-NAFTA components and maintain source records. The net cost method must be used for regional value calculations concerning automotive goods. Uniformity of tariff classification and origin decisions is promoted by NAFTA regulations, a common Certificate of Origin, and a trilateral working group.

Special rules of origin apply to free trade in textiles and apparel under NAFTA. For most products, a "yarn forward" rule applies. This means that the goods must be produced from yarn made in a NAFTA country. A similar "fiber forward" rule applies to cotton and man-made fiber yarns. Silk, linen and certain other fabrics in short supply within NAFTA are treated preferentially, as are yarns, fabrics and apparel covered by special tariff rate quotas. Safeguard import quotas and tariffs could be imposed during the transition period if a rise in textile and apparel trade caused serious damage. Other special rules of origin were created for electronics. For example, if the circuit board (motherboard) is made in North America and transformed in the region so as to change a tariff classification, the resulting computer may be freely traded.

Energy

Distinct rules govern energy and petrochemical products. Perhaps most notably, Mexico reserves to its state (as its Constitution provides) the oil, gas, refining, basic petrochemical, nuclear and electricity sectors. A limited range of new investment opportunities are created for non-basic petrochemicals, proprietary electricity facilities, co-generation and independent power production.

As under the GATT, minimum or maximum import or export price controls are prohibited on energy products, but licensing systems may be used. Trade quotas or other restraints are permissible only in limited circumstances, e.g. short supply conditions, and a general duty of national treatment applies. Mexico, unlike Canada, has not committed itself to energy sharing during times of shortage.

Food Products

A second set of distinct rules apply to agricultural trade. These are undertaken principally through separate bilateral agreements between the U.S. and Mexico and Canada and Mexico. The United States-Mexico agreement converts all nontariff trade barriers to tariffs or tariff rate quotas. These were phased out over a maximum of 15 years. Roughly half of the bilateral trade in agriculture was made duty-free immediately. Under special rules, trade in sugar was gradually liberalized with all restraints removed over 15 years after a major dispute before the WTO. All three countries agreed to combat agricultural export subsidies, including consultation and what amounts to joint action against third-country subsidies affecting any one of their markets. Special rules of origin apply in the agricultural sector and standards on pesticide residues and inspections are being harmonized.

Another food-related issue is sanitary and phytosanitary measures against health, diseases, contaminants or additives (collectively known as SPS protection). Each country retains the right to establish its own SPS levels of protection provided they are based upon scientific principles and a risk assessment, apply only as needed and do not result in unfair discrimination or disguised restrictions on trade.

Each NAFTA nation is committed to accepting the SPS measures of the others as equivalent to its own provided the exporting country demonstrates that its measures achieve the importing country's chosen level of protection. This is facilitated by procedural transparency rules requiring public notice of any SPS measure that may affect NAFTA trade. A committee on SPS measures strives to facilitate all of these principles and to resolve disputes.

Product Standards

Technical standards and certification procedures for products are classic nontariff trade barriers. The NAFTA reaffirms each country's commitment to the GATT Agreement on Technical Barriers to Trade (1979). In addition, each must provide national treatment and most favored nation treatment. As in the food products area, international standards will be used whenever possible, but each country may have more stringent requirements and scientific justification is not mandatory.

Procedural transparency rules and a committee on standards are also created. One innovation of note allows companies and other interested parties to participate directly in the development of new standards anywhere within NAFTA. All three countries agreed not to lower existing environmental, health and safety standards and to attempt to "upwardly harmonize" them.

Safeguards (Escape Clause Proceedings)

Escape clause rules and procedures are generally applicable to United States-Mexico trade under the NAFTA. These permit temporary trade relief against import surges subject to a right of compensation in the exporting nation. During a ten year transition period, escape clause relief could be undertaken as a result of NAFTA tariff reductions only once per product for a maximum in most cases of three years. The relief was the "snap-back" to pre-NAFTA tariffs. After the transition period, escape clause measures may only be undertaken by mutual consent.

If a global escape clause proceeding is pursued by one NAFTA partner, the others must be excluded unless their exports account for a substantial share of the imports in question (top five suppliers) and contribute importantly to the serious injury or threat thereof (rate of growth of NAFTA imports must not be appreciably lower than total imports). Exclusion of NAFTA partners from global escape clause

remedies has been ruled invalid by the WTO
Appellate Body.

Procurement

There are a variety of other areas of law impacted
by the NAFTA accord. Government procurement,
apart from defense and national security needs,
generally follows nondiscriminatory principles on the
supply of goods and services (including construction
services) to federal governments. The threshold for
the application of the NAFTA to such procurement is
$50,000 U.S. for goods and services, and $6.5 million
U.S. for construction services. When state
enterprises (e.g. PEMEX and CFE), not agencies, are
the buyers, thresholds of $250,000 U.S. and $8
million U.S. respectively apply.

The use of offsets or other requirements for local
purchases or suppliers are prohibited. Independent
bid challenge mechanisms must be created by each
member state and transparency in the bidding
process promoted by timely release of information.
These provisions are particularly important because
Mexico, unlike Canada, is not a signatory to the WTO
Procurement Code. They do not apply to state and
local procurement.

TRADE IN SERVICES

Cross-border trade in services is subject to national
treatment, including no less favorable treatment
than that most favorably given at federal, state or
local levels. No member state may require that a
service provider establish or maintain a residence,

local office or branch in its country as a condition to cross-border provision of services. However, a general standstill on existing discriminatory or limiting laws affecting cross-border services was adopted. Mutual recognition of professional licenses is encouraged (notably for legal consultants and engineers), but not made automatic. All citizenship or permanent residency requirements for professional licensing were eliminated.

Additionally, a NAFTA country may deny the benefits of the rules on cross-border provision of services if their source is in reality a third country without substantial business activities within the free trade area. For transport services, these benefits may be denied if the services are provided with equipment that is not registered within a NAFTA nation. Most air, maritime, basic tele-communications and social services are not covered by these rules, nor are those that are subject to special treatment elsewhere in the NAFTA (e.g. procurement, financing and energy).

Even so, the NAFTA considerably broadens the types of services covered by free trade principles: accounting, advertising, architecture, broadcasting, commercial education, construction, consulting, enhanced telecommunications, engineering, environmental science, health care, land transport, legal, publishing and tourism.

Whereas the CUSFTA allowed free trade in services only for those sectors that were positively listed in the agreement, the NAFTA adopts a broader "negative listing" approach. All services sectors are subject to free trade principles unless the NAFTA specifies otherwise.

Transport

Unlike CUSFTA, NAFTA created a timetable for the removal of barriers to cross-border land transport services and the establishment of compatible technical, environmental and safety standards. This extends to bus, trucking, port and rail services. It should eliminate the historic need to switch trailers to local transporters at the border.

In 1997, contrary to the NAFTA agreement, Mexico and the United States failed to establish border-free commercial trucking in contiguous states. Mexican and U.S. trucks serviced only narrow border bands in each country. This failure centered on United States perceptions of inadequate Mexican safety regulations for trucks and their personnel, and inadequate U.S. border-state enforcement capacity. Moreover, the powerful reality of Teamsters Union hostility to Mexican trucking in the United States cannot be ignored. Indeed, the Teamsters actually announced the U.S. refusal to implement the agreement in 1997 prior to the Department of Transportation.

Mexico's initial response was to exclude U.S. trailer trucks. By 1998, Mexico's patience and cooperative efforts were exhausted. It invoked its right to a Chapter 20 arbitration of the dispute. Complete cross-border point-to-point trucking was supposed to begin in 2000. Mexico has allowed minority NAFTA ownership of its cross-border trucking companies, and increasing ownership opportunities are scheduled for the future. By 2003, complete ownership in Mexican trucking companies should have been permitted.

In 2001, the trucking dispute Chapter 20 arbitration panel ruled unanimously in Mexico's favor. President George W. Bush indicated that the U.S. would comply, which after regulatory and litigation delays finally did happen as a "pilot program" in 2007. Congress and the Teamsters continued with challenges in the courts and appropriations bills, which bore fruit in the Obama economic stimulus bill. A provision that withdrew funding for the pilot program was buried in that 2009 law. Mexico, its patience exhausted, retaliated (as the NAFTA agreement anticipates) by imposing tariffs on a wide range of U.S. exports. Mexico notably used "carousel" tariffs, switching the goods to which they applied so as to amplify their negative impact on U.S. exports.

Late in 2010, Mexico and the U.S. reached accord on settling the trucking dispute. Mexico's compensatory tariffs on U.S. goods were removed. In 2011, the U.S. commenced a three-year pilot program allowing Mexican trucking firms that comply all U.S. regulations (safety, customs, immigration, vehicle registration and taxation) to operate anywhere in the United States. The Teamsters Union, asserting concerns with Mexican driver training and truck maintenance, attempted but failed in the courts to block this program. U.S. cross-border trucking restraints, finally at this writing appear ready to disappear completely.

Telecommunications

Public telecommunications networks and services must be opened on reasonable and nondiscriminatory terms for firms and individuals who need the networks to conduct business, such as intra-corporate communications or so-called enhanced tele-communications and information services. The "reasonableness" of Telmex connection fees was hotly contested in the United States, a dispute successfully taken to the WTO.

Cellular phone, data transmission, earth stations, fax, electronic mail, overlay networks and paging systems are open to Canadian and American investors, many of whom have entered the Mexican market, not always succeeding against Telmex's near monopoly power. Each NAFTA country must ensure reasonable access and use of leased private lines, terminal equipment attachments, private circuit interconnects, switching, signaling and processing functions and user-choice of operating protocols.

Conditions on access and use may only be imposed to safeguard the public responsibilities of network operators or to protect technical network integrity. Rates for public telecommunications transport services should reflect economic costs and flat-rate pricing is required for leased circuits. However, cross-subsidization between public transport services is not prohibited, nor are monopoly providers of public networks or services.

Such monopolies may not engage in anticompetitive conduct outside their monopoly areas with adverse effects on NAFTA nationals. Various rights of access to information on public networks and services are established, and the NAFTA limits the types of technical standards that can be imposed on the attachment of equipment to public networks.

Financial Services

Financial services provided by banking, insurance, securities and other firms are separately covered under the NAFTA. Trade in such services is generally subject to specific liberalization commitments and transition periods. Financial service providers, including non-NAFTA providers operating through subsidiaries in a NAFTA country, are entitled to establish themselves anywhere within NAFTA and service customers there (the right of "commercial presence"). Existing cross-border restraints on the provision of financial services were frozen and no new restraints may be imposed (subject to designated exceptions).

Providers of financial services in each NAFTA nation receive both national and most favored nation treatment. This includes equality of competitive opportunity, which is defined as avoidance of measures that disadvantage foreign providers relative to domestic providers. Various procedural transparency rules are established to facilitate the entry and equal opportunity of NAFTA providers of financial services. The host nation may legislate reasonable prudential requirements for such companies and, under limited circumstances, protect their balance of payments in ways which restrain financial providers.

The following are some of the more notable country-specific commitments on financial service made in the NAFTA:

United States—A grace period allowed Mexican banks already operating a securities firm in the U.S. to continue to do so until July of 1997.

Canada—The exemption granted U.S. companies under the Canada-U.S. FTA to hold more than 25 percent of the shares of a federally regulated Canadian financial institution was extended to Mexican firms, as was the suspension of Canada's 12 percent asset ceiling rules. Multiple branches may be opened in Canada without Ministry of Finance approval.

Mexico—Banking, securities and insurance companies from the U.S. and Canada are able to enter the Mexican market through subsidiaries and joint ventures (but not branches) subject to market share limits during a transition period that ended in the year 2000 (insurance) or 2004 (banking and securities). Finance companies are able to establish separate subsidiaries in Mexico to provide consumer, commercial, mortgage lending or credit card services, subject to a three percent aggregate asset limitation (which does not apply to lending by affiliates of automotive companies).

Existing U.S. and Canadian insurers could expand their ownership rights to 100 percent after 1996. No equity or market share requirements apply for warehousing and bonding, foreign exchange and mutual fund management enterprises.

CROSS-BORDER INVESTMENT AND INVESTOR-STATE ARBITRATIONS

Investment in the industrial and services sectors of the NAFTA nations is promoted through rules against nondiscriminatory and minimum standards of treatment that even benefit non-NAFTA investors with substantial business operations in a NAFTA nation. For example, an Asian or European subsidiary incorporated with substantial business operations in Canada will be treated as a Canadian investor for purposes of NAFTA. Investment, for these purposes, is broadly defined to cover virtually all forms of ownership and activity, including real estate, stocks, bonds, contracts and technologies.

Foreign Investor Rights

National and most favored treatment rights apply at the federal, state and local levels of government, and to state-owned enterprises (e.g. PEMEX, Canadian National Railway Corporation). Furthermore, each country is to treat NAFTA investors in accordance with "international law," including fair and equitable treatment and full protection and security. This is known as the "minimum standard" of treatment, officially interpreted as intended to embrace limited "customary" international law principles.

Performance requirements, e.g. specific export levels, minimum domestic content, domestic source preferences, trade balancing, technology transfer and product mandates are disallowed in all areas except government procurement, export promotion and foreign aid. Senior management positions may not be reserved by nationality, but NAFTA states may require that a majority of the board of directors or committees thereof be of a designated nationality or residence provided this does not impair the foreign investor's ability to exercise control. Joint ventures with local partners (common in Mexico) are no longer mandatory.

A general right to convert and transfer local currency at prevailing market rates for earnings, sale proceeds, loan repayments and other investment transactions has been established. But this right does not prevent good faith and nondiscriminatory restraints upon monetary transfers arising out of bankruptcy, insolvency, securities dealings, crimes, satisfaction of judgments and currency reporting duties.

Direct and indirect expropriations (and government measures "tantamount to" expropriation) of investments by NAFTA investors are precluded except for public purposes and if done on a nondiscriminatory basis following due process of law. A right of compensation without delay at fair market value plus interest is created.

Foreign Investment Exclusions

The NAFTA investment code does not apply to Mexican constitutionally-reserved sectors (e.g. energy, railroads and boundary and coastal real estate) nor to Canada's cultural industries. It did, however, remove Mexican foreign investment controls for U.S. and Canadian investors below an initial $25 million U.S. threshold phased-up to $150 million U.S. in 2004, and opened new Mexican mining ventures to NAFTA investors after 1998. Canadian review of direct U.S. investments in excess of $150 million U.S. and indirect investments in excess of $450 million (indexed for inflation from Jan. 1, 1993) will continue.

Maritime, airline, broadcasting, fishing, nuclear, basic telecommunications, and government-sponsored technology consortia are exempt from the NAFTA investment rules. All of the NAFTA countries agreed not to lower environmental standards to attract investment and permit (as Mexico requires) environmental impact statements for foreign investments. However, apart from consultations, there was no remedy in this area prior to the environmental side agreement discussed below.

Investor-State Arbitrations

In the event of a dispute, a NAFTA investor may (and quite a few have) elect as between monetary (but not punitive) damages through binding arbitration under the ICSID Convention (International Center for Settlement of Investment

Disputes (Washington, D.C.) if both nations are parties (not possible presently), the Additional Facility Rules of the ICSID if only one nation is a party to the Convention (most commonly used) or the UNCITRAL arbitration rules.

An arbitration tribunal for investment disputes will be established by the Secretary-General of ICSID if the parties are unable to select a panel by choosing one arbitrator each and collaborating on or having those arbitrators choose a third. However, there are no time limits for the arbitration and either side may appeal the award to the courts of the arbitration's situs, typically chosen with a view towards neutrality by the arbitrators. Alternatively, the investor may pursue judicial remedies in courts of the host state.

The number of investor-state arbitrations under Chapter 11 of NAFTA has exploded. Many of these proceedings challenge federal, state or local regulatory actions, such as Mexican rules for hazardous waste plants, Canadian and California controls over gasoline additives, and Mississippi punitive damages and appeal bond requirements. Mexico, after losing a court appeal of an award against it, was the first to pay an investor under Chapter 11 procedures.

Other arbitrations have settled favorably for NAFTA investors, provoking outcries from governments, NGOs and especially environmentalists that the entire process is skewed too heavily in favor of the interests of business. The three governments, collectively in defense, have issued a controversial restrictive interpretation of the "minimum standard" of treatment afforded cross-border investors under NAFTA.

Specific Chapter 11 arbitral decisions are summarized in my *Nutshell on NAFTA, Free Trade and Foreign Investment in The Americas.*

INTELLECTUAL PROPERTY

The NAFTA mandates adequate and effective intellectual property rights in all countries, including national treatment and effective internal and external enforcement rights. Specific commitments are made for virtually all types of intellectual property, including patents, copyrights, trademarks, plant breeds, industrial designs, trade secrets, semiconductor chips (directly and in goods incorporating them) and geographical indicators. NAFTA's coverage of trade secrets was a "first" internationally and was replicated in the WTO Trade-Related Intellectual Property Rights Agreement (TRIPs).

For copyright, the NAFTA obligates protection for computer programs, databases, computer program and sound recording rentals, and a 50 year term of protection for sound recordings. For patents, the NAFTA mandates a minimum 20 years of coverage (from date of filing) of nearly all products and processes including pharmaceuticals and agricultural chemicals. It also requires removal of any special or discriminatory patent regimes or availability of rights. Compulsory licensing is limited.

Service marks are treated equally with trademarks. Satellite signal poaching is illegal and trade secrets are generally protected (including from disclosure by governments). The NAFTA details member states' duties to provide damages, injunctive, antipiracy and general due process remedies in the intellectual property field. This has, for example, required major changes in Mexican law.

OTHER NAFTA PROVISIONS

Business Visas

The provisions on temporary entry visas for business persons found in the CUSFTA are extended under the NAFTA. These entry rights cover business persons, traders, investors, intra-company transferees and 63 designated professionals. Installers, after-sales repair and maintenance staff and managers performing services under a warranty or other service contract incidental to the sale of equipment or machinery are included, as are sales representatives, buyers, market researchers and financial service providers.

White collar business persons only need proof of citizenship and documentation of business purpose to work in another NAFTA country for up to five years. Many Canadians have taken advantage of NAFTA's special entry rights, particularly professionals obtaining TN visas. Apart from these provisions, no common market for the free movement of labor is undertaken.

State Monopolies and Antitrust

The NAFTA embraces a competition policy principally aimed at state enterprises and governmentally sanctioned monopolies, mostly found in Mexico. State owned or controlled businesses, at all levels of government, are required to act consistently with the NAFTA when exercising regulatory, administrative or governmental authority (e.g. when granting licenses). Governmentally-owned and privately-owned state-designated monopolies are obliged to follow commercial considerations in their transactions and avoid discrimination against goods or services of other NAFTA nations.

Furthermore, each country must ensure that such monopolies do not use their positions to engage in anticompetitive practices in non-monopoly markets. Since each NAFTA nation must adopt laws against anticompetitive business practices and cooperate in their enforcement, Mexico has revived its historically weak "antitrust" laws. A consultative Trade and Competition Committee reviews competition policy issues under the NAFTA.

Miscellaneous Provisions

Other notable provisions in the NAFTA include a general duty of legal transparency, fairness and due process regarding all laws affecting traders and investors with independent administrative or judicial review of government action. Generalized exceptions to the agreement cover action to protect national security and national interests such as public morals, health, national treasures, natural resources, or to enforce laws against deceptive or anticompetitive practices, short of arbitrary discriminations or disguised restraints on trade. Balance of payments trade restraints are governed by the rules of the International Monetary Fund.

Taxation issues are subject to bilateral double taxation treaties, including a new one between Mexico and the United States. The "cultural industry" reservations secured by the CUSFTA now cover Canada and Mexico, but are not extended to Mexican-U.S. trade. A right of compensatory retaliation through measures of equivalent commercial effect is granted when invocation of these reservations would have violated the Canada-U.S. FTA but for the cultural industries proviso.

Right of Withdrawal

The NAFTA is not forever. Any country may withdraw on six months' notice. Other countries or groups of countries may be admitted to the NAFTA if Canada, Mexico and the United States agree and domestic ratification follows. In December of 1994, Chile was invited to become the next member of the NAFTA. Negotiations stalled for want of U.S. Congressional fast track negotiating authority. By 2004, Chile had bilateral free trade agreements with Canada, Mexico and the United States.

DISPUTE SETTLEMENT UNDER NAFTA

The institutional dispute settlement arrangements accompanying the NAFTA are minimal. A trilateral Trade Commission (with Secretariat) comprised of ministerial or cabinet-level officials meets at least annually to ensure effective joint management of the NAFTA is established. The various intergovernmental committees established for specific areas of coverage of the NAFTA (e.g. competition policy) to oversee much of the work of making the free trade area function. These committees operate on the basis of consensus, referring contentious issues to the Trade Commission.

Forum Selection: NAFTA or WTO

Investment, dumping and subsidy, financial services, environmental-investment and standards disputes are subject to special dispute resolution procedures. A general NAFTA dispute settlement procedure is also established (Chapter 20). A right of consultation exists when one country's rights are thought to be affected. If consultations do not resolve the issue within 45 days, the complainant may convene a meeting of the Trade Commission. The Commission must seek to promptly settle the dispute and may use its good offices, mediation, conciliation or any other alternative means.

Absent resolution, the complaining country or countries ordinarily commence proceedings under the GATT/WTO or the NAFTA. Once selected, the chosen forum becomes exclusive. However, if the dispute concerns environmental, safety, health or conservation standards, or arises under specific environmental agreements, the responding nation may elect to have the dispute heard by a NAFTA panel. The U.S. tried and failed to do this in 2011 when Mexico filed a tuna labeling complaint with the WTO.

Chapter 20

Dispute settlement procedures under Chapter 20 involve nonbinding arbitration by five persons chosen in most cases from a trilaterally agreed roster of experts (not limited to NAFTA citizens), with a special roster established for disputes about financial services. A "reverse selection" process is used. The chair of the panel is first chosen by agreement or, failing agreement, by designation of one side selected by lot. The chair cannot be a citizen of the selecting side but must be a NAFTA national. Each side then selects two additional arbitrators who are citizens of the country or countries on the *other* side.

The Commission has approved rules of procedure including the opportunity for written submissions, rebuttals and at least one oral hearing. Expert advice on environmental and scientific matters may be given by special procedures accessing science boards. Strict time limits are created so as to keep the panel on track to a prompt resolution. Within 90 days an initial confidential report must be circulated, followed by 14 days for comment by the parties and 16 days for the final panel report to the Commission.

Early NAFTA Chapter 20 arbitrations concerned Canadian tariffication of agricultural quotas (upheld), U.S. escape clause relief from Mexican corn broom exports (rejected) and a Mexican challenge of the U.S. failure to implement cross-border trucking (upheld). Once the Trade Commission receives a final arbitration panel report, the NAFTA requires the disputing nations to agree within 30 days on a resolution (normally by conforming to the panel's recommendations). If a mutually agreed resolution does not occur at this stage, the complaining country may retaliate by suspending the application of equivalent benefits under the NAFTA. Any NAFTA country may invoke the arbitration panel process if it perceives that this retaliation is excessive.

When NAFTA interpretational issues are disputed before domestic tribunals or courts, the Trade Commission (if it can agree) can submit an interpretation to that body. In the absence of agreement within the Commission, any NAFTA country may intervene and submit its views as to the proper interpretation or application of the NAFTA to the national court or tribunal.

Antidumping or Subsidy Disputes

The unique independent binational review panel mechanism established in the CUSFTA for dumping and subsidy duties was carried over into NAFTA, along with the extraordinary challenge procedure to deal with allegations about the integrity of the panel review process. Chapter 19 panels are substituted for traditional judicial review at the national level of administrative dumping and countervailing duty orders. Mexico has undertaken major improvements to its law in this area. The procedures and rules for such panels generally follow those found in the

CUSFTA. They are limited to issues of the consistency of the national decisions with domestic law, and once again have been numerous.

In addition, a special committee may be requested by any country believing that another's domestic law has prevented the establishment, final decision or implementation of the decision by such a panel. A special committee may also be invoked if the opportunity for independent judicial review on a dumping or subsidy determination has been denied (a concern focused especially on Mexico). This committee's findings, if affirmative, will result in member state consultations. Absent resolution, the complainant may suspend the panel system or benefits under the NAFTA agreement.

THE SIDE AGREEMENTS ON LABOR AND THE ENVIRONMENT

The NAFTA side agreements on labor (NAALC) and the environment (NAAEC) do not create additional substantive regional rules. Rather the side agreements basically create law enforcement mechanisms. The side agreements commit each country to creation of environmental and labor bodies that monitor compliance with the adequacy and the enforcement of *domestic* law. The Commission for Environmental Cooperation (CEC)(Montreal) and three National Administrative Offices (NAO) concerning labor matters are empowered to receive complaints. Negotiations to resolve complaints first ensue.

Environmental Disputes

In the absence of a negotiated solution, the NAAEC establishes five environmental dispute settlement mechanisms. *First*, the CEC Secretariat may report on almost any environmental matter. *Second*, the Secretariat may develop a factual record in trade-related law enforcement disputes. *Third*, the CEC Council can release that record to the public. *Fourth*, if there is a persistent pattern of failure to enforce environmental law, the Council will mediate and conciliate. *Fifth*, if such efforts fail, the Council can send the matter to arbitration and awards can be enforced by monetary penalties. To date, no NAAEC disputes have gotten beyond the second Factual Record stage, and few have made it that far.

Labor Disputes

The NAALC labor law enforcement system is a calibrated four-tier series of dispute resolution mechanisms. *First*, the NAOs may review and report on eleven designated labor law enforcement matters that correspond to the NAALC Labor Principles. *Second*, ministerial consultations may follow when recommended by the NAO. *Third*, an Evaluation Committee of Experts can report on trade-related mutually recognized labor law enforcement patterns of practice concerning eight of the NAALC Labor Principles (excluding strikes, union organizing and collective bargaining). *Fourth*, persistent patterns of failure to enforce occupational health and safety, child labor or minimum wage laws can be arbitrated and awards enforced by monetary penalties. To date, no NAALC disputes have gone beyond the second Ministerial Consultations stage.

The NAAEC and NAALC law enforcement mechanisms have been invoked more frequently than many expected. Quite a few labor law enforcement complaints have focused on the organization of "independent" unions in Mexico. A major study explored pregnancy discrimination in the Mexican workplace. United States plant closings and treatment of immigrant workers have also been reviewed. Regarding the environment, a wide range of complaints have been filed asserting inadequate Canadian, Mexican and U.S. law enforcement. Nevertheless, in terms of enhancing environmental and labor law enforcement, the NAEEC and NAALC seem marginally relevant.

QUEBEC AND NAFTA

The Canadian Constitution of 1982 was adopted by an Act of the British Parliament. As such, the Act and Constitution of 1982 are thought to bind all Canadian provinces including Quebec. That province, however, has never formally ratified the Constitution of Canada. Since 1982 a series of negotiations have attempted to secure Quebec's ratification, and all have failed miserably.

In 1987, for example, the "Meech Lake Accord" was reached. This agreement recognized Quebec as a "distinct society" in Canada. What the practical consequences of this recognition would have been will never be known. Quebec's adherence to the Meech Lake Accord was nullified when Manitoba, New

Brunswick and ultimately Newfoundland failed to ratify the Accord. A second set of negotiations led in 1992 to the Charlottetown Accord which also acknowledged Quebec as a distinct society with its French language, unique culture and Civil Law tradition. This time a national referendum was held and its defeat was overwhelming. Quebec, five English-speaking Canadian provinces, and the Yukon territory voted against the Charlottetown Accord.

The failure of these Accords moved Quebec towards separation from Canada. In 1994, the Parti Quebecois came to power. It held a provincial referendum on separation in 1995. By the narrowest of margins, the people of Quebec rejected separation from Canada. Just exactly what "separation" would have meant was never entirely clear during the debate, perhaps deliberately so.

In 1998, Canada's Supreme Court ruled that Quebec could not "under the Constitution" withdraw unilaterally. To secede, Quebec would need to negotiate a constitutional amendment with the rest of Canada. The rest of Canada would, likewise, be obliged to enter into such negotiations if a "clear majority" of Quebec's voters approved a "clear question" on secession in a referendum. Subsequently, the Canadian Parliament legislated rules which will make it difficult for Quebec to separate, should it ever wish to do so. That prospect now seems more remote, particularly because the Parti Quebecois lost power in 2003 (although it was back in 2012).

If Quebec ever separates from Canada, this will raise fundamental issues about Quebec and NAFTA. Would Quebec be forced to negotiate for membership in NAFTA? If so, would English-speaking Canada veto its application? Might Quebec's relationship to Canada continue in some limited manner (such as for defense and international trade purposes) such that NAFTA is not an issue at all? Might Quebec automatically "succeed" to the NAFTA treaty, thus becoming a member without application?

Customary international practice maintains existing treaties when nations sub-divide. This practice was applied to the Czech Republic, Slovakia, and various states of the former Yugoslavia. Thus custom suggests that fears in Quebec about losing NAFTA benefits are exaggerated.

NAFTA COMPARED WITH THE WTO

The NAFTA Chapters chart below indicates the closest parallel WTO agreements. Recall that Chapter 20 allows a complaining NAFTA party to choose between NAFTA and WTO dispute settlement. For this choice to be effective, the subject matter of the complaint must fall within the scope of the WTO package of agreements noted below. An excellent example of the significance of opting in favor of WTO dispute settlement is the well-known *Sports Illustrated* dispute, which allowed the United States to overcome Canada's "cultural industries" exclusion under NAFTA.

NAFTA	WTO AGREEMENTS
Chapter 3, Trade in Goods	General Agreement on Tariffs and Trade 1994, Agreement on Textiles and Clothing
Chapter 4, Rules of Origin	Agreement on Rules of Origin
Chapter 5, Customs Procedures	No parallel
Chapter 6, Energy and Basic Petrochemicals	No parallel
Chapter 7, Agriculture and SPS Measures	Agreement on Agriculture, Agreement on SPS Measures
Chapter 8, Emergency Action	Agreement on Safeguards
Chapter 9, Product and Service Standards	Agreement on Technical Barriers to Trade
Chapter 10, Procurement	Agreement on Government Procurement (optional)
Chapter 11, Investment	Agreement on Trade-Related Investment Measures (TRIMs)
Chapter 12, Cross-Border Trade in Services	General Agreement on Trade in Services (GATS)
Chapter 13, Enhanced Telecommunications	See GATS, Basic Telecommunications Covered
Chapter 14, Financial Services	See GATS

NAFTA	WTO AGREEMENTS
Chapter 15, Competition Policy, Monopolies and State Enterprises	No parallel, but see Understanding on Interpretation of GATT Article XVII
Chapter 16, Temporary Entry for Business Persons	No parallel
Chapter 17, Intellectual Property	Agreement on Trade-Related Aspects of Intellectual Property Rights (TRIPs)
Chapter 18, Administrative Provisions	Not applicable
Chapter 19, Antidumping and Countervailing Duty Dispute Settlement	No parallel, but see DSU and Agreement on Implementation of GATT Article VI
Chapter 20, Dispute Settlement	Understanding on Rules and Procedures Governing the Settlement of Disputes (DSU)
Chapter 21, Exceptions	See GATT Articles XX, XXI and Understanding on GATT Balance of Payments Provisions
Agreement on Environmental Cooperation	No parallel
Agreement on Labor Cooperation	No parallel

NAFTA COMPARED WITH THE EUROPEAN UNION

Some of the most revealing aspects of the NAFTA agreement are found in what it does *not* provide. By comparison with the European Union, the NAFTA is politically, legislatively and judicially streamlined. There is no NAFTA Court of Justice, no NAFTA Parliament, nor a NAFTA Council of Ministers. The trilateral Trade Commission's powers pale in significance to those of the European Commission.

Substantively, the most dramatic differences are the absence of any free movement rights for workers or the citizenry at large, the lack of a common external tariff and a common international trade policy, the complete omission of any single currency and economic convergence goals, and the right of member state withdrawal upon six months' notice. Nor are there common NAFTA defense, foreign, internal affairs, regional development, research, technology transfer, education, taxation, company law, antitrust and social policies (to name only some of the areas in which the EU is quite active).

In short, when compared with European integration, the NAFTA is strikingly limited in its goals and techniques. This conclusion has a variety of implications for the future of North America. It suggests, on the one hand, that North America's limited trade and investment-oriented goals ought to be more obtainable than the grand panorama of European economic, social and political union undertaken in a treaty of unlimited duration.

The EU and NAFTA as Trade Policy Models

The European Union has served as a model for economic integration elsewhere in world. For example, the Andean Community (ANCOM) modeled itself on the EEC (as the EU was then called), as did the Southern African Customs Union (SACU), the Central American Common Market (CACM). These regional economic groups have suffered internal discord, economic stress and limited success. Yet, for the most part, they still aspire to become as comprehensive and effective as the European Union. MERCOSUR, established in 1991 by Brazil, Argentina, Paraguay, and Uruguay has probably come the closest to reproducing the EU model.

The EU trade policy model contrasts with the ASEAN (Association of Southeast Asian Nations) and LAFTA (now ALADI, the Latin American Integration Association) groups which have targeted more limited goals as free trade areas. Neither rises to the significance or depth of NAFTA (1994) or its 2005 sequel, CAFTA–DR (the Central American Free Trade Agreement between the United States, Costa Rica, Guatemala, Nicaragua, El Salvador, Honduras and the Dominican Republic). Hundreds of bilateral free trade agreements have been negotiated since NAFTA, including some by the European Union.

At this writing, the European Union and NAFTA present competing trade policy models that have each drawn adherents in the developing world. Apart from their core economic differences (customs union v. free trade area), the EU model embraces a remarkable legal superstructure to achieve economic integration. In contrast, the NAFTA/CAFTA model is minimalist. Multiple varieties of arbitration are used to resolve disputes, and there are no regional legislative or litigation systems.

Which model offers the best way forward? The Transatlantic Trade and Investment Partnership negotiations commenced in 2013 by the United States and the European Union are moving along a track that resembles NAFTA . . . but how could they do otherwise? With the apparent collapse of the Doha Round of World Trade Organization (WTO) negotiations, analysis of these questions has taken on added meaning.

POST-NAFTA U.S. FREE TRADE AGREEMENTS

United States free trade agreements since NAFTA (reviewed in Chapter 3) have evolved substantively under a policy known as "competitive liberalization." For example, coverage of labor law has been narrowed to core ILO principles: The rights of association, organization and collective bargaining; acceptable work conditions regarding minimum wages, hours and occupational health and safety; minimum age for employment of children and elimination of the worst forms of child labor; and a ban on forced or compulsory labor. Coverage of labor and environmental law enforcement is folded into the trade agreement (compare NAFTA's side agreements) and all remedies are intergovernmental (compare private and NGO "remedies" in the side agreements).

Other NAFTA-plus provisions have emerged. These are most evident regarding foreign investment and intellectual property. Regarding investor-state claims, for example, post-NAFTA U.S. free trade agreements insert the word "customary" before international law in defining the minimum standard of treatment to which foreign investors are entitled. This insertion tracks the official Interpretation issued in that regard under NAFTA. In addition, the contested terms "fair and equitable treatment" and "full protection and security" are defined for the first time:

> "fair and equitable treatment" includes the obligation not to deny justice in criminal, civil, or administrative adjudicatory proceedings in accordance with the principle of due process embodied in the principal legal systems of the world; and

> "full protection and security" requires each Party to provide the level of police protection required under customary international law.

More significantly perhaps, starting with the U.S.-Chile FTA, these agreements contain an Annex restricting the scope of "indirect expropriation" claims:

> Except in rare circumstances, nondiscriminatory regulatory actions by a Party that are designed and applied to protect legitimate public welfare objectives, such as public health, safety, and the environment, do not constitute indirect expropriations.

Hence the potential for succeeding with "regulatory takings" investor-state claims has been reduced. Moreover, the CAFTA-DR agreement anticipates creating an appellate body of some sort for investor-state arbitration decisions.

Regarding intellectual property, NAFTA-plus has moved into the Internet age. Protection of domain names, and adherence to the WIPO Internet treaties, are stipulated. E-commerce and free trade in digital products are embraced, copyrights extended to rights-management (encryption) and anti-circumvention (hacking) technology, protection against web music file sharing enhanced, and potential liability of Internet Service Providers detailed.

Less visibly, pharmaceutical patent owners obtain extensions of their patents to compensate for delays in the approval process, and greater control over their test data, making it harder for generic competition to emerge. They also gain "linkage," meaning local drug regulators must make sure generics are not patent-infringing before their release. In addition, adherence to the Patent Law Treaty (2000) and the Trademark Law Treaty (1994) is agreed. Anti-counterfeiting laws are tightened, particularly regarding destruction of counterfeit goods.

Other NAFTA-plus changes push further along the path of free trade in services and comprehensive customs law administration rules. Antidumping and countervailing duty laws remain applicable, but appeals from administrative determinations are taken in national courts, not binational panels. Except for limited provisions in the Chile-U.S. agreement, business visas drop completely out of U.S. free trade agreements, a NAFTA-minus development.

In sum, the United States has generally used its leverage with smaller trade partners to obtain more preferential treatment and expanded protection for its goods, services, technology and investors. It has given up relatively little in return, for example a modest increase in agricultural market openings.

THE TRANS-PACIFIC PARTNERSHIP (TPP)

U.S. fast track trade promotion authority was granted to President Obama in the summer of 2015. With all three NAFTA nations participating in the Trans-Pacific Partnership (TPP) negotiations, the NAFTA accords could effectively be updated via the TPP.

Late in 2015, a TPP agreement was reached and fully disclosed, with the NAFTA nations plus Peru, Chile, Brunei, Singapore, Malaysia, Vietnam, Japan, Australia and New Zealand (but not China) participating. These Pacific Rim partners comprise roughly 40% of world trade. The TPP contains notable developments on freer agricultural and food trade, trade in automobiles and auto parts, bio-similar pharmaceuticals, bans on use of investor-state arbitrations by tobacco companies, minimum wages and working hours, independent unions, technology protections, anti-corruption obligations, service sector openings, e-commerce and restraints on subsidies for state-owned enterprises. It contains minimal currency manipulation rules, a much debated topic.

South Korea, Thailand, The Philippines, Taiwan and Indonesia have expressed interest in joining the TPP, assuming it takes effect. Ratification in the U.S. under up or down fast track procedures (see Chapter 3) cannot occur prior to February 2016. With a number of leading candidates for the Presidency opposed to the TPP, U.S. ratification prior to the November 2016 elections seems unlikely. The TPP will take effect if all 12 nations ratify it within 2 years, or at least 6 nations comprising 85% of the GDP of the group (mandating USA and Japanese participation) do so.

INDEX

References are to Pages